Praise for
THE WATCHMAKERS

"A truly extraordinary book—one full of compassion, love, and hope in the midst of unimaginable suffering and despair—*The Watchmakers* is a humbling account, one that is both jaw-droppingly well-written and uplifting at the same time. It reads like a thriller, and revived my faith in the enduring quality and beauty of the human spirit, even when mired in the depths of darkness and crazed evil. Once I had finished the last page I only wanted to start reading it all over again. Unputdownable, despite the cruelty, brutality, barbarism, and sheer downright hatred visited upon the brothers at the heart of this epic tale. I will return to *The Watchmakers* again and again."

—DAMIEN LEWIS, #1 international bestselling author

"Inspiring. Exhilarating. Astonishing. An epic tale of brotherhood, ingenuity, and survival, told with the ticking precision of a wind-up watch. *The Watchmakers* reminds us of the importance of loyalty, how to persevere against aggression, and how well-timed and precisely measured audacity can ignite a hidden spark of humanity in the darkest of times."

—HEATHER DUNE MACADAM, international bestselling
author of 999: *The Extraordinary Young Women of the
First Official Jewish Transport to Auschwitz* and *Star
Crossed: A True Romeo and Juliet Story in Hitler's Paris*

"*The Watchmakers* is an astonishing testament to courage, guile, and brotherly devotion under impossible circumstances. Gripping as a thriller, deeply moving, it brings fresh urgency to a vitally important piece of history. Everyone should read it."

—JESSE KELLERMAN, bestselling author

"*The Watchmakers* is an extraordinary book—gripping, inspiring, and terrifying all at once. Each Holocaust survivor is a walking miracle. Many of them volunteered to testify to their lives in hell, but most did not manage to do so in time. We feel the loss of precious untold stories from the generation of survivors whose hard-earned physical existence will soon pass from this world. It is in that context that we honor this renewed literary genre of Holocaust testimony furthered by Scott Lenga, son of Harry Lenga. Harry speaks to us in his own voice captured from more than forty hours of interviews, notwithstanding the twenty-two years since his natural death. Here, Scott Lenga offers an empowering model for future generations of survivor descendants and delivers a harrowing saga of timeless values put to the test."

—BLU GREENBERG, author of *On Women and
Judaism: A View from Tradition* and *How to Run
a Traditional Jewish Household*, and founder of
the Jewish Orthodox Feminist Alliance

"A fascinating read. The horror of Nazi Germany will always haunt us, but like most traumas there is a temptation to file the era away and pay scant attention to the experience. *The Watchmakers* cuts through that and lays bare the utter inhumanity of what happened in appalling detail. Its focus on the day-to-day—indeed the moment-to-moment—struggle to survive strikes home vividly. Only occasionally does Harry Lenga stop to think about the wider implications, and I think that makes his experiences come across with an immediacy that is sometimes missing from other accounts. I really came to appreciate the life and death significance of something as simple as a pair of shoes, a battered metal soup bowl, or a shave. I found myself shocked, once again, by the mindless brutality and casual cruelty of the Nazi regime and its henchmen. As Harry notes, it could happen anywhere. *The Watchmakers* serves as a fresh warning of the dangers of ignoring history."

—SIMON SCARROW, *Sunday Times* bestselling author
of *Blackout* and the Eagles of the Empire series

"World War II and the Holocaust still have lessons to teach us, and stories yet to be told. *The Watchmakers* presents a unique survival story that will take its place in Holocaust literature alongside works by greats such as Elie Wiesel and Primo Levi."

—TOM YOUNG, author of *Silver Wings, Iron Cross*
and *Red Burning Sky*

"*The Watchmakers* is a beautiful tribute to the bond of brotherhood. Against all odds, Harry Lenga and his brothers managed to endure multiple concentration camps, ghettos, and a death march during the Holocaust. Their survival was largely based on making decisions as a team of brothers, their watchmaking abilities, and luck. Harry's son, Scott Lenga, does a wonderful job of incorporating his father's own words throughout the story. Additionally, the strong relationship between the brothers is undeniable as the author writes, 'The togetherness—the will to live—was so strong.' Even though the book documents the worst of mankind, I found their story compelling, as it manages to highlight the beautiful bond between brothers and the hope for a better tomorrow."

—ADENA BERNSTEIN ASTROWSKY, author of
Living among the Dead: My Grandmother's
Holocaust Survival Story of Love and Strength

"A must read! This is a story of broken family relationships that become unbreakable when put to the test. You feel their quickening heartbeat and the cut of the tightrope on their feet as they face death with every step. Inspiring and unforgettable."

—HADASSAH LIEBERMAN, author of *Hadassah: An*
American Story

"*The Watchmakers* is an intimate, powerful, and eloquent memoir. As told by Harry Lenga, the story is drenched in pain, brutality, and sadness, but with hardly a drop of hopelessness or despair. The focus required for precision watchmaking became a shield of resistance for Harry and his brothers in the Nazi slave labor and death camps. This craft learned from their father sustained their spirits, lifting them above the soul-crushing world of their captivity. Moreover, *The Watchmakers* teaches a lesson: when confronting a murderous evil, your biggest challenge is holding on to your own human decency."

—MICHAEL CLERIZO, author of *Masters of Contemporary Watchmaking* and *George Daniels: A Master Watchmaker and His Art*

"Scott Lenga's significant accomplishment was to capture his father's voice and portray his experience from early childhood as a young Chassidic boy into the gates of Auschwitz and beyond, from the death marches to life in postwar Germany and his re-settlement in St. Louis. Survivors often mistakenly say that the reason they survived was luck—they all knew someone smarter and wiser, braver and stronger, who was in the wrong place at the wrong time and did not make it through. Harry Lenga survived not merely by luck, but with his skill as a watchmaker, his audacity, and his ingenuity as he faced all but certain death time and again. He survived with his brothers because they too had skills, and they forged an iron bond to pull each other through. The work is compelling, the writing is riveting, and one comes away with deep gratitude to both father and son—father for telling the story to his son, and son for faithfully transmitting a story that must be told."

—MICHAEL BERENBAUM, Professor of Jewish Studies and Director of Sigi Ziering Institute, American Jewish University, Los Angeles

"A very personal life of a Polish Jew. *The Watchmakers* is an important account of Jewish life in Poland in the years preceding the Holocaust and the struggle for life during the Holocaust itself. It beautifully describes the strength of spirit that enabled some Jews to survive the Nazi onslaught."

—JOHN T. PAWLIKOWSKI, OSM, PhD, Professor Emeritus of Social Ethics, Catholic Theological Union, Chicago

"*The Watchmakers* is an amazing story of the family bond of three brothers enduring the Holocaust. Somehow, they were able to stay together as they were moved from camp to camp, and would depend on each other for survival. Their watchmaking skills enabled them to navigate through unbelievable hardships. Their will to live and ability to have optimism in the face of death is an incredible testament to those who faced that most terrible period of our history. Our father was fated to be a liberator of Ebensee, and the overwhelming images, stench of death, and emotions he encountered when his tank entered the concentration camp were etched into his memory. We feel that our father would have been honored to meet Harry Lenga. Like Harry, he began to share his experiences as a liberator in his later years. As he told it, 'Ebensee comes back and comes back. I can still see their eyes gazing at us and feel their crying need for help.' He had the opportunity to meet several other Ebensee survivors, and he marveled at 'how so many of the survivors have gone on to a very productive life after all of this suffering.' While he always stated that he did nothing extraordinary but was just following orders on May 6, 1945, we are very proud of his service and his willingness to share his story. We know his wish for 'Never Again' has impacted our lives and the lives of his grandchildren. We feel a connection to Harry and to all of the Ebensee survivors whose stories we have heard."

—ALAN PERSINGER, PEGGY GIANNANGELI, and LINDA OSIKOWICZ, children of U.S. Army Platoon Sergeant Robert Persinger, tank commander who liberated the Ebensee Concentration Camp

"I worked closely with Harry Lenga when I directed the Holocaust Museum and Education Center in St. Louis. He very often gave personal testimony about his Holocaust experiences to students in middle schools, high schools, and universities, and his articulate manner mesmerized his audiences. Harry's story comprises the entire gamut of atrocities perpetrated by the Nazis against Jews in Europe, and his story is replete with multiple examples of spiritual resistance as well as incredible bravery, moral and ethical courage, and altruistic behavior. *The Watchmakers* is a magnificent testimony to the strength that lies within the human spirit in the face of extreme adversity. This book should have a central place in every course that is taught on the Holocaust."

—RABBI ROBERT STERNBERG, founding director of
the St. Louis Holocaust Museum and co-author of
Jewish-Christian Relations in Light of the Holocaust

"Harry Lenga was the kindest person I ever met. He was always willing to speak to many of my classes about his experiences in the Holocaust. He would explain how he and his brothers were able to survive Auschwitz and other concentration camps by cleaning and fixing the watches of Nazi leaders and guards. He had to explain to my students that watches back then had movable parts. At the end of his talk, he would roll up his sleeve and show the students his prisoner number A-19367 that was tattooed on his left arm. My students were blessed to meet Harry and hear his explanation of how he survived the Holocaust. Harry's memoir *The Watchmakers* is an essential contribution to Holocaust education and research. As I read it, I could picture Harry talking to me and my students."

—DAVID C. OUGHTON, PhD, Associate Professor
of Religions of the World, Saint Louis University,
former religion teacher at Christian Brothers
College High School, St. Louis, and co-author of
Jewish-Christian Relations in Light of the Holocaust

"What's written in *The Watchmakers* is truly Harry Lenga's voice. I had the great privilege of interviewing Harry for the Oral History Project at the St. Louis Center for Holocaust Studies and accompanying him to different speaking engagements in the early 1980s. I vividly remember the powerful expressions on the faces of the students who listened and learned from this extraordinary man. Harry Lenga once said to students at Mehlville High School in St. Louis, Missouri, 'I hope you will repeat my stories to your children and then they will be eyewitnesses to tell future generations that things like this happened and never again should something like this happen.' The impact Harry Lenga made on the lives of these students and countless others was truly everlasting."

—VIDA "SISTER" GOLDMAN PRINCE, Chair, Oral History Project, St. Louis Holocaust Museum and Learning Center

"*The Watchmakers* is not only a powerful Holocaust survival story but an epic tale of courage, endurance, and grit on the scale of those heroic sagas dating back to *The Odyssey*. Indeed, Homer's description of Odysseus—strong, courageous, and ingenious— also describes Harry Lenga as he and his two brothers undertake a journey to freedom every bit as harrowing and brutal as the one taken by Odysseus. Just as Odysseus survived a series of increasingly dangerous monsters on his long voyage home, so, too, did this brave band of brothers survive the soul-crushing slave labor camps, the brutal Nazi taskmasters, and various death camps on their long voyage to liberation."

—MICHAEL A. KAHN, trial lawyer and award-winning author of *Bad Trust*

"Giving voice to his late father Harry, Scott Lenga has brought us a remarkable story of survival through ingenuity and mutual loyalty—brotherhood—that stands out even in the vast field of Holocaust memoir. Through a light-handed use of explanatory endnotes, *The Watchmakers* situates Harry Lenga's harrowing personal story in the broader historical context of the Holocaust period, making it exceptionally useful in any educational setting."

—RACHEL L. GREENBLATT, PhD, Judaica Librarian, Brandeis University, and Lecturer in Jewish Studies, Dartmouth College

"*The Watchmakers* is a vivid reminder of a Jewish world erased, miracles of survival, and lives of resilience—all characteristics of an extraordinary generation we are in danger of forgetting all too quickly."

—DANIEL GORDIS, Koret Distinguished Fellow, Shalem College, Jerusalem, and author of *Israel: A Concise History of a Nation Reborn*

"Both shocking and wonderful, this is a memoir you won't be able to forget. From his youth in a Chassidic community in Poland through the worst of the German Nazi horrors, we actually hear Harry Lenga's voice, masterfully curated by his son, Scott. Harry and his brothers—the Watchmakers—managed to stay alive through a combination of their craft and wits. Beautifully written and deeply researched, *The Watchmakers* is a book to be shared."

—JOSHUA TEITELBAUM, Professor of Middle Eastern Studies, Bar-Ilan University, Israel, and author of *Saudi Arabia and the New Strategic Landscape*

"Like so many chilling first-person accounts of the Shoah, *The Watchmakers* finds meaning in abject cruelty, subtle acts of kindness, and ambiguous interpersonal dilemmas. Harry Lenga's sharp and honest voice, curated lovingly by his son, presents a survivor's story that is full of high drama, but the narrative is equally attuned to the material details of everyday life before and after the war. Even those who have consumed hours and hours of survivor testimony will find Lenga's account moving and illuminating."

—DAVID HENKIN, Professor of History, University of California, Berkeley, and author of *The Week*

"Harry Lenga's first-person account, as told to his son Scott, takes the reader on the harrowing path Harry and his brothers endured through the ghettos in Poland and the Nazi death camps, to eventual liberation and reclamation of their freedom and independence in postwar Europe. Over and over, their close-knit fraternal bond, their watchmaking skills, and a fair share of luck enabled them to survive another day. *The Watchmakers* is an inspiring story of hope and resilience in the darkest of times, conveyed in a rarely found lively, relatable, and sober voice."

—NATHAN GUTTMAN, US Bureau Chief, Israeli Public TV

"Thanks to many hours of oral testimony of Harry Lenga as told to his son Scott, we are treated to a vivid Holocaust survivor memoir that gives us an eyewitness account of hell on earth. With the odds overwhelmingly stacked against them, three brothers maintained their commitment to each other and defied their fate. How Lenga and his brothers navigated their way amid the valley of death and emerged with their humanity intact is a story that needs to be read."

—DAVID MAKOVSKY, Ziegler Distinguished Fellow at the Washington Institute for Near East Policy and Adjunct Professor of Middle East Studies at Johns Hopkins University's Paul H. Nitze School of Advanced International Studies

"*The Watchmakers* is a well-written and engaging story of survival during the darkest years of the twentieth century. Scott Lenga and his father tell a story that starts in a Polish shtetl and travels through the Holocaust. It is a story ultimately about love, struggle, and resistance, and its message will resonate with many."

—ERIC LEE, author of *Operation Basalt*, *Night of the Bayonets*, and *How to Kill Hitler*

"Scott Lenga provides us with the personal story of his father and two uncles, who against all odds managed to survive six long years of war, deprivation, hunger, disease, and loss of their family members during the Holocaust. As an educator, I found this amazing story of resilience, chutzpah, and endurance to be a powerful message to every student in every classroom. There are numerous memoirs that have been published over the years; this one, written in the first person by Scott, is both powerful and engrossing and takes the reader through the most horrific events of the Holocaust without traumatizing the reader. Above all, it leaves us with hope—always the hope—that one needed in order to survive. Harry's ability to leverage his skills as a watchmaker is an inspiration. I highly recommend this memoir to any teacher who wants to provide his or her students with a firsthand account of the events of the Holocaust through this amazing story of the Lenga brothers."

—EPHRAIM KAYE, former Director for International Seminars for Educators at the International School for Holocaust Studies of Yad Vashem

The Watchmakers

HARRY LENGA AND SCOTT LENGA

CITADEL PRESS
Kensington Publishing Corp.
www.kensingtonbooks.com

CITADEL PRESS BOOKS are published by

Kensington Publishing Corp.
119 West 40th Street
New York, NY 10018

All Kensington titles, imprints, and distributed lines are available at special quantity discounts for bulk purchases for sales promotions, premiums, fund-raising, educational, or institutional use.

Special book excerpts or customized printings can also be created to fit specific needs. For details, write or phone the office of the Kensington sales manager: Kensington Publishing Corp., 119 West 40th Street, New York, NY 10018, attn: Sales Department; phone 1-800-221-2647.

CITADEL PRESS and the Citadel logo are Reg. U.S. Pat. & TM Off.

ISBN: 978-0-8065-4191-4

First Citadel hardcover printing: July 2022

10 9 8 7 6 5 4 3 2 1

Printed in the United States of America

Library of Congress Catalog Number: 2022931995

Electronic edition:

ISBN: 978-0-8065-4192-1 (e-book)

For Malke Reyle and Khana Lenga

Contents

Co-author's Note   xvii

Note on Transliteration   xxi

1. Childhood in the Chassidic Town of Kozhnitz
   (1919–30)   1

2. Teen Years and Watchmaking (1931–38)   21

3. Coming of Age in Warsaw (October 1938–
   September 1939)   35

4. German Occupation and the Warsaw Ghetto
   (October 1939–May 1941)   47

5. Kozhnitz Ghetto (June 1941–September 1942)   67

6. Gorczycki Camp at Wolka (October 1942)   85

7. Wolanow Slave Labor Camp (October 1942–
   June 1943)   97

8. Starachowice Slave Labor Camp (June 1943–
   July 1944)   127

9. Auschwitz (July 1944–January 1945)   137

10. Death March, Mauthausen, and Melk (Late January
    1945–April 1945)   169

11. Ebensee and Liberation (April 1945–October 1945)   191

12. Postwar Europe (October 1945–March 1949)   223

Afterword by Scott Lenga   237

Appendix A: My Search for Chassidic Context
             by Scott Lenga   245

Appendix B: The Tale of Laizer Yitzkhak
             Wildenberg   253

Appendix C: Conflicts Among the Kozhnitzer
             Rebbes and Their Followers   255

Appendix D: Jewish Religious and Political Groups
             in Prewar Kozhnitz   257

Appendix E: Testimony of Robert Persinger, the
             US Army Tank Commander Who
             Liberated Ebensee   259

Glossary   263

Sources   276

Endnotes   281

Photo Credits   305

Acknowledgments   311

Index   315

About the Autors   323

This is a true story.
No characters were invented, and no names were changed.

Co-author's Note

I CAN'T CLEARLY PLACE MY first childhood memory. Perhaps it was watching President John F. Kennedy's funeral on our black-and-white TV in November 1963. I was two months shy of my third birthday. President Kennedy's son John-John was about my age, and my family made a big deal out of that when John-John walked in the funeral procession and saluted his father's coffin.

But I'm sure that even before the Kennedy assassination, I knew that my dad, Harry Lenga, was from a small town called Kozhnitz and that his mother had died in childbirth when he was around four years old. That event marked the end of his childhood and continued to reverberate through mine.

At five, I didn't know what a concentration camp was, but I knew that my dad had a blue number tattooed on his arm from a place called Auschwitz. Sometimes I used to stare at it when he sat at his workbench fixing watches or when he reached for his glass of soda on a hot summer day. It was not something that eventually seemed normal or that I ever stopped noticing, like a mole or a scar.

Many *Shoah*—that is, Holocaust—survivors were not able to speak about what happened to them during World War II. My dad was on the opposite end of the spectrum. Around 1960, eleven years after he had moved to the United States, he started to have terrible nightmares about the concentration camps. He used to cry and yell for help, and my mom would shake him out of the dream. "Harry, you are here in America!" she would tell him. "You are in bed! You're a free person!" One day, he ran into another Shoah survivor, and they shared some wartime memories. That night, he didn't have any nightmares. From then on, he never stopped telling us his stories at the dinner table or during evening walks around our suburban neighborhood in St. Louis, Missouri.

From listening to these stories, I understood that I shouldn't complain to my dad about uncomfortable dress shoes, a choking tie, or other difficulties at school that didn't measure up to the sufferings of his childhood. Even as he belittled my problems—"These are problems!?"—he also viewed them as a source of pride. We were not living in poverty or in fear of persecution. I was growing up in America. In his eyes, that meant I could do anything.

In my teens, I continued to listen to my dad's stories with respect and found them interesting, but the Shoah and Jewish identity wasn't "my thing." I was busy trying to carve out a self-image as a regular American kid. That changed in my late twenties and early thirties as I learned to embrace my legacy as the son of a Shoah survivor.

I also grew to appreciate how rare and important my dad's stories are in the context of both the existing Holocaust literature and the larger historical record. Of the 3.4 million Jews living in prewar Poland, some 320,000 survived—the only remnant of the vibrant Jewish culture that had developed there for over a thousand years. Of the 320,000 survivors, only 40,000 to 50,000 had been stuck in the German-occupation zone in Poland. My dad and his brothers were part of this small group. Their ability to fix watches enabled them to create windows of opportunity in the black-market economy of the German camps and became a powerful key to their survival. Unlike the vast majority of prisoners, they could influence their fate. Moreover, they were willing to take harrowing risks to stay together.

From 1989 to 1993, when my dad was in his early seventies, I interviewed him for some thirty-seven hours to record the stories I had heard over the years and to fill in the context that would make them fit together as a coherent, detailed account. He told everyone we were writing a book. I wasn't so sure. Then he fell ill and passed away in the year 2000.

For the next fifteen years, I was content to tell my kids stories about the *zadie* (grandfather) whom they never really knew. From the time my daughter, Orli, was about ten years old, she had been threatening to write this book herself if I didn't take up the challenge. In my early fifties, I finally harnessed the maturity as well as the inspiration from Orli to take on this project.

This book is written in my dad's first-person voice and style of communication. It is the voice of a father telling his extraordinary life story to his son. Filtering his interviews through my narrative voice would have diluted the graphic passion of his will to survive. The deeper messages couched in his simple, un-adorned language would have been lost.

The process of "translating" his Yiddish-English from the interview transcripts and editing this book in my dad's first-person voice injects an aspect of editorial license that a ghost writer would normally employ. Sadly, my dad was not available to confirm the final text, but the stories are his alone. Considerable effort was made to remain true to my dad's account of his upbringing in a Chassidic family of watchmakers in the 1920s and 1930s and how he and his brothers managed to survive the years of fury in German-occupied Poland and Austria (1939–45).

Every Shoah survivor faces the question, "Why was I the one to survive?" My dad could not answer the *why*, but he spoke very clearly about the decisions that somehow enabled him to survive another day. In my dad's estimation, the emotional and spiritual tools that he activated in the Shoah were no less im-portant than his watchmaking tools. He spoke of hope and optimism as indispensable:

We worked hard to keep hope in our minds and not to become meshuga. And the more you talked yourself into it, the more you believed in that hope. If a hungry person believes that he'll find something to eat later, he can last longer. If he thinks, *It's pointless, and I won't survive,* he dies faster. I saw it happen many times. Pessimism is a terrible sickness. You destroy yourself. You have to have optimism all the time.

My dad's ability to marshal these qualities in the most extreme circumstances remains a complete mystery to me—the stuff of miracles at a time when the desperate cries of millions were met with silence and cruel abandon from God and their fellow men. All the more so because when I was growing up in America, my dad seemed quite ordinary and I never knew him to be particularly hopeful or optimistic.

This book shines a light on daily life in dark times that only got darker and on how a regular kid discovered his survival instinct and the hidden resources within himself to face the test.

—Scott Lenga

Note on Transliteration

NON-ENGLISH WORDS HAVE BEEN TRANSLITERATED to enable the English reader to easily read them aloud in a manner that reflects the sound of the original spoken word. In most cases, the guttural *h* in Yiddish, Hebrew, and German is denoted with the letters *kh*. However, certain non-English words which are more familiar to the English reader (e.g., Chassidim and challah) are spelled with a common English spelling that uses '*ch*' for the guttural '*h*.' Polish language names of cities, towns and slave labor camps are spelled with the Polish '*w*,' which is pronounced like the English '*v*' and the Polish '*c*,' which is pronounced like the English '*ts*.'

Non-English words and phrases that are not generally familiar to the English reader are italicized with a brief translation in the text the first time they are used. Expanded definitions are provided in the Glossary.

THE WATCHMAKERS

This map of prewar Poland (1924–1938) identifies Kozhnitz and other small towns and cities that were significant in the course of Harry Lenga's life in Poland before the war.

CHAPTER I

Childhood in the Chassidic Town of Kozhnitz (1919–30)

H ERE, IN AMERICA, EVEN MY brother calls me Harry. I named myself after President Harry Truman when my ship arrived in New Orleans in 1949. It was an identity that the Americans would understand. A new life. I was thirty at the time, and World War II had ended several years before. The world of my childhood—the Jewish world of Poland—had been severed from the physical world. A phantom limb.

I was born Yekhiel Ben Tzion—Khil, for short—in a small town in the Polish countryside about eighty kilometers southeast of Warsaw. The Jews called it "Kozhnitz." All of the Polish towns had separate Yiddish names. At that time in 1919, the total population was just under seven thousand, of which more than half were Jews.

My father, Mikhoel Lenga, was a watchmaker from Warsaw who moved to Kozhnitz as a young man because he was a devoted follower of the Kozhnitzer sect of Chassidim. He told me that his great-great-great-grandmother had been betrothed and perhaps briefly married to the great Chassidic *Rebbe* known as the Maggid of Kozhnitz (1733–1814).[1] For a young man new to the town and looking to marry, even this tenuous family connection to the great Maggid increased his prospects for a good match.

My mother came from a well-known Chassidic family in Kozhnitz. Her maiden name was Malke Reyle Wildenberg. There was family lore that her great-great-grandfather, Laizer Yitzkhak Wildenberg, almost became the second Rebbe of the Gerer Chassidim.[2]

Well, that's not so important to me anymore. In my childhood years, it was important because I was real religious, and this *yikhus* (noble ancestry) conferred status in our community. I believed that a Chassidic Rebbe was the closest to God. Now I believe that a Rebbe may be more educated, but a simple man can sometimes be closer to God than a Rebbe.

🕰 🕰 🕰

MY PARENTS MARRIED in 1910 and used the money from my mother's dowry to open a jewelry store in Kozhnitz and rent an apartment above the store. In 1913, my oldest brother was born. They named him Yitzkhak—Itshele, for short.

When World War I broke out a year later, Kozhnitz was gripped with fear that the German army would destroy the town on its march through Poland to attack Russia, so my parents fled to Radom, about forty kilometers to the southeast. Before they left, my father took all the merchandise from the store and the furniture from their apartment to a neighbor's basement for safekeeping.

The German army did occupy Kozhnitz in World War I, but they did not destroy or plunder anything in the town; there was no danger to the Jews or other locals. When my parents heard the good news, they returned to German-occupied Kozhnitz with the baby after just a few weeks, only to find that all their possessions had been stolen by local thieves, even the furniture. On top of that, they had to move out of the apartment they were renting. The landlord needed it back for his daughter, who had gotten married, though he did agree to let my parents live in the small room at the back of the store until the war was over.

That room had a stove to burn coal or wood, a sink, and three beds. There was no running water, but that was normal. Small Polish towns like Kozhnitz didn't have running water in those days. There was a *vasser treyger* (water carrier) who carried a pole across his shoulders with a bucket on each side, and we would pay him three or four *groshen* (a coin worth 0.01 *zloty*) each time he brought us two buckets of water from the well.

By the time my little brother, Moishele, was born, eight years later in 1922, we were a family of seven, and we were still living in the back room of that store. That single burglary in World War I drove our family into a cycle of poverty from which we never recovered. Perhaps it would have been different if we hadn't lost our mother.

🕐 🕐 🕐

IT WAS THE winter of 1924, and my mother was about to have another baby. She started to experience labor pains one Thursday afternoon and went to her mother's, my *Bubbishe* Feyge's house for the birth, just as she had with the rest of us. They called the midwife and sent the five of us children to stay at my Uncle Fishel's home.

Thursday passed. Then Friday, Saturday, and Sunday . . . the baby didn't come. There was no doctor with them, and the midwife probably didn't know what to do.

I'll never forget that Sunday night, when my mother called us in to see her. Moishele, our older sister Khanale, and I were dressed up, but our mother was in her pajamas. She took Moishele, who was two at the time, into the bed with her, and when she saw that I was jealous, said, "Khiltshu, come in, too." She shared with me the soup she was eating. Then she put a piece of cake on her stomach and asked if I could make it disappear. She looked away when I grabbed it and pretended to be surprised when it was gone.

I hugged her and clung to her. I cried. I was only four years old and Khanale was six, but I understood that something was not right. My mother kissed us, and tears fell from her eyes. Then my father took us back to Uncle Fishel's house.

It was only when we were older that we heard the details of what happened. My grandmother had told my parents to go to Radom and find a doctor named Peshka, who was an expert in delivering babies and knew how to perform caesarean operations.

The only way to reach Radom was by bus, and there was only one bus per day. There were no taxis in those days. My father asked my mother to go, but she refused. She had already been in labor for seventy-two hours. It wore her out too much.

They waited another day, and on Monday morning, my mother said, "I cannot stand it anymore. I don't care what you do! Try to get the baby! Try to get the baby!"

So, my father decided to call the only doctor in our town. He was a new doctor—a young man who had just finished medical school—but there was no other option at that point. The doctor said the baby had a big head, so it couldn't fit through the birth canal, and he suggested we sacrifice the baby to save my mother's life. When he put in the instruments, he pierced the baby's back and lungs. Only then he understood that the baby was lying sideways—he turned it, and pulled it out, dead.

Maybe from that alone my mother couldn't bear to live. She called to my father, "Mikhoel, I'm dying! I can tell. I'm in terrible pain!" She didn't get sedatives or anesthesia. Nothing. She was fully cognizant and had seen everything. She died right there.

My father and my two older brothers, Itshele and Mailekh, were standing there in the room with her when it happened. Bubbishe's house only had one room.

Meanwhile, that night, Khanale, Moishele, and I were at Uncle Fishel's, lying together in one bed, when our father came in crying and knocking on his head with his fists. I remember it like it happened today. He said, "Children, you don't have a mother anymore. Your mother died. She died."

I had a hard time accepting that my mother was really dead. I hadn't seen her dead. I had just seen her alive the previous night when she took me into her bed. Tuesday was the funeral. Moishele, Khanale, and I were not allowed to attend. Kids didn't go to funerals until they were about nine or ten years old. My two older brothers went.

The next thing I remember is sitting *shiva*, the traditional seven-day mourning period under Jewish law, in my grandmother's house, where we had all been sleeping. My father brought us candies so we'd behave when people came to *daven* or pray, and console the family. They didn't talk to me, but everybody who came cried. I overheard their conversations, but I still couldn't digest exactly what was going on.

No relatives visited my father after the shiva. Later, I was told that my grandmother blamed my father for my mother's death. She believed that he was too stingy to take her to Radom on the bus.

My father didn't accept full responsibility for her death. He hadn't known she needed a caesarean surgery to deliver the baby, and my mother had refused to go to Radom. They didn't think there would be time. If he had known her life was in such danger, of course, he would have taken her.

My mother died on 16 Shvat on the Jewish calendar. It was in late January. One month later, on Purim, my father sent Itshele and Mailekh with a cake for *shalakh munes*, a traditional Purim gift of food, to my grandmother's house, where Moishele and I were still staying. When they delivered the holiday greeting from my father, my grandmother said to them, "A *gutten* [good] Purim. Take that cake to your mother in the cemetery. I don't want anything from him." So, my brothers went back to my father with the cake and her message.

My father was enraged. It was unforgivable that she said such a thing to the children.

After that, Moishele and I moved back home. My father and grandmother didn't talk to each other anymore, and they didn't see each other. Nothing. My uncles and aunts also cut off all contact with my father. Their relationship with him was finished. It became an abiding hatred. My father felt that he was forsaken by everybody. It was a terrible thing for him. He didn't have any family in Kozhnitz. The only relatives we had were from my mother's side.

When I was older, I would discover that my older brothers also blamed our father for her death. They thought he should have taken her to Radom no matter what, that he shouldn't have listened to her because she was in too much pain and too exhausted to decide for herself. Of course, it's easy to look back and say what should have been done.

The tragedy of my mother's death hung over every aspect of our family life and followed me into adulthood. I don't have many memories from when she was alive, but I do remember when I was three years old and everybody had to be dressed in new clothes for Passover. My mother bought me a sailor's uniform with a big collar and a hat with ribbons and a tie. Oh, that was beautiful. I was really very happy.

⏱ ⏱ ⏱

MY FATHER WAS left with five children under the age of eleven, and he didn't have anybody. He tended the store, and at night he cooked and took care of Moishele.

Passover came thirty days after Purim, and my father did everything to prepare for the holiday all by himself.[3] It was just him and us kids at the Seder—the first without our mother. The next day, after *shul* (synagogue), my father was tired. He told me and my sister to take care of Moishele, and he went to take a nap. It was a nice day, and the three of us sat outside, playing. Moishele was a mess with a full diaper, but Khanale and I didn't know how to do anything. What can you expect from a six-year-old girl and a four-year-old boy?

A neighbor came by and saw what was going on, and she fed the baby and took off his *fercockta* [soiled] diaper. Then she went to tell my grandmother about it.

My Bubbishe came over and found us outside. "I'm going to take the baby, and from now on, he will be with me," she said. My sister had the *sekhel*, or good sense, to say, "Why are you doing this? Our father told us to watch the baby before he went to lie down. He'll wake up and won't see Moishele. I'm going to tell my father."

Bubbishe replied, "Don't wake him up. Don't say nothing to him." Then she grabbed the baby and left. We knew that our father and Bubbishe didn't like each other. But for me and my sister, she was still our grandmother. We belonged to her family. Our father told us not to visit her, but we sometimes did anyway without his knowledge.

When our father woke up, we told him that Bubbishe had come and taken Moishele. He started to yell, unleashing on us all the pain that was in his bitter heart. Then he sent us to bring back Moishele. We cried to her, "Bubbishe, give us back the baby because our father will kill us." She said, "He won't kill you. He'll be glad that somebody is taking care of the baby. The baby is better off staying with me and that's all. Tell him not to send you anymore. If he wants to come, I'll give him what's coming to him. He didn't have any business going to sleep and leaving little babies to take care of a baby." So, we told him what she said, and that was the end of it. Moishele was staying with her.

I thought it was wise that she should take Moishele. My sister was glad, too. As young as we were, we understood that he would be better taken care of by Bubbishe and our aunt Perla, who wasn't married yet and still lived at home. Before that, my sister and I had the responsibility of taking care of Moishele all day while our father worked in the store.

Later, when Moishele could walk and talk a little more, Bubbishe would send him to our house every morning with a linen sack hanging from his neck to get some bread rolls from us. He would announce, "I came here for the rolls. You are supposed to give me rolls." When my father put in the rolls, he'd run outside to where Bubbishe was waiting for him. It was a chance for him to have a little contact with the family.

A FEW MONTHS later, in the summer of 1924, my father's friends convinced him to send Mailekh and Itshele to yeshiva in a different town called Shedlitz. They said it was too much for him to take care of so many children. It would be easier for the time being. In our home, everything was always for the time being.

Itshele was eleven and attended the third grade in public school. Mailekh was nine and was in the second grade. Most religious people, especially Chassidim, didn't want to send their children to the *goyishe* (non-Jewish) public schools. My father believed that it was good to have a secular education in addition to the Jewish education, but now, my brothers would go to a faraway town and receive only a strict religious education in a famous yeshiva. They cried.

The yeshiva found a different family to host them for a meal every day as charity, and they slept on a bench in the *beis medrish*, the study hall. That's how it was for poor kids in yeshiva. After a while, fewer families were giving them meals, and my brothers had to search for food themselves. They didn't have any money.

Itshele and Mailekh would come home for the high holidays in the autumn—for Rosh Hashanah, Yom Kippur, and Sukkes—and sometimes for Passover in the spring. That was it. Twice a year. I cried when they told me about the misery they endured in that yeshiva.

WHEN I WAS three years old and my mother was still alive, I started *kheder* to learn Hebrew and religious subjects. The word *kheder* literally means "room" in Hebrew. That's exactly what it was—schooling in the main kitchen-dining room of the teacher's apartment. While we studied, his wife watched their younger kids play on the floor, and their baby lay in the crib.

When my father first took me to kheder, I was scared to death. My brothers had told me how the teachers discipline you to study all the time and beat you if you don't behave. My father never asked me if I was scared, and I was afraid to tell him. It was not something you discussed with adults. So while for him it was a happy day—he brought a candy for every child in the room—the first thing I wanted to learn was the size of the teacher's whip.

The teacher was strict, and the wooden handle on his whip had strips of leather connected to it that were long enough to strike a child sitting at the other end of the table. Most of the time, though, he'd miss. Maybe intentionally. I don't remember him ever actually hitting me, or anyone else, with that whip.

The first thing they taught us was to recite the *Shema*,[4] so we could pray. When a woman gave birth, they used to bring our class of three- and four-year-olds to her house to chant the Shema for the mother and baby. That was supposed to bring good luck and protection against any demons that could be lingering in their house. We looked forward to that ritual. They would give us candies.

We also learned the Hebrew letters and vowel sounds. We used to sing a folk song called "Oyfn Pripetchik" about learning the *aleph-beis*. It is translated as follows:

> *On the hearth, a fire burns, and in the house it is warm.*
> *The rabbi is teaching little children the aleph-beis.*
> *See, children, remember, dear ones*
> *What you learn here, repeat and repeat yet again, "Ko-*
>   *mets aleph: o!"*
> *Don't be afraid. Every beginning is hard.*
> *Lucky is the one who has learned Torah. What more does*
>   *a person need?*

*When you grow older, children, you will understand by
    yourselves*
How many tears lie in these letters, and how much lament.
*When you, children, will bear the exile, and will be ex-
    hausted*
*May you derive strength from these letters. Look in at
    them*

If it was raining or cold, some mothers brought their children a little late or let them stay home. The mothers were caring and loving and liked to comfort their children. I didn't have that privilege after my mother died, so in my eyes, those children were spoiled.

At five, we could read Hebrew and graduated to the next class with a different rabbi. I liked him. He taught us to read and interpret *Khumash*, the Five Books of Moses. I especially liked his wife, the rebbitzen. She would give me food that the other children did not finish. I didn't want to accept it at first, but she was very discreet and didn't do it in front of the others. She treated me with *rakhmunes* (compassion) because I didn't have a mother.

By that time, I had *peyis,* or sidelocks, hanging below my cheeks and wore a long black Chassidic coat with a little round cap. I felt proud to be dressed like a little Jew. I had advanced to be a *mensch.* Not all of the kids dressed that way. There were a lot of Jews in our city who weren't Chassidic, but we all attended the same kheders. Even the parents who weren't religious put their kids through kheder to get a Jewish education in the early years.

I was the best student in the class, and the rabbi taught me a speech to give at a celebration for a rich kid from the kheder whose family owned a candy factory. I did such a good job, but I left right away after I finished delivering the speech. Apparently, they had looked for me and expected that I would stay for the meal. Oy, was I angry at myself! They served the best meal, and I could have used it. I was only five. Anyway, that speech made me famous in Kozhnitz. Whoever was at that party would call me into their store and ask me to recite that speech. In the begin-

ning, I did it for the honor, but then I got smart and asked for five
groshen. They paid me, so I had money to buy candies. Later, I
raised my price. I saw it was a good business.

⏱ ⏱ ⏱

MY FATHER HAD to be the businessman, the father, the mother,
the cook—everything. It was too much for him. Suddenly, he got
sick. It was about a year after my mother's death, before Passover in 1925. It turned into pneumonia, and he started to cough
up blood.

Only Khanale and I were there in the house with him. Mailekh and Itshele were away at yeshiva in Shedlitz. Moishele was
still living with our grandmother. My sister and I were so scared.
We thought he was going to die. "We'll be *yusemim* [orphans].
We won't have nobody. What will happen to us? Thank God we
have a grandmother." At five years old, I was already thinking like
a grown-up.

My father's friends helped. They brought us something to eat
every day. My grandmother wanted us to come live with her, but
we refused. "You remember how much he went through when
you took Moishele away. If you take us away, too, he will die for
sure, and we cannot allow that to happen." She understood, but
she didn't try to help my father. They were completely *broyges*
(embittered and unreconcilable) with each other.

We didn't have a doctor or any money for a doctor. My father
had a good friend, Ezra Rosen, who took care of him. He even
brought a *feldsher* to treat him. Feldshers were healers whom
people in our town used for most medical problems. They
weren't real doctors, but they knew all the folk remedies.[5]

My father was sick for several weeks. My grandmother came
for us again, but still we refused. Khanale was the talker. She understood more than I did. Thank God, he recovered. For us, it
was a miracle. After that, his friends would cook for us and
wouldn't let him cook anymore. I used to carry the warm meal

home from their houses every day. One time, I dropped the pot, and the food spilled out. I started to cry because we wouldn't have anything to eat. Neighbors noticed and said, "Don't worry. Come in, we'll give you more food. Don't tell your father you dropped it."

It was a hard life for us, I'm telling you. All of my father's friends told him he should get married.

🕐 🕐 🕐

MY FATHER DID remarry in 1926 to a woman who was also named Malke, like my mother. I was six or seven years old. I met her before they got married. My father had left me and Khanale in the store while he went on a date with her at a neighbor's house. That neighbor was good friends with my father, and my future stepmother was close friends with my mother's younger sister, Perla. She had known my mother, too.

I was an inquisitive little *mamzeru* (mischief maker). I said to my sister, "If I go up to them now and ask him for money to buy a *khale mit yagdes*, he'll give it to me because he'll feel embarrassed in front of that lady." A khale mit yagdes was a big three-cornered cake filled with blueberries. It was so delicious. And it used to cost ten groshen.

I'll never forget that. I went to the neighbor's house four doors away, and his wife said they were sitting in the room upstairs.

I found the two of them there, drinking tea. My father said, "This is Miss Wilczek," and I went over and shook her hand. He told me to give her a kiss, so I kissed her hand, as he'd always taught us to do when being introduced to a lady from the family. She was very friendly and asked me my name. She told me that her beloved brother who had died was also named Khil.

My father asked, "Well, would you like that she should become your mother?" I said, "Sure. That would be terrific." Then he asked why I was there. "Is there a customer in the store? Do you need me?"

"No. I just thought maybe you could give me ten groshen to buy myself a khale mit yagdes." He couldn't refuse. "Okay, but you could have waited." Then *she* opened her purse and gave me fifty groshen. That was a lot of money for me. My father told me to bring back the change. She said, "No, no. Buy for all the money."

I liked her. She liked me, too. Again, I gave her a kiss on the hand and ran to tell my sister what I'd accomplished.

My father asked me later what I thought. I said, "*Tateshe*, she'll make a good *Mameshe*." My sister didn't like it. She asked me, "What are you so happy about? It's not your mother!" I told her, "It's not our mother. But we need a mother, don't we? Let's be happy that our father wants to get us a mother."

After they married, my father told us to call her Mameshe. Khanale, Moishele, and I complied, but my two older brothers didn't want to. She told them to call her Mima—stepmother. They didn't like that either because if they called her Mima and we called her Mameshe, it didn't sound right. So they just avoided calling her by name.

My father was about thirty-eight. She was a few years younger than him, and it was her second marriage, too. She had been married to a man from Kozhnitz who got sick and died. They didn't have any children, and she didn't have any children with my father, either. It was okay. He didn't need any more children.

Around that time, my father hired a shoemaker to make a new pair of shoes for me. Maybe it was for their wedding. In those days, you did not buy ready-made shoes in a store; you had them custom-made for you by a shoemaker. It was expensive, so this was an especially big deal for a poor family. When I got the shoes, they were too small for my feet, but my father had already paid for them, so I walked in pain until they wore out and never told my father.

We all lived in that one room at the back of the store. The room was divided with some boards that didn't reach the ceiling. The two beds for the adults were in one half of the room, so they could have a little privacy. The beds for all the children were on the other side. It was supposed to have been a temporary arrangement during World War I. But a short time became a whole lifetime that we lived in that store together, with a little dividing wall.

☼ ☼ ☼

MOISHELE GOT SICK with some kind of throat infection a few months after my father remarried. It was serious. Such bad blisters formed in his throat that Moishele's life was in danger from choking.[6] He needed hospital care in Radom. My grandmother and stepmother took Moishele and got the bus driver to take them to Radom immediately. My stepmother still had a good relationship with my grandmother, and she was still friends with my Aunt Perla. The marriage with my father hadn't changed that. When Moishele recovered and they returned to Kozhnitz, my stepmother talked things over with them, and Moishele came back to live with us.

☼ ☼ ☼

ITSHELE AND MAILEKH came home for Passover after my father got remarried. It was probably 1928. They had been away at yeshiva for three years and hated it. Itshele studied and learned the religious texts, but he didn't believe because he was forced into it. At the Seder, he started to cry. "Tateshe. No more. I won't go back." But my father wouldn't hear of it. He wanted them to be advanced Torah scholars, *talmidey khakhomim.* His only aim in life was to educate his children in the Jewish tradition.[7]

My older brothers went to my grandmother for help. She suggested they stay in Kozhnitz and learn a trade. "You'll make your own money, and your father won't be able to tell you what to do." She gave them the courage to defy my father and set them up in a place to learn to be *gemashmakhers,* tradesmen who cut the leather uppers for shoes. When my father found out . . . ooh, he almost jumped out of his skin from anger.

My stepmother intervened. "Mikhoel, I won't let you send them back. They don't deserve that kind of a life—looking for a meal from somebody's table. It's no good for them." And they never went back to the yeshiva. My stepmother was a giving person and had rakhmunes for us children. My brothers had come home with head lice and clothes lice. Everything was dirty, and she took care of everything for them. We loved her for that.

ŏ ŏ ŏ

MOST OF THE Jews in our town were either shoemakers or leather-cutters. My brothers decided to become leather-cutters, and while the trade was considered to be more *aydele* (refined) than shoemaking, it was a *shonda* (embarrassment) for my father nonetheless.

But they needed to make a few zlotys. We didn't have enough food to eat. Sometimes we had to wait until 4:00 P.M. for my father to make enough money in his watchmaking shop to buy our family a loaf of bread to eat for that day. The sign on the store said we sold jewelry, but my father didn't have money to buy merchandise.

My brothers worked for the first few months without pay as they learned the trade. Mailekh had a sharp mind and quickly became a skilled leather-cutter. He learned how to cut forms in a way that saved leather and how to sew the leather upper with a sewing machine. It was the early 1930s, and there was a terrible depression in Europe, especially in Poland. Shoes were sold on credit, so his boss couldn't pay salaries until customers paid for the shoes.

At one point, Mailekh's employer owed him more than six hundred zlotys. That was a fortune! Finally, he got smart and left that job. When his employer came complaining to my father that Mailekh had quit, my father said, "Get out, you *gonef* (thief). You'd better pay him, or I'll sue you."

Mailekh never got paid, and my father never sued his former boss.

My stepmother was friendly and nice and beautiful, too. She got along with all of us except for my sister. Khanale didn't want a stepmother and always looked for ways to resist. One female with another . . . you know how it is. But Khanale had to learn to live with it.

Things grew worse when my stepmother's mother, who lived in another town called Tsozmer, started to have problems with her eyes. Her vision got worse and worse, but she didn't want to give up her store. The first time my stepmother went to help, she stayed about a week until her mother got better. The next time, it was two weeks, and then it became months, and sometimes it came to half a year that my stepmother was away. Each time she returned to us, her mother sent a letter or a telegram claiming something else was wrong, even if it wasn't true, and each time, my stepmother packed a suitcase and ran to Tsozmer.

Meanwhile, my father didn't have a wife with him, and we didn't have a mother. The responsibility fell to my sister to be the woman of the house—too much responsibility for a young girl. She was unhappy about it, but she cooked and did everything. Sometimes I also cooked. Or Moishele cooked.

It went on for years like that. In the beginning, my stepmother would come home for holidays, but later, she didn't even do that most of the time. I think it would have been a different story if we were her real children.

One time, she took me and Moishele to Tsozmer with her. My stepmother wanted to move the whole family to Tsozmer.

She told my father he couldn't make a good living in Kozhnitz. Tsozmer was a richer town with more people. He could open a jewelry store and have a better chance. It sounded good to me, but my father was stubborn. Afraid. He didn't want to be dependent on his mother-in-law, who criticized him all the time. My stepmother would *shtokh* (jab) him with her mother's barbs whenever they fought. We heard all of it.

My father was depressed about the way his life was going. He had lost his will and initiative to make a change. He was always giving advice to everyone in town, but he could not help himself.

We didn't understand at the time, but now I understand why my stepmother stayed away so much. She was a good-looking young woman from a very nice family. Her mother had a home with a store. With us, she was crowded into one room with a husband and five kids, living in hunger and poverty.

She and my father managed the situation as best they could. They treated each other with respect, and they loved each other. They wrote each other letters every day. Every day. But he didn't move to Tsozmer, and she hardly came back.

🕰 🕰 🕰

I WAS ENROLLED in the public school for boys in 1927. I was in school from 8:00 A.M. until 1:00 P.M. Then we would go to kheder until 8:00 in the evening, often later. We went to kheder the whole year round, even in the summer when we had vacation from public school.

By that time in kheder, I had already been learning the Talmud with commentaries for about a year. These were difficult texts. I had to go home and read the assigned chapters over and over again to be ready for the next day.

However, in public school, I was only starting the first grade. Like most Jewish children, I spoke broken Polish because we spoke only Yiddish at home. I didn't start to speak Polish well until I was in the fifth or sixth grade.

There was a big cross hanging in the entry hall to the school. It was like walking into a church. The day started with a roll call. Then everybody had to stand up and say a Catholic prayer to Jesus in Polish. The school administration and the government wanted the Jewish kids to say it, too. The Jewish parents fought with the school about that, and the teachers agreed to let us be silent or say "Blessed be God" in place of "Blessed be Jesus Christ."

But we couldn't wear a hat or a *yarmulke*, as required under Jewish law. You had to stand for their prayers and sit in class without any head covering. Public school was a difficult adjustment.

There was a recess between classes. The gentile kids never played with us and never accepted us as equals. The Jewish kids would congregate in one corner and play together in a group. The other kids called us dirty words and looked for all kinds of different ways to attack us, to beat us up, even while the teacher was watching. They didn't target specific Jewish boys; they just picked on whoever happened to be close to them.

I could have beaten up some of the Polish kids. They weren't so strong. But we would rather take a blow quietly than hit someone else because whenever a fight broke out between a Jewish kid and a Christian kid, the teachers always took the side of the Christian boy and blamed us. The teachers had an unwritten rule that justice could never side with the Jewish kid in a fight.

Of course, some of the Polish kids were nicer and we got along with them, but we all stayed in our separate groups.

Our parents expected us to be good Chassidic boys. We didn't play sports like the other kids. Why would you waste time playing with a ball when you could sit by the table and study the Torah? That was the idea. That was the tradition. I resented it when I saw the other kids having fun playing, but of course, I didn't complain. If I had told my father that I would like to go out and play, he would have thought I'd gone crazy.

We did have a class called "gymnastics," where we played sports like soccer or handball. The Polish kids would pick on us and hit us with the ball. If the teacher saw that the Jewish boys were getting too many points in a competition, he would stop the game.

In the classroom, we didn't *have* to separate ourselves from the Polish kids, but the Jewish boys sat together quietly in the last rows. Some teachers were nice, but most of them were antisemites. For example, if there was story that included a bad character, they would compare him to a Jew. One teacher who taught us to use woodworking tools explained to the class that the handle of a hand plane—used to shave a board to make it smooth—was like a Jewish nose. A full 40 percent or 50 percent of the class were Jewish boys, yet they always made us feel like unwelcome outsiders.

Saturday was a regular school day. Jewish children didn't have to come because it was our Shabbos, or Sabbath. But they would teach material on Saturday and give a test on it when we came back on Monday. When we complained that we didn't have a fair chance, they said, "That's not my business. You should have come on Saturday."

There was a Polish boy named Kashie Sikolowski who lived very close to me. He was a nice kid. His family owned a tavern. Sometimes we would do homework together at my house, and he always gave me the Saturday lessons. My father suggested that I give him candies for helping me. Kashie would have done it without the candies, but I needed his help every week, so it seemed right to give him something for it.

CHAPTER 2

Teen Years and Watchmaking (1931–38)

There are four types among those who sit before the
sages:
A sponge, a funnel, a strainer and a sieve.
A sponge, which soaks up everything;
A funnel, which takes in at one end and lets out at
the other;
A strainer, which lets out the wine and retains the
sediment; and
A sieve, which lets out the coarse meal and retains
the choice flour.
—Mishnah, Pirkei Avos, 5:15

WHEN I WAS IN THE fifth grade, the school made a rule that students could not come to classes in long Chassidic coats and peyis. The Polish government was trying to adopt this as a formal law in the parliament. My father refused to go along with the school's requirement. He didn't believe the law would pass, and as he said, "Even if it passes, I won't allow you to dress differently. I'll just take you out of school."

But I really wanted to finish public school. It was there that I learned what I needed to live in Poland: Polish reading, writing and literature, history, math, geography, physics, and chemistry. I didn't want to be like the other Jews who lived completely separate from the gentile world around us. I wanted to learn the language and to be treated like a regular citizen. So I cut off my peyis. I knew that I would eat *tsures* (lit., eat trouble) for doing that. I cried when I got home and argued with my father. In any case, my peyis were already cut, and a law had recently been passed that every child has to attend school at least through the seventh grade. So, he conceded.

The rest of the Jewish boys had already changed the way they dressed, but I continued to wear the long black coat to school. There were two other Chassidic boys who still wore the long coats, too, but by the next school year, those two boys had dropped out. I was the only one left. Of course, the Christian kids made fun of me. Finally, the teacher called me aside and said, "Listen, Lenga, I'm telling you for your own good. You're the only one in school with a long coat. You'd better not come to school like that because I won't be responsible for the consequences."

I decided that I couldn't discuss this with my father. My brother Itshele, who had started to call himself Izak, had been wearing a regular short jacket around town, and when my father heard about it from a friend, he threw Izak out of the house for seven weeks. I knew that my father wouldn't back down and would pull me out of school over that coat.

So what did I do? I borrowed a short jacket from my best friend, Khamaira Salzberg. Khamaira was a strong, muscular kid whose family owned a bakery. They were religious people, but not Chassidic. It was an old jacket, but it wasn't torn. In the morning, I left my house dressed in my long coat. On the way to school, I went to Khamaira's house and changed into the short jacket. After school, I went back again, changed into my long coat, and went to kheder.

I was very careful that my father shouldn't find out, but he must have known. His friends had to have seen me walking in that short jacket—especially in the summer. But my father didn't say nothing, and I didn't say nothing ... It was a kind of gentlemen's agreement.

Outside of school, we also had problems when we strayed from the Jewish neighborhoods. Sometimes I would bring Moishele to visit my real mother's brother, Uncle Aharon, and we had to walk through a Polish neighborhood to get there. I didn't like to go there alone because there were some Polish kids who would beat me up on the way.

One time, when I was by myself, I thought, *Why should I be afraid to walk there? To hell with it.* A group of kids came up to me, and one called me a *zhid* (a derogatory name for a Jew). That wasn't a big deal, but then one tried to hit me. When I grabbed a stone, he started to run, so I threw it, and it landed right on his head. Those boys left me alone after that.

The Poles would call us Christ killers. I knew better—that we didn't kill Christ. One summer when I was twelve, I wanted to go swimming in the river just outside of town. Khamaira and my other friends were busy, so I decided to take a risk and go by myself. A Polish peasant in his twenties came toward me, and as he started to raise his arms to hit me, I said, "Wait a minute. Why do you do this to me?" He stopped and said, "I don't know." The conversation went like this:

KHIL: "You must have a reason. Did I hurt you? Did anybody that belongs to me hurt you? Tell me, why do you want to hit me?"

POLISH PEASANT: "You killed Christ."

KHIL: "I killed Christ? How long ago did this happen?"

POLISH PEASANT: "I don't know."

KHIL: "But tell me, was it a month ago, a year ago?"

POLISH PEASANT: "Oh, no, no, it was a long, long time ago."

KHIL: "How long? Was it one hundred years ago?"

POLISH PEASANT: "It must have been one hundred years ago."

KHIL: "All right, how old do you think I am?"

POLISH PEASANT: "I don't know."

KHIL: "Take a guess."

POLISH PEASANT: "Oh, maybe you are ten or twelve or fifteen years old."

KHIL: "Now how could I have killed Christ? You say it's one hundred years since Christ was killed, and let's say I'm fifteen years old."

POLISH PEASANT: "You know, you're right."

When I started to see that he was thinking about it, I took off and ran away.

I never told my father about these interactions. Because whatever happened, he always blamed us—his own kids. "You shouldn't have gone there," he would say. "You shouldn't have gotten involved." That was his way. That was the culture.

It was not easy at all to be a Jew in Poland, but you just had to face it. You were reminded minute by minute that you didn't belong. The Poles hated us. All the Jews felt it—even in the good times. But I never felt inferior. I pitied them for their ignorance.

🕐 🕐 🕐

WE LIVED SIDE by side with the Poles in separate civilizations, but it was different on market days, when everyone came to buy and sell. One time, when my father sent me to the market with money to buy food for the family, I saw people standing around a guy who was playing three-card monte.[1] I watched the game closely while others played. They were losing their bets, but each time, I knew what the card was before he turned it over. I could have won.

I was a young kid and didn't understand that the other players were working with the guy who was running the game. He didn't use sleight of hand to switch the cards in those rounds, and the players were losing intentionally to trick observers like me into placing bets. Finally, I couldn't resist the opportunity. I was sure that I knew which card to choose. I put my finger on the wrong card and lost all the money.

I was so upset that our food money was gone and scared of what would happen when I told my father. I was sure that he would beat the hell out of me. But he didn't raise his voice. He didn't even get angry. He said it was worth it to lose that money if I learned my lesson not to be a gambler.

I was surprised. Usually, my father was a very nervous-type person. He was strict, impatient. Every little thing aggravated him. He always found reasons to criticize our behavior in order to make us menschen. We were all afraid of him when we were young. Many times, he hit us if we did something we shouldn't. I don't think he was always that way, and he acted differently around people outside of our family. I can understand him better now than I could when I was a kid. I'm glad he was strict because he kept us in line.

Although my father wasn't ordained as a rabbi, he was very educated in the Torah, the Talmud, and the Chassidic teachings. He was religious and refined, but not extreme in his piety. As poor as he was, he dressed nicely. His boots were always polished—shining—and his beard was trimmed. He could speak Polish well, and he read the Yiddish newspaper from Warsaw to stay informed. Most of the local Chassidim didn't do that. He was well liked, and friends used to come to *kibbitz* (chitchat) with him in the store.

Neither my father nor my stepmother had any family in Kozhnitz, but he was respected in the circle of Reb Mailekh, the Kozhnitzer Rebbe of his generation. My father was a good friend of his. Sometimes when they got together, my father brought me along, and I played with Reb Mailekh's little boy. I was about twelve years old, and he was about three or four.

My father also had prestige in the larger Jewish community, which elected him to serve as a member of the *Geminder* (Jewish council).

In each town, the Jewish population elected a Geminder that was responsible for the institutions of Jewish community life. If you were rich, you had to donate money to the Geminder so they could support the poor and take care of the synagogues, the schools, the Jewish cemetery, the *chevra kadisha* (burial service), and the *mikve* (ritual bath). The Geminder also made sure that a *shoykhet* would be in the town to slaughter animals for meat in a kosher way, and they would hire a rabbi to *paskin shaylas*—that is, give authoritative answers to questions of Jewish law that came up in daily life. For example, if someone opened a chicken and it had blisters inside, you would bring it to that rabbi to determine if it was kosher. Those routine questions were important, but that rabbi was not a spiritual leader like a Chassidic Rebbe. That was something completely different.

The Kozhnitzer Rebbes were *tzadikkim* (holy men). But they had conflicts too—and plenty.[2]

🕐 🕐 🕐

SHABBOS WAS IMPORTANT for us and was strictly observed in our community. An hour and a half before sunset on Friday night, the *shames* (caretaker of the synagogue) used to go from door to door and knock three times with his wooden hammer. That was an old tradition from earlier times when people didn't have their own clocks or watches. All the Jewish merchants would lock up their stores, run home, wash themselves, go to immerse in the *mikve,* and dress for shul to welcome the Shabbos.

On Friday nights, only the men went to shul. Our family went to the *shtiebel* (a small synagogue) of the Kozhnitzer Chassidim. Every group of Chassidim had their own little shteibel.

Our family used to sing *zmiroys* (religious songs) after dinner. It was a beautiful thing. We lived at 35 Radomska, right on the *mistraza* (walking street) where the local townspeople came to stroll in the evenings. They used to stop and listen to our songs, especially in the summertime when the windows were open. My father was famous in the town for that.

The Kozhnitzer Rebbe made a *tish* (a Chassidic community gathering for song and blessings) for his Chassidim every Friday night, after everyone had finished dinner in their own homes. My father used to bring me along to sit and listen to the Rebbe's Torah and Chassidus.

My stepmother was a good cook. When she was home, she would put a *cholent* (bean and barley stew) and a *kugel* (sweet noodle casserole) in the oven at Khamaira Salzberg's bakery to stay hot overnight because it is forbidden under Jewish law to make a fire or cook on Shabbos. When I was a child, I would run over after shul on Saturday morning to bring home the pot of food for our lunch. It was delicious. I miss that . . . even now.

After our Saturday lunch, my father quizzed each child, starting with the oldest, to see what we had learned that week and how our studies were progressing. That was difficult. You couldn't say, "I don't want to do this today." There was no such thing. The rabbi at kheder was more lenient than my father.

Then he used to sit and study Talmud by himself or sometimes with us. Usually, we had to go back to kheder on Saturday afternoon to learn until it was time to go to shul for *minkha* and *ma'ariv*, the afternoon and evening prayer services.

All of the stores had to be closed on Sunday for the Christian Sabbath. That was the law. Poland was a Catholic country, and the police enforced the Sunday closures very strictly. But some of the Jewish merchants, like my father, worked in their stores with the doors locked. Polish people from the surrounding farms and villages came to town for Sunday morning mass, and after church, they often would buy supplies at the Jewish stores or bring us a watch to fix. If they knocked on our door, we let them in.

You DIDN'T HAVE big bar mitzvah celebrations in Poland, especially in Kozhnitz, when you didn't have any money. When a boy turned thirteen, he read from the weekly portion of the Torah and the Haftarah, which is a selection from the Prophets, and after the davening was over, the family made a *kiddish*, which was a blessing over wine after the Saturday morning prayer service and was followed by a snack. That's all. I spent a long time at kheder learning a speech with a rabbi who liked me very much. It was a terrific speech with interpretations and quotes from the Talmud, but I didn't get to deliver it because my father didn't make a kiddish for the congregation.

I was shocked and disappointed. He knew about the speech I had prepared, and it hurt me deeply. He didn't say anything, and I didn't say anything. I cried about it in private.

I don't know what happened. He loved me, and he liked me. I never doubted that. Maybe he didn't have the money. Also, he was probably disturbed. My stepmother wasn't there. She was away more than at home. But I was afraid to complain. He was the only one we had. I felt sorry for him and for what had become of his life.

I didn't talk about it with my sister or Moishele or even my older brothers. I didn't want to make them hate my father. I didn't want to make myself hate him, either. I didn't hate him. I said, "*Opt knikht tsures,*" which means, "Don't need more troubles." Nobody asked about it, and that's how it was.

Kheder and public school both ended when I was fourteen. My father wanted me to continue learning in the beis medrish, where married men and teenage boys sat and studied the Talmud constantly. The older ones answered questions and gave explanations to the younger students. I didn't like it so much, and when I was fifteen, I decided that I'd had enough and stopped attending. I thought it would be better to learn a trade.

🕰 🕰 🕰

MY FATHER NEVER told us to become watchmakers or tried to teach us the trade. If we wanted to learn how to fix watches, we had to have our own initiative.

I didn't want to be a gemashmakher like my older brothers. I didn't particularly care for the trade, and my father hated it. If I wasn't going to be a Torah scholar, at least I wouldn't be a gemashmakher. Also, I figured that if I learned watchmaking, I could go to Warsaw one day and make something of myself.

In the evenings after work, my older brother Mailekh would go over to the workbench and try to take apart a watch or a clock. Moishele and I did the same thing after school, and when I stopped studying at the beis medrish, I took it upon myself to stand at my father's bench during the day and watch him work. When I asked him a question, he always answered. He noticed that I was taking an interest and let me try to fix broken alarm clocks.

I was very glad that he gave me a chance. Of course, I wasn't good at the beginning. I made mistakes and broke some parts. But he was very patient and lenient with me. He didn't yell or hit me like he usually did when I misbehaved. He corrected my errors and showed me the right way to work.

I became more confident. Whenever he left the workbench, like when he went to the shtiebel for afternoon prayers, I would sit down in his place and try to take apart a regular clock and fix it. When I succeeded, I showed it to him, and he was very pleased. Eventually, he gave me the responsibility to handle all of the clock repairs that came into the store. I'd still ask him questions when I had difficulties. Later, I started to take watches apart. He appreciated that I was trying to learn.

WHEN I USED to sit with my father in his watchmaking shop, he would give *tzedoka* (charity) to people who came into the store. That was a normal thing. Without it, you didn't feel like a mensch.

Poor people would come in to get a handout, and he used to give five or ten groshen. Also, people came in to collect money for someone else who got into tsures—somebody lost his wife or got sick and needed help with medicine or doctor bills. My father was always openhanded.

I didn't like it, to tell you the truth. There was a depression all through the 1930s, and we were living in terrible poverty. Many times, he gave away money we needed to just to buy a loaf of bread. He told me God would provide.

Fridays were the worst. On Friday evening and Saturday, it was against Jewish law to make a fire. If you didn't have food prepared before Shabbos, you wouldn't have anything to eat for that night and all the next day. We bought our *challahs* (twisted loaves of bread) from Khamaira's bakery. When it was thirty minutes before sunset and Khamaira's mother noticed that we hadn't come for our challahs, she sent them to us. We would go to the dairy store for yogurt; that was the cheapest option. All we had for Shabbos were the challahs with a little yogurt. We didn't even have any wine for kiddish, so we made the Friday night kiddish over the challahs.

That happened many times, but nobody else knew about it. We had to keep it secret. My father was too proud to let anybody give him a handout, God forbid. He wouldn't allow it. We would boil pots of water on the stove just so people would see the steam coming out of the windows and assume we were cooking for Shabbos.

On the rare occasions when my stepmother was home and we didn't have money for food, she bought on credit. This made my father jump out of his skin. He would rather fast than have debts. But my stepmother didn't care, and it made me like her more.

One Friday, we got lucky. My father had given a coin to a guy who came in asking for charity. It was the only money we had. Later, when we still had a few minutes to run out and buy something before Shabbos, a Christian guy came into the store with a watch he needed repaired right away. He didn't ask, "How much do I owe you?" Instead, he just opened his wallet and gave us two zlotys. That was an unusual thing. Nobody knew who he was, and we never saw him again. We thought that he must have been Elijah the Prophet and that God had sent him. No kidding. We used to think that way.

For the rest of my life, I resented my father's readiness to give charity to other people despite the immediate and cruel expense to our family. But it was this religious discipline and poverty that would later translate into valuable survival skills when I needed them during the war. My father's true reward for his suffering and his commitment to charity was not the two zlotys from a strange customer but rather that his four sons would survive the Shoah.

IT WAS 1933 when I finished public school and kheder—the same year Hitler came to power in Germany—and over the next year, I began to understand myself in new ways. I became cool to the Chassidic life, though to please our father, my brothers and I still put on *tfilin* (phylacteries) and davened every morning. In our house, you had to daven before you could eat. I started to attend meetings of the *Noar Hatzioni* with Khamaira Salzberg. The Noar Hatzioni was the youth group for the General Zionist organization started by Theodore Herzl. They preached diplomacy as the only way for the Jews to establish a state in *Eretz Yisroel* (the Land of Israel), which differed from Betar, the youth group of the Revisionist Zionist movement led by Zev Jabotinsky. He preached that realpolitik and military force would also be required. The General Zionists were not religious, but they liked to recruit the religious kids. We were educated and disciplined young boys and girls with strong Jewish values.

My father didn't like that I had joined the General Zionists, but he didn't oppose it strongly. We could all feel and smell how antisemitism increased in Poland with the rise of Hitler. Around

1936, the Polish government started to make antisemitism an official policy. The prime minister said in a speech that it's not nice to kill the Jews, just don't buy from them. That was his official statement in the Polish Parliament. The newspapers reported it, and they played it on the radio everywhere. People were talking about it on the street.[3] I knew that we had to get out of Poland. That was the most important thing. We thought maybe we could go to Eretz Yisroel. By the time we were eighteen, Khamaira and I had become leaders in the General Zionist organization and were training the younger ones. My older brothers and sister were already leaders in the Betar youth movement.

We knew what the Nazis were doing to the Jews in Germany. Of course, we didn't imagine how bad it would get.

$$\textŏ \quad \textŏ \quad \textŏ$$

MAILEKH AND IZAK had already moved to Warsaw by that time. They came home to visit for Passover in 1938 and told us what was going on there.

Polish university students from the Endeks Party (National Antisemitic Democratic Party) would go out in groups to attack Jews in the streets of Warsaw. They were right-wing Polish nationalists who wanted to rid Poland of the Jews, but they were not tied to the Nazis. After these attacks, the police would arrest the Jews who fought back and let the Endek students go free, without punishment.

Izak happened to be walking on the street when the Endeks were running wild through the Jewish Quarter in Warsaw. One guy came with a knife and tried to stab him in the neck. Izak grabbed that knife with his bare hand and twisted it out of the attacker's hand by force. It cut deep into Izak's whole palm, but he grabbed that Endek by the throat with the other hand and knocked his head against a gate until that guy lost consciousness. He fell down, and Izak ran away. Later, the newspaper reported that somebody had almost killed a university student and that he was lying in the hospital for several weeks with a brain concussion. If Izak had been caught, they would have killed him.

But the Passover Seder was beautiful. We read the Haggadah, and my father told stories from the *Midrash* (interpretive legends) and gave all kinds of deeper explanations. We asked questions and held terrific discussions. Every year, it felt like something new. I really miss that.

By this time, my older brothers weren't so interested in religious things. Around my father, they pretended that everything was like it had been. When he said let's daven or say a *bracha* (blessing), they joined out of respect. But inside, they didn't feel like it was necessary.

CHAPTER 3

Coming of Age in Warsaw (October 1938–September 1939)

If I am not for myself, who will be for me?
And when I am for myself only, what am I?
And if not now, when?
            —HILLEL, *Mishnah, Pirkei Avos*, 1:14

I LEFT KOZHNITZ AT NINETEEN. I wasn't a perfect watch-maker, but it was time for me to become independent—to try to get a job in Warsaw.[1] My two older brothers were already living there, so what could I lose?

My father didn't like the idea. He said that I wasn't a good enough watchmaker yet to work for someone else and that I would be back in a few days. He had told my brothers the same thing when they'd left home. It was his way to criticize us all the time. I understood that.

I was worried to leave my father alone in the store, but Moishe was already grown and was happy to be there with him.

When it was time to say goodbye, my father embraced me. I was surprised, actually. He was crying and said, "I'm losing another son." He never hugged us or showed much emotion. We used to shake hands. It hurt me so much to leave him. But I had made up my mind; I had to go, and I was glad to be taking off on my own.

In those days, it was common for religious boys to get married at seventeen or eighteen years old. But nobody my age was thinking about marriage. There was something in the air. We knew something was going on with Hitler coming to power. It was the fall of 1938, after the *Sukkes* holiday—one year before the war. I was wearing the long black Chassidic coat when I left.

My brother Mailekh was the first pioneer. He had left for Warsaw when he was nineteen and started his own business. He cut the upper parts of the shoe, sewed them, and sold them to shoemakers and shoe factories, which assembled the complete shoe. About two years after Mailekh left home, he invited my oldest brother, Izak, to join him in Warsaw, and they became partners. They managed to buy two sewing machines on credit, and they even hired two employees to help them.

Now, three years after Izak left Kozhnitz, I traveled to Warsaw on a ferry down the Vistula River. That was the cheapest way. I only had enough money to pay for my boat ticket and figured that my brothers would help me out until I found a job. And they sure did. They had an open tab in a restaurant and paid for my suppers there at the beginning.

Every day, I went around to look for work. After the first week, my brothers told me they would give me another week to find a job and start supporting myself. If not, I would have to go back home. I agreed. After another few days, they were ready to send me back. But I was stubborn, and I got a job before the end of that second week.

I didn't want to work with my brothers. I could see they weren't doing so well. They were supporting themselves, and they had a book of business, but their customers weren't paying. Each month was a struggle to collect even a small amount of what they were owed. Those were hard times in Poland. The Depression was still going on.

Mailekh and Izak lived together in a one-room place. They worked on their shoemaking machines in the kitchen and slept on a field cot that they folded up in the morning. There wasn't room for me. They hardly had room for themselves.

At that time, my cousin Khayala from Kozhnitz was living in Warsaw, too, and she took me in. I told her it would be just for a few days until I got a job. She wasn't married yet, and her mother and brother were staying with her, too. I slept with her brother in one field cot. After a short time, her mother decided to return to Kozhnitz with the brother, and Khayala told me I had to leave. It wouldn't have been proper for me to live alone in an apartment with a single woman. I saw a room in the paper for two zlotys a week. For me, it was a *metsiye* (bargain). It was in a very bad neighborhood, but who cared about the neighborhood? The landlord was a Jewish guy. After asking me a few questions, he said, "Listen, from talking to you and looking at you, you're not the material that belongs here." I asked why, and he replied, "It's enough that I tell you. Don't do it. I'm telling you as a friend." I persisted, and finally, he agreed to rent to me.

I didn't know what he was talking about. I was naïve. It turned out that was the place where all the whores stood on the corners, even his own daughters! When I came in, the girls tried to proposition me. Well, I didn't like it, and I stayed away from them.

The landlord and his wife had rakhmunes on me. He told me right away to stay away from the girls. I told him that I had never had sex in my life and didn't have it in my mind to chase after such things. I needed work just to buy food for myself.

Anyway, I didn't stay there long.

The first job I found was in a jewelry store. They hired me as a replacement for another guy who had left after a misunderstanding with the boss.

The boss didn't want me to use a Jewish name in the store, and he decided to call me Kheniek, which was a regular Polish name. Jewish people in the big cities like Warsaw took Polish names to assimilate. So, I began to use the name Kheniek in business.

When I met people privately, though, I used my real name: Khil or Khilik, which is a Yiddish variation with a little flavor of Polish.

I was relieved to finally have a job. But after just one week, they told me I had to leave. The guy I replaced had worked there for many years, and he had a poor mother to support. He came begging for his job with tears in his eyes, and the boss couldn't refuse him. The boss sent me away with some encouraging words, saying that I did good work for him and that he would do what he could to help.

That first job made me believe in myself. The salary for that week wasn't much, but I had tasted that first little bit of money and independence. I resolved to stay in Warsaw no matter what. I went around to watchmakers day after day, but I still couldn't find a job. Then I saw an ad in the paper for a sleeper in a jewelry store on the Shendlet, which was a beautiful neighborhood in Warsaw.

Most of the jewelry stores had someone sleeping there for security. The sleeper could pull the alarm if something happened, and the police would come running. They didn't have automatic alarms in those days. Burglars paid attention and would not break in if they knew somebody was in the store. Either the owners slept in the store themselves or they had to pay someone to be a sleeper.

It wasn't considered a nice job. It was a job you looked for when you didn't have another way to live. But for me, being a sleeper was a good opportunity. During the day, I could pick up watch work that I could do at night while I was locked up in the store.

I went to that jewelry store and met the owner, Mr. Auerbach. He called my boss from the first job for a reference, and that guy gave me a good recommendation. Auerbach offered to hire me for ten zlotys a month. I would have to come into the store at 7:00 P.M., when it closed, and stay overnight until 9:00 A.M., when the store was opened. I couldn't go out of the store during that time, and I had to polish the floor by hand with paste wax before they opened in the morning.

I agreed to everything. I also told him I was a watchmaker and asked if I could use his workbench to fix watches while I was locked up in the store at night. He said, "Oh, you're a watchmaker. I'll do better than that. I'll hire you as a watchmaker to help my store manager. I'll give you dinner every day. You'll come to my house, where I live. Breakfast and lunch you'll have to manage on your own, but dinner you'll get from me."

We made an agreement, and it worked out. He didn't pay me much, but the Auerbachs were beautiful people. When his wife gave me dinner every day, she saw that I was hungry and anxious to eat, and she always gave me another portion. I was very much impressed by her generosity.

Auerbach was also the president of the watchmakers' organization in Warsaw. I hadn't known that before. Can you imagine? If I could say that I worked for him, anybody would hire me or give me watch work because he was so well-known.

I couldn't have been happier. Things were going my way for about six weeks. Then Auerbach sold his store, and I had to move on.

🕐 🕐 🕐

ANOTHER JEWELRY STORE put an ad in the paper for a sleeper. When I got there, I talked a little bit with the salesgirl, and she said, "You know something? I think Mr. Weiss will like you." Then a man walked in, and she introduced me.

His name was Khil Weiss, and I had met him at Auerbach's many times. He was the secretary of the watchmakers' trade organization, and when I saw him, I felt ashamed that I was asking for a sleeper job. Weiss apparently knew all about me already— who I was and what I was. He knew my name, too. He said, "Kheniek, you want to sleep? You got it. Everybody else who works as a sleeper has to be locked up from 7:00 P.M., when we close the store. But you don't have to come until later because I know you. You'll get your own set of keys, and I want you to be in the store by 11:00 P.M. until we open at 8:00 in the morning. Saturday night, I'll give you two hours extra so you can go out to a show or something. You won't need to be in the store until 1:00 A.M." I hadn't even thought about going to shows. He was speaking to me like someone he had known for years.

He offered ten zlotys a month, the same that Auerbach had paid me, and his watchmaking bench and tools would be open to me in the evening. Having a place where I could sit and fix watches at night was my biggest treasure. The community already knew me a little bit, so other jewelry stores gave me watch work. With that arrangement, I could exist financially on my own. Not to live well, but to get by.

Weiss's store didn't have a name. The sign just said JEWELRY STORE. They didn't want to advertise a Jewish name because then the goyim wouldn't come in. Especially in that neighborhood. It was on Bednarski Street, close to the Krakowska, a very beautiful neighborhood where all the consulates were located.

⏱ ⏱ ⏱

MEANWHILE, I GOT a day job working at a wholesale store that sold watch parts to all the watchmakers in Warsaw. It was a big, beautiful store packed with merchandise. The owner, Levinson, contacted me through my brothers. He had heard about me from the guy who hired me for the first job and fired me a week later. The job was to sell materials and fix watches when the store wasn't busy. He asked how much I wanted per week. Before, I had been paid so little, so I asked for twenty zlotys. We agreed on eighteen.

Eighteen zlotys per week was enough for me to live on while I was sleeping at Weiss's store, but it wasn't enough to rent my own place. The price for a decent dinner at that time was one zloty. Rent was much higher.

But the salary didn't matter. Why? There were only three stores that supplied watch parts, so all the watchmakers in Warsaw had to come to Levinson's store. When they'd see me there, I'd ask them for watch repair work to do at night. Soon, all the watchmakers knew me. I was lucky to get that job. I never dreamt that I'd be able to work for Levinson. He was too *groyse artik* (distinguished).

The second week on the job, a terrible tragedy occurred. Levinson's son went for a Sunday outing with his girlfriend, and a tree fell on them during a thunderstorm. She was injured, and it smashed his brain—*nebekh* (such a pity). He was in the hospital for several days, and then he died. That's all the family Levinson had. His wife had passed away years before. Levinson's son was a terrific boy. He had finished university—that was a big deal in those days—and was in the business, too.

I cried. They were such good people.

When his son died, Levinson needed me much more. He raised my salary to twenty zlotys a week and started to treat me almost like a son.

🕑 🕑 🕑

I DIDN'T HAVE much time to spend with my brothers. Sometimes I would visit them on a Sunday, but that's about it. They would go out at night and meet people, but I was too young to be invited into their circle of friends. They were already in their mid-twenties; I was only nineteen.

One Sunday, about three weeks before the war broke out, I decided to go swimming in the Vistula, a river that runs through the city, and I broke my ankle. I didn't have a friend with me and there were no public telephones, so I flagged down the first empty *droshke* (horse-drawn carriage). The driver helped me get in, and suddenly I realized, *My gosh, I don't have a home where I can go lay down.* I couldn't be at Weiss's store during the day. Then I remembered that Weiss's wife and his son had gone on vacation and that Weiss was staying by himself in the room they rented from another family on Bednarski Street. So, I told the coachman to take me there.

Weiss wasn't home. Adela, the salesgirl who had told Weiss to hire me as a sleeper, answered the door and invited me in. Her family lived there and rented a room to the Weiss family. Adela took me to Weiss's room and put me in his bed. I was in terrible pain. When Weiss came home, he was very gracious and invited me to stay with him for a few weeks until his wife and son returned from vacation.

Adela introduced me to her parents and her younger sister, Lola, who were all living in the apartment. They had a phone, and I was able to contact my brothers by calling the store next to their apartment. My brothers didn't have a phone; only rich people had phones in their homes.

The next morning, Mailekh came with a droshke and took me to a hospital. I had health insurance from my job at Levinson's—there was a law that companies had to insure their employees for health—so the hospital didn't cost me anything. The hospital took an x-ray and diagnosed that my ankle was fractured. The nurses put my leg in a cast up to the knee and gave me crutches. Then I went back to Weiss's place and called Mr. Levinson.

Levinson told me to take a week off, until the cast came off. I told him that even if I had to take a droshke, I would come to work. He said, "Listen, I like that idea. You'll come in a droshke, and I'll pay the fare."

I got to work that first day around lunchtime. When I arrived at the store, Levinson called me over and invited me to join him for lunch. That had never happened to me before. He took me to a first-class restaurant and ordered the same thing for me that he ordered for himself. I had never eaten such good food. It was not a kosher place. He wasn't a religious guy, but he had a Jewish heart.

And that's how it continued. Every day, Levinson paid for a coach to bring me to and from work, and he took me out for lunch. Other people would have stayed in bed, but I came. I couldn't stand behind the counter and wait on customers, but I could sit by the watchmaker's bench and put in a jewel, which

Levinson's son had taught me how to do before he died.[2] Levinson's store was the only place in Warsaw that had the equipment to find the right-sized jewel and set it in the watch. It was precision work, and you had to be careful or you could easily break a jewel. So, I was a big help for Levinson's customers even with my broken ankle. My father didn't give me that kind of work in Kozhnitz. When he saw that a jewel was broken, he became nervous. He didn't have real jewels, so he had to improvise with the material that was available to him. He would make a replacement jewel from a little, round piece of brass. He drilled a small hole, put it in like a jewel would be set, and the watch would run. My father was a highly skilled watchmaker. Of course, the brass wore out faster than a real jewel.

In Warsaw, we didn't have to make our own "jewels" from brass. Levinson had Swiss jewels made from glass, which were much cheaper than jewels made from rubies. He charged a zloty and a half to put in a glass jewel.

All because I broke my ankle, I became closer with both Weiss and Levinson and learned more about watchmaking. That was a blessing. I'm telling you, I had *mazel* (luck).

⏱ ⏱ ⏱

ONE FRIDAY, I was at the store with Mr. Levinson when we heard over the radio that the German army had crossed the Polish border and was on its way to Warsaw. It was September 1, 1939.

The year before, Germany had taken over Austria and Czechoslovakia,[3] and the world hadn't done anything. If the other world powers had stopped Hitler then, there wouldn't have been a war at all. We had heard that the British and French were still trying to negotiate with Hitler. Just then, we saw planes cruising over the skies. Everyone thought they were our Polish planes. We were mistaken.

The Germans dropped the first bombs on Pilsudski Street, where Levinson's store was located. It was the most exclusive neighborhood in Warsaw. The high government officials and Polish royalty lived there. It was not a Jewish area.

At noon, they dropped bombs on a primary school and killed fifty-six young children. We knew then that the war was on. Schools and hospitals in Warsaw had the Red Cross painted on the roof so an enemy would know that those places could not be bombed. That was one of the laws according to the Geneva Convention. Hitler, that dog, didn't obey those laws at all.

We all waited in Levinson's store for the rest of the day. In the evening, I took a droshke back to Weiss's house. His wife was still on vacation, but she came back about two days later, and I started sleeping in their second store. Another watchmaker used to sleep there, a Jewish guy, but he was a Polish soldier and had been mobilized to fight in the war. I never saw him again.

At that time, Polish boys were drafted to the army at age eighteen if they were physically capable. I didn't have to join the army because that hadn't been the law when I'd turned eighteen two years before.

For the next two days, the Germans bombed Warsaw constantly. Nobody could go outside. Everybody was crying and scared to death about what would happen to the Jews. We had heard what they were doing to the Jews in Austria and Czechoslovakia.

One night, the Germans firebombed the building where Izak and Mailekh lived. My brothers ran outside in the middle of the night and came to me in their underwear. The next day, I took out money that I had saved up from my sleeper salary and gave it to them to buy new clothes. Everything they owned had been burned up—completely destroyed.

🕰 🕰 🕰

THE GERMANS MARCHED into Poland with tanks and motorized armies. Within a week, they took over all of western Poland, except for Warsaw. Overall, the Polish army was no match for the Germans. However, Warsaw was the only place where the Polish army was prepared with heavy artillery, and they held back the German invaders. We heard on the radio that the Germans were occupying the suburbs outside of Warsaw and had completely surrounded the city. Warsaw was *baleygert* (under siege) and fighting.[4]

By the third day, the Germans had destroyed the machinery that delivered water to the houses. They had also bombed the electric company machinery and the gas distribution system. There was no running water, no electricity, no gas. Nothing. Warsaw was in flames.

People didn't know where to go. Many went down to their basements, but that was a big mistake. When a bomb fell, the whole building collapsed on top of them. Nobody could get them out.

I was the only one besides Levinson who came to work at his store during that time. Bombs were falling in the streets, shrapnel was flying, and I went to work by foot! We couldn't even get a droshke in those days. Levinson scolded me: "Kheniek, why did you do that? You could have been killed!" I said, "You're too good to me that I should let you stay alone." I could tell he appreciated that.

Then suddenly, Russia invaded Poland from the east side. That's when we found out about the secret Molotov-Ribbentrop Pact between Hitler and Stalin to invade Poland from opposite sides and divide the country between Germany and Russia. Everyone was so surprised that communism and fascism would join together in the war. The siege of Warsaw continued for four weeks. Finally, the Polish government surrendered on October 1, 1939, and the Germans marched in.

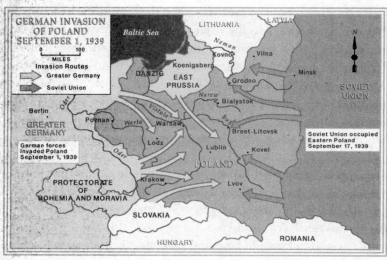

In August 1939, the Germans and the Russians signed the Molotov-Ribbentrop Pact, which divided Poland between them, setting the stage for the German army to invade Poland from the West on September 1, 1939, and the Soviet army to invade Poland from the East on September 17, 1939. The invasions ended with Germany occupying western Poland and the Russians occupying eastern Poland. The border between them was the Bug River.[5]

CHAPTER 4

German Occupation and the Warsaw Ghetto (October 1939–May 1941)

Nobody had any food, and we hardly had any water when the German army marched into Warsaw. I was on my way to Levinson's store that morning when I saw people walking with bread. A Polish guy told me where the Germans were giving it out. When I came to the place, there were two trucks and people standing in a long, long line. I'm telling you, the line went for two and a half miles (four kilometers)!

I got in the line, and just a few minutes later there was already a long line of people behind me. It took about six or seven hours until I got close to those trucks. All the while, I prayed that they would still have bread when I got to the front of the line. When I finally came up to the truck, the German soldier bent down to get bread for me, and the Polish guy who was standing behind me in that six-hour line pointed at me and yelled, "Jude, Jude, Jude."

When that German heard the word *Jude,* he threw down the bread and reached for his rifle on the floor of the truck. I didn't wait to see what he was planning to do. I ran away in a zigzag and prayed to God. I heard one shot and kept running.

This happened in the Polish neighborhood where I worked. Jewish people didn't live there. I don't know if I could have passed for being Polish in the eyes of that German soldier, but that lousy antisemite Pole behind me could tell that I was a Jew. I was surprised. I imagined that the German aggressors were the common enemy of the Jews and the Poles. This was the first incident showing me that, in this war, the Jews were going to be treated as the common enemy of the Germans and the Poles. I heard later that German soldiers had killed quite a few Jews that day just for trying to get a loaf of bread.

⏱ ⏱ ⏱

THE GERMANS STARTED to issue laws against the Jews on the second or third day after they entered Warsaw. All Jewish bank accounts would be frozen, and withdrawals were limited to one hundred zlotys. Any Jew who had more than one hundred zlotys in his possession had to surrender the money. Any Jew who was caught with more than one hundred zlotys would be shot.

Jews could not have radios. We couldn't have gold or silver or any valuables. We couldn't have any coffee. The Jews had to give up everything they owned.

About a week later, the Germans issued a new order that all the Jews had to wear a white armband on their left arm. It had to be ten centimeters wide with a blue Jewish star. They hung up notices on walls and broadcast it over the radio. The notices said that whoever was caught on the street or in his house without the armband—man, woman, or child, no matter what age—would be shot dead immediately. We heard about this over the radio in Weiss's store, where I was sleeping. Not many people still had radios at that time.

In the beginning, we rushed to cut a piece of linen and drew a star on it with a piece of crayon. Later, Jewish factories started to produce armbands made from plastic or linen with the star made from blue tape.

These laws were only for the Jews.

Despite the laws, people didn't surrender all their money. They tried to hide it. So the Germans used to go around and search Jewish homes in the middle of the night. They called that an *"aktzion."* Three or four of them would come in with their guns. You jumped out of bed, and they lined you up with your face to the wall. If they found things like money or jewelry that you were supposed to have surrendered, they would confiscate it, and maybe they would take one or more people from your family and kill them right in front of you. They made a lot of aktzions and killed a lot of Jews.

🕐 🕐 🕐

GERMAN GENDARMES (MILITARY police) would be out on the road with their motorbikes and would stop streetcars to grab Jews for work. If you tried to resist, they beat you up. If you started to run, they would shoot you on the spot. That's how it was every single day.

One morning, several weeks after the Germans entered Warsaw, they grabbed me off the streetcar in the Jewish Quarter. I had to wait while they grabbed more and more men. All of us were about eighteen to thirty-five years old. Then they brought trucks and took us to the Polish Parliament building on Pilsudski Street, which was far away from the Jewish area.

With bayonets on their rifles, they marched us into the building at about 9:00 A.M. and told us to line up with our faces to the wall. We stood waiting like that for hours. We had to be completely silent with our hands down and our heads back. I couldn't even raise my hand to wipe my nose. Behind me was another row of Jewish men and more rows behind them. We heard each new group of people line up as they arrived.

When the guards came and hit your shoulder with a wooden nightstick, you had to turn around and follow them. When they finally hit my shoulder at about 1:00 P.M., I turned around and saw about four hundred Jews standing against the wall.

The guards walked me down the hall and led me into a room, where three SS men in their late twenties or early thirties were drinking beer. One sat by a typewriter facing me. One of the others pushed me and told me to stand in front of the table.

The guy with the typewriter asked for my *ausweis* (ID card). He looked at my photo and started to ask me questions. "What is your name? How do you spell it? How old are you? Where do you live?" I answered him with the same information that was on the ID card.

The ID card had my old address from when I was sleeping at Auerbach's store before the war. That building had been completely bombed out by German planes and was not in a part of the city where Jews lived. But I had never gotten a new ID with my new address at Weiss's store. I figured the Germans wouldn't know which addresses had been bombed and which were not in the Jewish Quarter. Inside, my heart was beating hard with fear. It was a dangerous risk.

After I answered all the questions and he finished typing everything, one of the others came over—a big tall guy. He put his hand in my hair and said, "You have beautiful hair." Then he picked me up by the hair, raised me up toward the ceiling, and dropped me. I was able to land on my feet.

Then the two guys took turns punching me in the face—a few hits from one side, then a few hits from the other. Several times, they repeated it. I felt blood rolling down my face. Then one of them threw my passport to the ceiling toward me. I knew instinctively that I had to catch it, that if it fell on the floor and I bent down, they'd start to kick me with their heavy boots and beat me to death. My mind was still clear.

So I clapped on that ID with two hands to catch it before it fell. They picked me up and threw me down a second time, and again I landed on my feet. Then they punched me several more times in my eyes and my head. Finally, they said, "You can go now, but tomorrow you have to come here at 8:00 A.M. for work. You'll be working here for sixty days." And I said, "Yes, sir!"

Then one of them grabbed my hair and pulled me along. I was walking backward after him until he stopped and left me standing there with my face against the wall. I thought, *Thank God I'm still alive.*

Blood was still flowing from my eyes and nose. When the SS guy had walked far enough away that I couldn't hear him anymore, I glanced to my sides, and standing there were all the Jews who had already been interrogated, blood running from their mouths, noses, ears, and other parts of their bodies. Some of them had their teeth knocked out. It scared me to death! I didn't know how bad I was. I started to touch my face. Everything was still in its place—not so much blood. I saw that I was lucky compared to the others.

I decided right then that I wasn't going to return to that place for work. We stood there for another several hours, and at about 5:00 P.M., they marched us out of the building. Before they let us go, they reminded us that we needed to report back the next morning. They said, "We have your addresses. We have your names. If you don't show up, know for sure that you won't be alive the next day."

I went back to Weiss's store and looked at my swollen, bloody face in the mirror. Some of the blood had already dried. I washed up and sat down with Mr. Weiss to tell him what happened and that I wasn't going back. This could have been a dangerous situation for Weiss, too, if the Germans came searching for me in his store.

It took me about three days to recover. I was scared to go outside, but I was still going to work every day. Every night I slept at a different place, just in case they were searching for me. I stayed with friends. I also stayed with Izak, who was living with his girlfriend's family.

Levinson wasn't worried about my situation because I couldn't be traced to his watch parts store through any government records.

I asked around, and people told me that the Germans had ways to find me if they wanted. If I were somebody important, they could call the Polish police and start to investigate. But I was nothing to them—just a worker who didn't show up. They could easily grab another Jew off the street to replace me.

I lived in fear like this for about six or seven weeks. Then I heard that the whole division of German soldiers who were stationed in the Parliament building had been shipped out of Warsaw. After that, I became more relaxed.

I wondered where those soldiers went, but I didn't look into it. I didn't try to find out about other kinds of things that were going on, either. I felt that the more information I'd get, the worse off I'd be.

Looking back on it now, it's unbelievable what happened in that room in the Parliament building. If a Polish guy wanted to beat up a Jew, he would yell at you first. He would call you "dirty Jew" or "Christ killer" or something like that. He would beat you only after he made himself angry. But those German guys were not even angry. They didn't call me a dirty Jew or any other name. They were completely without emotion, without rakhmunes, without anything. Even when they saw the blood on me, it didn't affect them. It was just their job, and they were enjoying it. The guy at the typewriter had been laughing. For him, it was entertainment, a comedy. They were doing those beatings the whole day, one after another. I don't know if those same guys were beating people all day long. Maybe they worked in shifts to beat Jews.

Their violence was combined with bureaucracy to the last detail. They were such capable murderers, yet everything had to be perfectly in order. All of us were wondering how this was possible.

⏱ ⏱ ⏱

I WENT BACK to sleeping at Weiss's store. During the day, his family lived and cooked their meals in the room behind the store and often invited me to join them. He had money, so they lived a little better than I did, but it wasn't a groyse artik dinner.

It was rice with a little fried onion or something like that. It helped me a lot.

Lola, the younger sister of the salesgirl whose house I lived in with Weiss, started to try to become close with me. I didn't have this in my mind at all, but she was a good-looking girl and it was convenient to be accepted by her family. They used to invite me for meals, too.

We used to go out for walks. Sometimes we would kiss, but that was all. I didn't want to get too close. I didn't promise her anything. We didn't talk about a future together. We just tried to get by for the time being. That's how our lives were.

Then Weiss went out of business, and both his store and my sleeping job were finished. He left Lola's family's apartment, but Lola's family invited me to stay. They didn't have a separate room for me, so I slept on a field cot in their dining room. I folded it up and put it away every morning.

In October 1940, the Germans issued an order that all Jews had to move into the Ghetto. The area was about twenty or twenty-five city blocks—mostly in the Jewish Quarter of the city. It was sudden—no advance notice.

Mailekh left Warsaw for Kozhnitz right away. At that time, Jews could still use the public transportation system to travel to other cities. I gave him money to buy a bus ticket and told him to leave while it was still possible. I stayed because I had a job working for Levinson. Izak stayed because he had a girlfriend and lived with her family.

All Jewish businesses were banned from areas outside the Ghetto. Levinson had to give up his store on Pilsudski Street. I remember standing in the dark, packing his merchandise in boxes, pushing whatever we could into a rented coach to bring to his house in the Ghetto.

In the Ghetto, Levinson rented a store, and I continued to work for him. He tried to help me as much as he could, paying money to the *Judenrat* (Jewish council) for me to have papers saying that I had an important job so the Germans shouldn't grab me off the street. Levinson didn't make much money after the war started. Bullets were flying, and very few people came to buy watch materials. But he had money. I imagine he withdrew it before they froze all the Jewish bank accounts.

Lola's family had to move out of the apartment they owned because it was in a Christian neighborhood. They lost everything and got nothing! Not a single zloty.

They rented a two-room apartment in the Ghetto and invited me to live with them. The parents and the two girls, Adela and Lola, slept in one room, and I stayed in the other. We had running water and toilet facilities and electricity. This sounds normal now, but it was a rare thing in the Ghetto. It was common for three or four families to be crowded into one apartment. People took shifts through the night just to be able to lay down and sleep.

I paid Lola's family rent in the Ghetto. Her mother tried to refuse, but I insisted. I knew how a zloty could help them, too, and I had my salary from Levinson.

⏱ ⏱ ⏱

WHEN THEY FIRST pushed all the Jews into the Ghetto, Jews could travel all over Warsaw. We could travel on streetcars. We just had to be in the Ghetto before the curfew at nightfall. After curfew, everybody had to be off the streets all over the city.

They built a brick wall around the Ghetto, with barbed wire on top. Three circles of police guarded those walls. On the inside, there were Jewish police. Outside the wall were Polish police, and German SS patrolled a circle around the Polish police. At each gate to enter and leave the Ghetto, approximately four German military police stood guard, day and night.

German soldiers also patrolled inside the Ghetto. There was a law that you had to take off your hat when you saw a German. When I walked on the streets, that was always the top thing on my mind. If you messed up and didn't take off your hat, that German could come up and hit you. If he was a killer, he might kill you. Nobody would accuse him of doing something wrong.

The main day-to-day security inside the Ghetto was in the hands of the Jewish police, who had dark blue uniforms with a Jewish star. People were scared of them, too. They were paid and controlled by the Judenrat, which was controlled by the Germans. Before the war, the Jewish community in each town had a Geminder registered with the Polish government to provide social services. The Germans took complete control over the Geminder in Warsaw and renamed it the Judenrat. They wanted a cooperative Jewish authority to carry out their policies in an orderly way. It was a big organization and was responsible for taking care of all the basic services in the Ghetto.

Adam Czerniaków, the president of the Judenrat, was the most important personality in the Ghetto. Everybody talked about him. We believed that Czerniaków tried to refuse that job, but he was forced to take it. Later, he committed suicide in the Ghetto.[1]

I didn't have any interactions with the Jewish police or the Judenrat, except for the employment tax that Levinson paid for me. I always tried to keep quiet and not to be noticed. If you became popular, you were sure to end up dead. I went to work and came home. That's all. I avoided talking to anybody I didn't know because the Germans had recruited Jewish spies to work for them in exchange for things they needed, like bread or medicine. The Germans killed the spies later, just like the other Jews.

When they sealed the Ghetto in November 1940, they would shoot any Jew who was caught outside the Ghetto without a permit from the German military authority. It was very difficult to get a permit to go in and out of the Ghetto. I didn't know anybody who had one.

IZAK CAME TO me one Saturday evening, thirty minutes before the curfew, to tell me he was getting married that same night. He wanted me at the wedding, but I wouldn't have been able to come back afterward because of the curfew. It was too late to arrange somewhere else to sleep, so I couldn't go. He understood. Life was already completely different. We didn't live normally.

It was the fall of 1940, maybe a week after the Germans issued the law forcing all the Jews of Warsaw into the Ghetto.

Izak's bride was a very fine girl, from a nice family, too. Her father owned a shoe factory, which was in his house, and he had about fifteen employees. Izak used to sell him the upper parts for shoes. That's how he met her. Izak lived with her family, and I sometimes visited them. I had gotten to know her very well, but I can no longer remember her name.

About three weeks after he got married, Izak decided to go to the Russian side of Poland. I wanted to go with him, even though I had a job. But he wanted to go alone and check out the situation. If he saw that it was good, he was going to come back to get his wife and me. He was afraid they would close the border crossing at the River Bug and we wouldn't be able to get out, so he had to move fast.

A lot of Jews were fleeing across the border to the Russian side of Poland. Polish people could live on one side of the border and commute back and forth to work on the other side. Germany and Russia were allies at that time, and they cooperated at the border.

For Jews, it was still possible to cross the border, but it wasn't legal and it wasn't easy to get there. First, you had to smuggle yourself out of the Ghetto. Then you had to get to the train out of Warsaw. If you didn't get caught on the train and you made it to the border, the Germans were not so strict there. They looked away, you walked across the bridge, and suddenly, you were in Russia.

Maybe a week after Izak left, they issued a new law that Jews couldn't travel on trains anymore without a travel permit from the German authorities. He wrote to his wife that he couldn't return to the German zone but that she should try to get out.

Levinson still had a phone in his store, and somehow, Izak's wife called to tell me she was going to leave.

I decided not to go with her. The risk was too high, and I wanted to go home to my family in Kozhnitz. If I went to Russia, I might never see them again. Also, I still had a job with Levinson. It was a lucky and rare thing to have a job in the Ghetto. I felt that I should continue to work as long as I could.

Izak's wife took a big risk and left by herself. It was winter 1941, and the Ghetto was already sealed. She had to smuggle herself out of the Ghetto, travel on foot through the forests in German-occupied Poland, and cross the border. Izak knew she was coming, but she didn't arrive. We never saw her again or found out what happened to her.

We had no idea what happened to Izak, either. All we knew was that he was in Russia. We heard rumors that the Russians were rounding up Jews who had escaped from the German side and sending them to Siberia. We figured that Izak was probably there.

🕐 🕐 🕐

WE WERE LIVING under terrible pressure. The only thing we talked about and hoped and prayed for was that the war would end. And food.

Food in the Ghetto was rationed. Under the law, you couldn't have food supplies for more than three days, and any additional food that you accumulated would be confiscated.

Everyone had to register with the Judenrat, and each person got a ration card every month. The Judenrat called that ration card the "bonus." The lyrics of a popular song in the Ghetto said that if you died, you had to give away the bonus. It became a joke. Instead of saying someone died, you said, "He gave away the bonus." There were a lot of jokes, but I can't remember them. No matter how bad it was, we still had a little humor to tell a joke and share a smile.[2]

The bonus card gave a monthly ration for each member of a family, consisting of half a loaf of bread (1.1 pounds or 0.5 kilo) and some other basic food items. You couldn't survive on that. Bread was a luxury in the Ghetto. Before the war, you could buy a 2.2 pound (1 kilo) loaf of bread for forty or fifty groshen (about US 10¢ at the time, which was roughly equivalent to $1.76 in 2018). But in the Ghetto, the price for a loaf of bread on the black market was about 25 zlotys (US $5 at the time, which was roughly equivalent to US $88.00 in 2018).

Usually, people didn't eat bread. Instead, we ate turnips, potatoes, or onions, which were cheaper. A typical meal was potatoes fried with a little onion and a bit of oil. Then you boiled it in water, and it was a soup. If you also had flour to mix with the potatoes, you could make noodles. The people who had that were lucky.

I never saw meat. We never talked about meat. There were no rations for that, and nobody could afford to buy it. There were no animals for meat in the Ghetto. The only thing that you could slaughter was a horse that belonged to somebody who was lucky enough to still have a live horse. But first of all, a Jew cannot eat horse meat. And second, the owner of the horse would kill you before you killed that horse!

My weight was going down and down and down. And I was one of the lucky ones. I had meals every day—potatoes and water. Soups! I lived and worked with rich people. I didn't eat what they ate, but they helped me. I felt that God was giving me mazel and opportunities. My father taught me that the word *mazel* (מזל) (Hebrew for "luck") is an acrostic. The first letter, מ (M), stands for the word מקום (*makom*), which is Hebrew for "place." The second letter, ז (z), stands for the word זמן (*zman*), which is Hebrew for "time." And the final letter, ל (L), stands for the word לימוד (*limud*), which is Hebrew for "study" or "learning." So, the deeper meaning of *mazel* is: to be in the right place at the right time, and to understand the opportunity and how to act on it. I developed confidence that I could get by in this world, even as the Germans were trying to destroy my world of Jews and Jewish values. The little bit of money that I had saved up and my salary from Levinson was enough for me to get by. I didn't live groyse artik, but I was not starving to death like other people.

People played music on the Ghetto streets to earn a few pennies to buy something to eat. That stopped later, when things got worse and nobody had money to give.

The first victims of starvation were the poor people who didn't have money to pay the high prices for food on the black market. The streets were lined with people who were half dead and already dead from hunger. The ones who were still alive were sitting and lying on the sidewalks, praying and begging that somebody would give them something to eat. More and more people died every day.

One day, I came upon an elderly woman sitting on the street, more dead than alive, her feet swollen with pus. She was crying and could hardly speak. As I walked by, I heard her soft, weak voice: "Please, somebody have rakhmunes. Give me something to eat. I'm dying."

I had a piece of hard candy in my pocket. Candy was easy to come by in the Ghetto. Most of the candy makers had been in the Jewish Quarter, and when the Germans started to confiscate everything, the candy factories opened their doors and told people to come fill their pockets. I had grabbed a lot of candy.

I bent down and placed a candy to her mouth, and at that same moment, she died with that piece of candy sticking on her lips, her eyes looking up at me, frozen in an expression of gratitude as the soul left her body.

Every evening around six o'clock, the Judenrat workers came to pick up the bodies. People died on the streets, and others brought out corpses from their houses. I saw how the workers piled up the bodies onto those little wagons. Then they took them in horse-drawn vans to the cemetery. I didn't see it, but I heard that they threw all the bodies into one mass grave. We didn't know how lucky they were, that they still had the honor of being buried.

⏱ ⏱ ⏱

EACH DAY, WE lived on the hope that maybe tomorrow would be better. We knew something was not right; they grabbed people off the street constantly, and when a person was taken away, we never heard from him again. Not me, but other people had a father or son who was taken away. You figured that if a person is alive, somehow he will send you a message. The mail was still working. We could send a letter to anywhere in Poland or Germany. Maybe the letter was censored, but it was delivered.

My father wrote me letters in Warsaw. In the beginning, I would receive a letter from him every week. We only wrote simple, permitted messages like, "I hope everything is all right with you, I'm well, I have enough to eat," and things like that. Even if it wasn't true. We didn't talk about politics or any of the bad things that were happening. We had to be careful because they would open the letters. Even a Yiddish letter could have been read by the censors. But somehow, we were able to communicate.

My father had information about what was going on in Warsaw, and he wrote me to do whatever I could to get out of the Ghetto and come back to Kozhnitz because the longer I stayed, the worse it would be. Still, he left it up to me to decide. I was lucky to have a place to run to. Most people didn't have anywhere to go, even if they could escape.

Things were getting tighter and tighter. Escape from the Ghetto was a suicide mission. Levinson also advised me to go. His business had gotten too difficult in the Ghetto, and he couldn't employ me anymore, but he gave me five hundred zlotys to pay a guy who could organize an escape with forged travel papers. If it worked, it worked. If not, I would die. But I was willing to take the chance to be together with my family. Levinson didn't have to give me that five hundred zlotys. It was a fortune.

I found a guy who was smuggling Jews out of the Ghetto and taking them to Radom, which was very close to Kozhnitz. His price included the passport, a permit to travel outside of the

Ghetto, and all the logistical arrangements. I don't know how he did it. There were a few of them who worked together—Jewish guys who got things done, *makhers*. I paid him that five hundred zlotys and prayed to God that I was doing the right thing.

The makher chose his clients based on the ages on the passports he had access to. The passport he gave me was for a watchmaker with a date of birth in 1920. I was born in 1919, so it was perfect. My new passport had someone else's name and fingerprint, but no photo. I had to memorize the new name, birth date, occupation, and city of birth.

I sewed my real passport into the lining of my overcoat behind a heavy pocket so no one would notice it. I needed my real passport for when I got back to Kozhnitz. Everyone knew me there, and I couldn't live under a false name.

The plan was to jump over the Ghetto wall that same night. I had to be at a certain place in the Ghetto at 7:00 P.M., just before curfew, and wait there. One of those makhers would then guide a group of us over to the other side. In the morning, a coach would take us to the railroad station, where we could use the travel permit to buy a ticket to Radom.

I didn't know if I could trust the makher, but that was my only chance to escape. I said goodbye to Levinson and told Lola I was going to leave that day. Later, I would learn that he had gotten remarried in the Ghetto. At least he was not alone. Levinson did not survive the war.

When I came to the designated address that evening, we were a group of seven—two women and five men, including me and the makher. We stayed inside until the middle of the night, when the makher told us to move. He had bribed the Jewish police patrolling inside the Ghetto and the Polish police who were guarding outside the wall.

The makher was with us the whole time, and he instructed us what to do. We had to climb over barbed wire in one corner of the Ghetto on Krolewska Street, where it was dark and overgrown with trees. Each of us had to jump over the wall at that

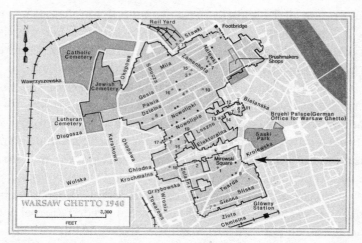

*The border at Krolewska Street in the lower right (southeast)
section of this map was the meeting place and point of escape
from the Warsaw Ghetto at the end of May 1941.*

spot. On the other side, we had to hide inside a bombed-out building across the street. I went first. Then the others came, and we were lying there waiting all night.

A coach waited for us on the highway at ten o'clock the next morning, when there was heavy traffic, so it would seem possible that we had exited the main gate of the Ghetto that morning. From our hiding place in the building, we could see that a coach had stopped and that the driver looked *a hare* and *a hin* (this way and that). He kept looking toward our hiding place.

The makher walked out to the coach and got in. He had a code word to make sure that the driver was the right guy. Then he called us over. We all walked out to the sidewalk as Jews with our armbands and got in the coach. The driver called our assumed names, and we showed our travel permits. Then he started to argue with the makher over the amount he should get paid. They'd already had an agreement on the price, and now the driver tried to raise it by four or five times. The makher didn't have enough money to meet the driver's demands, even if he'd wanted to. In response, the driver threatened to take us to the *gendarmerie* (German military police station) and turned the corner to head in that direction.

Outside the Ghetto walls, on the street or at the train station, it wasn't as convenient for the police to investigate suspicious papers. If we were taken to the German gendarmerie, though, they could look more closely. This was a very dangerous situation.

Two German gendarmes on patrol stopped us while the makher was still arguing with the driver. The driver couldn't speak or understand German at all, so the conversation with the Germans was short. Our makher was the translator. The driver said in Polish, "I picked them up on the street, and they wanted to go to the railroad station." It was good that he said that; it was consistent with our story. The driver must have been afraid for himself, too. He had been threatening us, but I don't think he expected to get stopped by the Germans. If he was found to be involved in the illegal smuggling of Jews, he would have been shot to death.

The Germans took us off the coach and told the driver to leave. They brought us to their police headquarters and called us in one at a time while the rest of us stood in another room. We heard yelling and beating and crying, but each one made it through because the passports seemed legitimate and matched our ages. All except one.

One guy was about forty-nine years old, and he had a passport saying that he was twenty-nine. It was a twenty-year difference, and the Germans didn't buy it. They beat him up terribly while we stood in the next room and listened. But he was smart. He let them beat him up and then said, "Okay, I'm going to tell you the truth." He told them that he grew up in a place far away from the city and that when he was born, they didn't know you had to make a birth certificate. Later, when he was ready to go to the army, they assessed how old he was and gave him that passport. He told this story in a way that sounded believable. They threatened him and beat him some more, but he stuck to his story. Eventually, they lost interest and let him go. Thank God.

Then it was my turn. My passport said that my occupation was watchmaking. I told them that my father had a watchmaking shop, that he worked for the Germans, and that the commandant gave us that permit so I could go to Warsaw to buy parts.

They gave me a few *potches* (slaps) in my face, but it wasn't too bad, and they quickly became distracted by my watch parts. One guy saw the gold-colored watch hands in my bag and said, "Look! That guy has gold!" I told them it's not gold, and he asked how I can prove it. I told him that real gold would not get dark if you put a little flame on it. If it's just gilded or painted gold, a flame from a match would burn the paint off and it would become dark. It's true. So, they took out a whole bunch of watch hands and lit a match to them. It happened like I said: the gold paint burned off and it became blue. Then they believed me.

They hit me several more times on my head and face, and they made me take off all my clothes so they could check if I had any other valuables. It was a miracle from God that they didn't find my real passport. Even though it was sewn in behind a heavy pocket of my overcoat, you could feel it if you were paying attention.

They let us go. It was such a close call. That son-of-a-bitch driver almost got us all killed. We had to walk from the police station to the main railroad station. We walked together through heavy traffic with our armbands on. It took about forty-five minutes.

When we arrived at the railroad station, our makher told us if we entered as a group, it would look suspicious. So we each approached the ticket window separately and bought our tickets to Radom. I had to show them the permit to prove I had permission from the German authorities to travel. I got my ticket and went straight onto the train. We didn't sit together. We didn't even look at each other.

The train arrived in Radom at about five o'clock in the afternoon. From Radom, everybody departed to different towns. I was the only one traveling to Kozhnitz. I gave my fake passport back to that makher, according to our agreement, and went to wait for the Kozhnitz bus with my real passport. I could be Khil Lenga once again.

CHAPTER 5

Kozhnitz Ghetto (June 1941–September 1942)

THE BUS DROPPED ME OFF at the bus station close to my house in Kozhnitz. Germans were walking around everywhere. I was terrified that they might catch me on the street—like what had happened on the way to the train station in Warsaw. So, I asked someone I knew at the bus station to go to my family and tell them to come get me.

My brother Moishe came running and guided me back. Like in Warsaw, whenever you saw a German on the sidewalk, you had to take off your hat and step down onto the road so he could pass by. But unlike Warsaw, these were the streets and walkways of my childhood, and here was Moishele, already a man but still my little brother, calming my fears and explaining the rules to get me back home.

My father, stepmother, and Mailekh were there to greet me and Moishe upon arrival. My stepmother's mother, Slova, was also there. She had also moved in with us a few years before the war. We were so happy to be together. They said I looked like a skeleton from eating so little. We sat down, and everyone cried when I told them what I'd gone through in Warsaw and how close I'd come to getting shot on the way back. Then my father told me what had happened in Kozhnitz.

When the Germans first marched in on September 8, 1939, all of the Kozhnitzer Jews were hiding. Our family hid in a basement. The Germans found everyone that first day and pushed all of the Jews, several thousand people, into a fenced-in churchyard in the center of town. The Germans didn't give the Jews anything to eat. Some people had brought food with them. Those who didn't fasted until someone had rakhmunes and shared a little of whatever they had.

The Germans also forced as many Jews as would fit inside the church itself and locked the doors. Eventually, of course, those people had to relieve themselves, but there were no toilets inside the church. The Germans instructed them to do it wherever they wanted in the church and refused to let them out.

After four days and three nights of this torture, the Germans finally opened the church doors and allowed all the Jews to go home. Then they called in the Polish Christians and showed them what the "damned Jews" had done to their church—how it was defiled with urine and feces. They did this to whip up Polish hatred. The local Poles, for the most part, didn't blame the Kozhnitzer Jews. They had seen what happened, and they knew our community from before the war. But the Germans wanted them to *say* that the Jews had disrespected the church, and the Poles danced the dance even though they didn't believe it. The Poles who had already hated the Jews now had a reason to hate us more.

After the Jews were permitted to leave the churchyard, the Germans assembled the most honored Jews of the town and demanded they bring about twenty thousand zlotys as a communal tax to their new German overlords. My father was among that group because he was a member of the Kozhnitz Geminder.

The Germans took some of them and cut clumps of hair off their beards with violent strokes of a knife or scissors. They did you a favor if they didn't cut off a piece of skin with the beard. Many went away bleeding. German soldiers came into my father's store one day and cut off his beard just for fun. After that, my father started to shave to avoid that abuse.

Some days later, the Germans lit a bonfire in front of the main shul and beis medrish of the Kozhnitzer Chassidim and forced the Jews to remove all of the books and throw them into the fire. Then the Germans commanded them to remove the Torah scrolls from the special cabinet where they were kept (*aron koydesh*) and asked for the rabbi. When he stepped forward, they ordered him to take the scrolls and throw them into the fire. The SS men commanded him again and again to throw the scrolls in, but he stood there, frozen. Eventually, one of the Germans hit him over the head and pushed him into the fire. The Torah scrolls fell out of his arms into the flames, and a few Jews standing close by pulled the rabbi to safety.

But it wasn't over yet. The SS men told the rabbi to dance and sing happy songs. They didn't like the way he danced, so they beat him terribly and pushed him back into the fire, where he was burned to death.

Then they ordered other Jews who were standing close by to dance in circles around the fire. Finally, the Germans threw gasoline and set fire to the shul and the beis medrish.[1]

My stepmother, Moishele, and Khanale were there with my father that day, along with the rest of the Jews in Kozhnitz. The Poles came, too. It was a big event in the town.

THE GERMANS HAD taken over the Kozhnitz Geminder and renamed it the Judenrat. Just like in Warsaw, they imposed restrictions on the Jews with regard to money, valuables, coffee, and sugar. The Germans would dictate laws, policies, and forced-labor quotas to the Judenrat, and the Judenrat established a Jewish police force to enforce them on the Jews of the town. The Germans ordered the Judenrat to deliver men for slave labor, and the Jewish police grabbed Jews off the Ghetto streets or from their houses. At the beginning, they took a few people to work inside the town. In some places, the Germans made them clean toilets with their tongues.

Right after the Germans burned the rabbi to death, my father resigned from the Judenrat. When other members threatened that they would have to report his resignation to the Germans, he replied that he would rather be killed than be a stooge for the Germans. I was proud of my father when I heard about that. Thank God that someone else filled his post right away. I don't think the other members ever notified the German authorities about my father's resignation.

About 80 percent of the council members from before the war resigned. The new members of the Judenrat were not such high-quality people, and they became the leaders of the Jewish community. My father knew them all and avoided them.

🕐 🕐 🕐

EARLIER IN THE war, when I was still living in Warsaw, my sister, Khanale, met a young man named Toyvia. His father owned a big wholesale store in Schidlovitz that supplied leather to the Kozhnitz shoe factories, and Toyvia came personally to make sure that his customers had enough business to support the cost of those wholesale supplies. That's when he met my sister. My father invited Toyvia to spend Shabbos with our family, and they sat by the table and sang zmiroys together. My father liked Toyvia. Everyone liked him.

After he left, Khanale and Toyvia wrote letters to each other, and they fell in love. Toyvia wanted to hold the wedding in Schidlovitz, but it was already the period of the Ghetto, and it was against the law to travel between cities without a permit. Khanale could have been killed if she'd tried to go there.

But my father had a plan, and he told the whole story to the captain of the Polish police in Kozhnitz, who was a steady customer of ours for many years. They were good friends, and he used to come in our store to kibbitz. He was a Volksdeutsche, an ethnic German who was born and raised in Kozhnitz. The Jews had good relations with the Volksdeutsche before the war. They even spoke Yiddish with us sometimes because they knew German.[2] After the Germans marched into town, most of the Volksdeutsche became enthusiastic Nazi antisemites overnight, and many, like this police captain, were appointed to key jobs to support and enforce the German occupation. But Kozhnitz was a small town, and sometimes a personal relationship created space for an exception if you knew how and when to ask. The two of them agreed that the police captain would handcuff my sister and smuggle her to Schidlovitz as if she were a prisoner. My father paid him something for that. As soon as he returned, he told us that she was in the Schidlovitz Ghetto and everything was all right.

Of course, no one else from our family could travel to Schidlovitz for the wedding. All of this happened before I returned home from Warsaw. Khanale never came back to Kozhnitz.

🕐 🕐 🕐

MY FATHER TOLD me about all these events only after I returned to Kozhnitz. He never wrote about them in his letters. My father was a learned man, and I wanted to hear his interpretation of the German onslaught against us. He spoke about the German occupation of Kozhnitz during the First World War, only twenty-three years earlier. He remembered the Germans as nice, gentle people—educated and cultured. They were especially friendly with the Jews because every Jew could speak German, and every German could understand Yiddish, more or less.

We had a lot of experience with antisemitism, and German antisemitism was nothing new. But our current situation with the Germans was unbelievable, astonishing. Something completely different from the antisemitism we had known in the past. Still, my father believed—he had a strong desire to believe—that each new level of German atrocities was as bad as it would get. If we could wait it out, the situation would get better when the passion that drove their violence quieted down. That was how European Jews had been trained to think. That's how we had endured pogroms and other violent outbursts of antisemitism throughout the generations.

My father dismissed the rumors that the Germans were planning to destroy us. In Poland, there were 3.4 million Jews out of a total population of 32 million—more than 10 percent. In Warsaw and Krakow, more than 25 percent of the population was Jewish. About 50 percent of the people in Kozhnitz and many other Polish towns were Jews. My father argued, "What could they do? Kill all of us? How would such a thing even be possible?"

🕰 🕰 🕰

WHEN I RETURNED from Warsaw, there was a Jewish Ghetto in Kozhnitz, but it was not sealed, and we could still move around the town. All of us were helping my father in the store, and we had a lot of watch repair work. There was only one other watchmaker in town. He was also a Jew. At the beginning of the war, Polish soldiers came to our town, and they were quickly replaced by lots of German troops. All of them had watches that they had brought from home or stolen from Jews and other locals during their occupation of Poland. My father made a better living during the war than before. We had plenty of food to eat. We even had enough to share with somebody less fortunate than us.

On June 22, 1941, just a few weeks after I arrived in Kozhnitz, Germany launched a surprise attack on Russia. At first, we thought that the war would end soon, but it didn't. The German forces pushed deep inside Russia, and we heard that German military units were shooting whole villages of Jewish people like cattle in the Ukraine, Latvia, and Lithuania. We prayed that Izak had been sent away from those areas to Siberia, like other Jews who had escaped from Warsaw to the Russian zone of occupied Poland, and we prayed that a miracle would come and that Hitler would be defeated in Russia just like Napoleon was defeated a century before.[3]

🕰 🕰 🕰

THEN THE GERMANS increased their demands for Jewish forced labor. They started to take Jewish men in trucks to other places and keep them there for a day or a week or more. You never knew where they were taking you or how long it would be.

I was sent to a lumber mill. Sometimes they had us cut down trees in the forest to send the wood to Germany. Other times they just told us to pick up rocks or trees or lumber from one place and put them down at another place. And the next day, they would tell us to put it all back in the same place where we took it from the day before—just to keep us doing hard labor. When they drove us back in the evening, our hands were bleeding from the work.

Sometimes we hid in the attic of our house and removed the ladder to the attic so they couldn't catch us. At first, we were lucky, and it worked. But the Jewish police knew how to search the houses, and eventually they found our hiding place. There weren't too many places to hide in the Ghetto. They never took my father for forced labor because he was a watchmaker and they needed him to do that work.

🕰 🕰 🕰

THE JEWISH POLICE were controlled by the Judenrat. They volunteered for the job because they were promised better treatment than the other Jews. Most of the Jewish police tried to show their loyalty to the Germans by going above and beyond their required duties to oppress the Kozhnitzer Jews.

One guy who had been a good friend of mine before the war, Moishe Bronshtein, became the worst *shtick dreck* (piece of shit)! When Khamaira Salzburg and I belonged to the Zionist Youth Organization as teenagers, Bronshtein had been our *madrikh* (counselor), and we worked very closely with him. He was about eight years older than us. We looked up to him and liked him very much. He was an intelligent guy—no doubt about that.

When I returned from Warsaw, I heard the stories. Bron-shtein had become the *gansa makher* (the most important big shot) in the Judenrat. The Jewish police were under his command. When I saw him in action, I couldn't believe my own eyes. I was afraid and tried to avoid him, but he came up to shake hands and talk with me, like he was still my friend.

Bronshtein sold out the Jews of the town. The Germans or-dered him to do whatever they wanted, and he delivered. When the Germans told him to collect money from the Jews, Bron-shtein acted with force. He didn't say, "Please help me and give me some money because we have to pay the Germans." Instead, he would demand the money and would back up his demand with a threat to inform the Germans of how much money you had so they would come and take everything from you. That's how he handled it.[4]

We were surprised at how some people became collaborators, and we hated them for it. Everyone knew each other in the town, and that made it even worse.

🕐 🕐 🕐

Around September 1941, the Germans sealed us in the Ghetto with a barbed wire fence and imposed a tighter curfew. After 7:00 P.M., no Jew could be out in the streets. During the day, start-ing at 7:00 A.M., we could walk around only inside the Ghetto. Gatherings of ten or more people weren't allowed, and there were no more newspapers.

We knew this was a calculated step in a larger plan, but of course, we didn't know what the Germans were planning or when. Rumors circulated that the Ghetto was sealed as a preparation—to keep us together under their control so that when they were ready, they would be able to grab us and destroy us more easily.

The Ghetto was divided into two separated areas, with Lubelski Street running down the middle. Jews could not go from one side to the other without a permit. The Jewish neighborhood was on both sides of Lubelski Street, but Lubelski Street had to be outside the Ghetto because it was a main street of the town, and it ran to the railroad station.

My friend Khamaira Salzberg lived on the other side of the Ghetto, so we hardly could see each other anymore. You couldn't get a permit to cross the line unless you had to work for the Germans or had another good reason.

The Ghetto was about two and a half kilometers from one end to the other—more than half the size of Kozhnitz. There was only one gate to go in and out, and it was guarded by two German soldiers at all times. No Jew could leave the Ghetto without a permit from the Germans. Some tried to leave and smuggle things at night. Many of them were caught and shot.

The Germans made aktzions in the middle of the night on Jewish homes to terrorize us, but they never did this to my father. I don't know why. They said they were looking for arms, but they knew that the Jews didn't have arms. Nobody had arms. They shot people for any little thing that wasn't obeyed. If they broke down your door at 2:00 A.M. and found a fur coat, they shot the whole family in the house and left them lying there. A tiny folded piece of paper with a little bit of coffee in it was a reason to kill.

At that stage, people in the Kozhnitz Ghetto were not starving to death like the people in Warsaw. Kozhnitz wasn't as crowded, and it was close to the countryside, so people from the nearby farms could come and trade with the Kozhnitzer Jews on the black market.

⏱ ⏱ ⏱

ON THE MORNING before Yom Kippur in October 1941, the Jewish police came to our house and grabbed me, Mailekh, and Moishe out of the attic. That evening, the Yom Kippur fast would

begin at sunset. My "good friend" Moishe Bronshtein was standing right there supervising when they dragged us down and
loaded us onto trucks that took us to an electric power plant in
Pionki. We had to shovel coal into little railroad cars and then
push the cars to the furnace and throw the coal into the fire. They
brought us home the same day, about 10:00 P.M.

My stepmother had kept food warm for us even though it was
after the Yom Kippur fast had already started. We were so hungry. We hadn't eaten anything the whole day, but we were afraid
of our father's reaction if we ate on Yom Kippur. We asked our
stepmother what would happen if he woke up and saw us eating.
She told us to eat and not to worry about it.

Later, she told me that my father had been awake and had told
her to feed us. He knew it was the right thing to do, even under
Jewish law. And yet, he acted like he didn't know, and we never
spoke about it with him.

I can imagine that it was a tragedy for him. But eating that
meal wasn't a tragedy for us. We agreed among ourselves that if
God wanted us to fast, why didn't he protect us from this abuse?

The next day, my brothers and I accompanied our father to
Yom Kippur prayers that were held in secret at a private home
with thirty or forty people. My father had the honor to serve as
khazzan (cantor) for the morning prayer service. If the Germans
would have found us, they would have killed the worshipers in
that house. People took chances to observe the high holidays.

THE GERMANS STILL needed my father to continue working for
them as a watchmaker, so they made us move out of our place on
Radomska Street and put us in a corner house on the border of
the Ghetto. The entrance to the house was inside the Ghetto, and
in the back, there was a window that faced outside the Ghetto on
Lubelski Street. That was lucky for us. All of the other Ghetto
windows and doors that faced that street were boarded up, but

my father had special permission so that the Germans and Poles could come up to our open window on Lubelski to get their watches fixed.

When my father fixed watches for the Poles, he got paid for his work. We didn't ask the Germans to pay. Once in a while, one behaved more like a gentleman and would ask what he owed us. We always said, "Whatever you want to give will be all right." Usually, a German would throw down two or three zlotys, just a token amount that wasn't the real price.

But there was one German gendarme, named Kalisch—I will never forget his name—who was not like the other Germans. He had a little sympathy for the Jews and insisted on paying the going rate when we fixed his watch. He told my father, "I'm ashamed that I'm a German, but I cannot do anything. So far, I haven't killed a Jew. I don't know what will happen tomorrow."

We were worried he might be baiting us into saying something bad about the Germans. So my father simply said, "Please, don't speak to me about politics." Kalisch actually said, "I'm sorry, Herr Lenga." It was unheard of to receive an apology from a German.

There was gossip in the town that Kalisch liked Jewish girls and had a Jewish girlfriend. We never dared to ask him or talk about it. God forbid. It was not our business. It was against the law for Germans to have sex with Jews, and if the other Germans had learned he had relations with a Jewish girl, they would have finished him off along with the girl and her family.

But we knew about it. I wouldn't say that his girlfriend was an official prostitute. I don't think they had Jewish girls working as real prostitutes in Kozhnitz, but there were loose, promiscuous girls, and they could get food and other things in exchange for sex.

When Polish peasants came from the villages to get their watches fixed, my father told them not to bring money but something to eat from their farms—flour, onions, eggs, potatoes, a chicken. Whatever they brought was good enough.

WE WERE BETTER off than most because my father had a trade that was valuable to the Germans. Other people had trades like shoemaking that the Germans didn't care about, and those people quickly fell into poverty and starvation. Shoemaking was the only real industry in Kozhnitz, and that work dried up completely. Small groups of Jews in the Ghetto organized as much as possible to support those who didn't have any food. The Judenrat also tried to help, but by the time they started to give subsidies, it was too little, too late. A lot of people died from hunger.

The Jews took whatever valuables they had kept hidden from the Germans and started to sell them to the Christians to survive. My father's business also declined, and he wasn't making enough to feed our family.

Then a typhus epidemic broke out in the Ghetto, and people started to die by the hundreds. To respond, the Jewish community formed a makeshift hospital where the Jewish doctors and others volunteered. There wasn't enough medicine. I, myself, got sick. My stepmother took care of me and called the doctor to see me several times. Somehow, she got medicine and I recovered.

Despite all this going on and the laws against public meetings, we went to weddings of family friends that were held in the Ghetto. They weren't celebrated like a wedding should be, but people got married. It was a time-honored practice for Jews to continue to marry and bring children into the world, even in the darkest times.[5] All of the weddings were in the daytime because of the curfew.

🕑 🕑 🕑

MY STEPMOTHER VOLUNTEERED around the Ghetto to try and heal the sick. She dedicated herself to helping people and knew all the folk remedies. It used to be that when someone had a cold, she would heat up little glass cups and put them on his back. It created a kind of suction. One time, when I was a small child before the war, I pulled a pot off the stove and boiling water splashed all over me. My stepmother quickly put me in a bathtub, and all the neighborhood women came to peel potatoes on me until I was covered with potato peelings. I never had a mark from that burn.

By the time I returned from Warsaw, my stepmother's mother, Slova, was blind and paralyzed and couldn't get out of bed to go outside to the bathroom. My stepmother had to move her and clean her and wash her all the time.

Not only that, my stepmother also would sneak out of the Ghetto at night to sell rings and other jewelry to the Christians. My father still had some merchandise and gold hidden. We had a customer who had a big *tzukerinian* (nightclub) where the Germans would come to have expensive chocolate and cocktails. He would buy jewelry for himself and for other Poles, but he was afraid to enter the Ghetto, so the transactions were only possible if someone could come to his house.

My stepmother would push herself through a gap in the barbed wire fence that surrounded the Ghetto. She did it many times. We were scared to death that she would be caught. She took off her armband, and for that alone she would have received the death penalty. Fear didn't stop her, though. She was smart and really knew how to do business.

My father couldn't have gone himself, even if he wanted to. Everyone in the town knew him because he was the watchmaker, and any Pole who didn't know him could take one look at his face and be sure that he was a Jew. But my stepmother was not so well-known, and she didn't look Jewish.

My father used to call her *meshuga* (crazy) to risk sacrificing her life to make a zloty. He told her not to go. All of us told her, but she didn't listen. That's how she was. I guess she wanted to show that she was also responsible for bringing food into our house.

In addition to her mother, her youngest sister, Liba, also lived with us at that time. We all lived in one big room with a partition to create a little privacy.

Liba had escaped from the Warsaw Ghetto. She had blond hair and looked like a Christian, so she had traveled to Kozhnitz without the armband. My father used to say that my step-mother's family "didn't have any real blood in their veins" to take such chances.

THE GERMANS TIGHTENED up everything, a little at a time. We never knew what was going to happen next. They had convinced us that they needed us for labor and that this work would be the key to our survival. So, Moishe volunteered for forced labor—digging canals in a place called Wolka to regulate the overflow of a river for irrigation and to turn waterwheels that drove two flour mills. Before the war, that project had been run by a Polish company called Gorczycki, and the Germans gave them a permit to continue operating. It was a good idea for Moishe to volunteer for the Gorczycki camp. They didn't beat you up so much. Moishe was about twenty years old and strong. The project was close to Kozhnitz, and he had the privilege of going back home every day after work. They gave him ration cards to buy food. Those were better than money at that time. Also, Moishe had a permit from the German authorities to show that he was working at Gorczycki, so the Germans would let him go when they stopped him on the street.

My father didn't actively tell us what to do. We talked about our situation with him, and he tried to give us advice about how to be careful and not to get killed. But each son decided what to do on his own, and my father supported our decisions.

NOT LONG AFTER I recovered from typhus, the Germans made a decree that all of the Jews would be resettled in the German-occupied Russian and Ukrainian territories. They claimed that they were taking us to work there and that the children would be taken care of. They didn't say when.

We heard what had happened already in other towns. The Germans would empty out all the Jews from a town, load them onto trains, take them away, and nothing was heard about them afterward. We were waiting for it to happen to us, but we didn't actually know what was going on. So, each of us chose what he wanted to believe. The pessimists tried to explain that the Germans would take those people to their deaths, that they were destroying us. But the majority—including my father—were optimists who still couldn't believe it was possible for human beings to act like that.

In the meantime, every single day the Jewish police grabbed Jews off the street and took them away. The police caught Mailekh one day and sent him to a slave camp in Pionki where they manufactured war ammunitions. They kept him for about four weeks but then sent him back because they had too many workers. The Poles were still the big makhers in that factory, so Jews paid a lot of money to be taken there. The idea was that whoever was working in Pionki wouldn't be taken away by the Germans when they liquidated the Ghetto.

People would joke and say, "Don't worry, tomorrow you'll probably go on the train without having to pay for a ticket." Even though we were living in deep and constant fear of today and what tomorrow might bring, we were still telling jokes.

Around Yom Kippur in late September 1942, we heard that they took away the Jews of Schidlovitz, where my sister was living. We felt that something was going to happen any day in Kozhnitz.

⏲ ⏲ ⏲

ON THE SECOND night of Sukkes, September 26, 1942, at around 6:00 P.M., the captain of the Polish police—the same one who had taken Khanale in handcuffs to Schidlovitz to get married—came to our house in the Ghetto. Our store wasn't open because of the holiday, but he made a special visit to pick up a watch that he had left with my father to be fixed. I'll never forget. It was Saturday night, already dark, and I was sitting with my father.

He greeted us and said, "Mr. Lenga, why don't you tell your son to leave the room?" With a quick glance, my father sent me out. After the police captain had left, my father's face had turned ashen and white. The captain had told him that at midnight the Germans would surround the town, and in the morning, they were going to evacuate the Jews from Kozhnitz. He said, "If you love your boys, tell them to leave this evening before 8:00 P.M. Otherwise it'll be too late." He explained that if we left before 8:00 P.M., we wouldn't get caught because the gendarmes were not patrolling. They needed to rest and prepare themselves for the big aktzion the next day. Then he left.

Before, my father hadn't believed the rumors, but at that moment, he knew for sure that it was going to happen. He said, "Don't ask questions, don't ask nothing. Just get Moishele and Mailekh, gather together whatever you can, and leave right away to the Gorczycki camp. The sooner you do it, the better chance you'll have. Of course, there's a high probability that you'll be captured and shot by the Germans. But it's worth the risk."

🕑 🕑 🕑

MOISHE WAS HOME, but Mailekh was out somewhere in the Ghetto talking to people about the rumors. Earlier that day, he had already said that we should run away, so we knew he would be coming soon.

In the meantime, Moishe Bronshtein came to our house and invited me outside for a private conversation. "Khiltshu," he told me, "I'm going to Pionki in a taxi. If you want to come, I'll take you. The Germans will take all the Jews away and kill them off. I'm giving you a chance." I told him that I would stay and die together with my family if that was our fate. I didn't tell him anything about our plan to leave.

Finally, Mailekh came back at about 7:00 P.M. and said, "We are leaving right now or we will lose our chance to escape." We asked my father to come with us, but he refused, saying, "I want to be with my people . . . wherever my people go, I go." Of course, there was another factor involved. My stepmother wouldn't leave her mother. Her sister, Liba, said she couldn't leave their mother with her sister. My father said he couldn't go away and leave his wife with her mother. And that's how it was. One felt responsible for the other. But all of them agreed that we three should take the chance.

I would probably have done the same thing if I were in my father's shoes. He was already fifty-five years old at that time, and he wouldn't have been able to do hard labor or withstand the beatings and hunger.

My father told us to go to the Gorczycki camp and find Lescinski, the supervisor. "Wake him up whenever you reach there and tell him that you are Lenga the watchmaker's sons. Hopefully, he'll take you in." Lescinski's father was my father's good friend. He was a railroad conductor who used to bring us watches to fix. Moishe was already working in that camp and was registered, so the supervisor would know him.

And you know what my father did next? He got together whatever he had and gave it to us—watchmaking tools, watch parts, watches, and money. I said, "Tata, you can't give us everything. You need it, too." He said, "Where I am going, I won't need it. You're still young. You have a chance. So, you take it and use it." We took it. You can't imagine how much that helped us later. He bought our lives many times over with those tools and watch parts.

We all knew for sure that it was the end of Kozhnitz and that we would probably never see each other again. We were all deeply depressed in the midst of frantic activity. My father was making sure we left quickly, even as he passively accepted the cruel fate awaiting him and the rest of our family. He cried, I cried, Mailekh and Moishe cried, my stepmother cried, her sister,

Liba, cried. It was the second night of Sukkes, and everything was ready for kiddish and for a *yontiff dika* meal (a meal worthy of a holiday). It was so tempting to remain. We kissed each other and embraced one last time. It was less than thirty minutes after Mailekh had returned. My father was praying to God for our safety as we left the house.

CHAPTER 6

Gorczycki Camp at Wolka (October 1942)

W E WALKED OUT THE MAIN gate of the Ghetto. No Jewish police, no Polish police, no German police. It was open, just like the police captain had informed my father. He was a true friend to our family at a critical moment. At the same time, he had a leadership role in the Polish collaborationist police that had persecuted our family for years and was about to help the Germans evacuate them and all of the Kozhnitzer Jews from our town.

My father had loaded us up with more than we could easily carry. When we made it outside the Ghetto, my brothers wanted to go back and grab the rest of the tools. I was against it, but they insisted we still had time and left me to wait for them. They came back with another filled valise. My father didn't let them leave anything behind.

We had to cross a small stream to get to the highway. The water reached almost to our knees. Then we took off our arm-bands and waited on the highway for a peasant going by in a horse-drawn cart. I stopped the first one and asked the driver if he would take us down the highway a few kilometers. I offered him ten zlotys, and he wanted twenty. I agreed. I didn't make any *kintsim* (bargaining). We put our stuff in and climbed onto the open wagon.

We didn't tell him where we were going or for what purpose. Even though he had to have known we were Jewish, he acted like he didn't know. That was lucky for us.

We told him where to drop us off on the highway and then walked a few kilometers on a rocky, pitted road in the direction of the camp. It wasn't an easy walk because we had too much to carry—a suitcase, sacks, and a box.

The suitcase was about two and a half feet (seventy-six centimeters) long, and it was heavy—packed with watchmaking tools. We even had a machine to make a plastic watch crystal (the clear cover on the face of the watch) by hand. It was about the size of a tea kettle. You would measure the watch, put in a piece of celluloid to cut a circle to size, and press the handles with your hands like a pair of pliers to make the shape of the crystal. It was a terrific tool. The plastic crystal didn't crack so fast like a glass crystal. We used to sell a lot of glass watch crystals before the unbreakable plastic crystals came into existence. They were a better product, but that was also worse for us because we didn't sell so many crystals anymore.

Besides that suitcase, we also had a smaller box with all the watchmaking materials. We didn't have so many watches that were running—mostly old watches, movements, hands, balance staffs, and other parts.

We took only the pants and shoes that we were wearing and a couple of shirts and a jacket. Mailekh and I had a pair of good leather shoes with laces that reached above our ankles. Moishe had leather boots that were good for working in water. They reached almost to his knees. I also had a round hat with the little *doshik* (visor). We didn't take extra clothes because we had saved all the room for watchmaking tools and materials. They were our hold on life. We knew we would be able to exist if we had those tools.

My stepmother had made sure we each took a *perna* (down comforter) and a pillow. The perna was filled with down and was very light, so we could pack it small. I don't remember taking winter coats, but we must have, because I do remember that each of one us had a good coat when it got cold. It wasn't cold when we left home. It was a warm September evening.

🕐 🕐 🕐

AFTER THE LONG walk, we arrived at the entrance of the Gorczycki camp. There were no guards. No security. We just walked through the open gate with all our bags. Nobody looked at us. We came to a barrack, and there were people lying outside because the barrack was full. It was dark, and everybody was sleeping.

We put our things down and went to look for Lescinski, the supervisor. It took a while to find where he was sleeping. Moishe woke him up and asked him to register us right then. We thought maybe the German gendarmes would come to the camp, too, and we were afraid to wait. He said, "I understand. We'll take you in. I can't do anything now. But don't worry. So far, I haven't heard anything. Go lie down and sleep wherever you can. Tomorrow morning we'll register you two in the books so you will belong in this camp. We'll see to it."

We didn't look for a place to lie down. We talked quietly the whole night about what was going to happen at home. Which rumors were true? Will the aktzion happen or not? When the first light of morning appeared, we stood by the wire fence at the edge of the camp and watched as peasants in nice clothes walked toward Kozhnitz. It was Sunday, and we understood that they were going to church.

About a half hour later, we saw the same people returning. We called out to them through the fence and asked, "Why are you coming back home so early? Usually, when you go to church it takes about two and a half hours for a mass, and here it is only thirty minutes, and you are already walking back." We had a good idea of the answer, but we wanted to know for sure. Some of them didn't want to talk to us. But three guys with a woman stopped and with tears in their eyes told us what they had heard. "The whole city was surrounded with Gestapo, and they didn't let anybody in or out. Terrible things are going on in the Ghetto."

We cried. My friend Khamaira Salzberg also ended up at the same camp, and he was together with us. Everybody in the camp stood and cried that Sunday morning. We didn't know what else to do. Some said they were taking everyone from the Ghetto to work in the east. Others said it's the end of those people. Of course, there were rumors right away that the Germans were going to come after us, too. Our camp was not too far from the railroad tracks. At 12:00 noon, we heard the whistle as the train went by. We knew then that we'd never see our parents again. We didn't know how long until we met the same fate.[1]

Lescinski registered us as workers at the Gorczycki camp that morning just like he'd promised. The next day, Monday, was a "regular" workday. We heard from the Poles who commuted back and forth from Kozhnitz that the Germans had dragged all the Jews out from their homes in the Ghetto and lined them up in the street. They let each Jew have only one little suitcase. Then they marched them to the railroad station and packed them like herrings into boxcars. The sick ones who couldn't get out of bed, like women who had just delivered a baby, were shot by the Germans right in their beds. Kozhnitz was *Judenrein* (cleansed of Jews),[2] except for about 150 young men they kept back to remove the things from the vacated Jewish homes.

The project at Gorczycki was to dredge the bottom of a river and build up the river's banks so it wouldn't overflow during the rainy season. Channels going out from the river were also dug to irrigate the fields.

Every morning, we stood in the water and dug with a shovel. It was hard for me. There were about twenty-five men in each work group, and there was one Polish guy and one Jewish guy overseeing each group. The Pole was like the engineer. The Jewish guy was making sure that we did the work. They used to beat us a little bit, but it wasn't too bad. They didn't carry a club or a whip.

Gorczycki was under Polish administration, and it was only for Kozhnitz laborers. There were no Germans there. Actually, it wasn't equipped and organized like a camp should be, and you could walk wherever you wanted. You could run away, anything. The food was bad in Gorczycki. It was never hot, and there wasn't enough. But at least you could buy more food on your own from the Poles.

When we arrived, there were about two hundred Kozhnitzers working there—mostly Jews. In the days and weeks before the evacuation, Gorczycki had received a big inflow of new workers like us who had come there to protect themselves. It was chaotic.

The camp didn't have enough barracks to house us, so we often slept outside under the chilly October sky with the pernas from our stepmother to keep us warm.

⏱ ⏱ ⏱

WE DIDN'T KNOW anything about Treblinka. We knew that something was going on with the trains full of Jews from each town that was evacuated, and there were always rumors, but nobody came and said "I saw it myself" or had heard the information from somebody else who had directly witnessed what happened to those people.

About ten or twelve days after we arrived at Gorczycki, two young men smuggled themselves into our camp in the middle of the night. I knew one of them from the Polish public school. They told us they had been taken to the train when the Germans liquidated the Kozhnitz Ghetto.

That train left with all the Kozhnitz Jews—over ten thousand. Young and old. Men and women. They traveled quite a distance toward Russia—several hundred kilometers. The train stopped at a camp with a sign that read TREBLINKA. The SS opened the doors, yelling, *"Raus, Raus,"* (out, out) as they shot their guns into the air and into the crowded train cars.

After the Kozhnitz Jews got off the train, the Germans lined them up and delivered a speech:

"You are brought here to work. Anything that you have with you—money, gold, diamonds, jewelry—throw it down in front of you. Don't leave anything in your pockets. You'll have to take off the clothing that you are wearing now and leave them where you're standing. You're going to be taken into a shower room. We'll give you a shower and give you new clothing. Then you'll be taken into a camp. In that camp, the children under ten will be taken away from you, and they'll be held in special schools. At 7:00 P.M. you'll be united with your children. Each one of you will have to work twelve hours a day, except the children under ten. But you are the lucky ones to have come here, and you'll survive the war."

The Germans picked out two hundred Jewish men, including those two guys, between ages eighteen and twenty-five and ordered them to gather the clothing that the people took off and throw it back into the empty train cars. They warned, "Don't pick up anything. Don't look in pockets. Because if you do, you'll be shot!"

While those two hundred guys were throwing the clothes in the boxcars, they watched as the Germans told the others to march—ten thousand men and women and children together, naked—a little way to a big building that looked like a barn. Two doors opened, and it was like a huge hangar—large enough to take in all of those ten thousand people. The SS hit and pushed the Jews with sticks and guns and shot into the crowd so everybody was terrorized into escaping deep into the chamber, until it was so packed with people that nobody else could go in anymore. Then the SS locked the doors.

Those two hundred men who were working didn't know it was a gas chamber at that time.

The two guys told us about the voices and the screams that they heard when the poison gas started pouring into that sealed hangar—terrible! It took about half an hour until they were all

"Oh, I have a broken clock. If you can make it to my house, I'll give you something to eat if you'll fix it for me."

I went there and fixed his clock. He gave me food, and when I asked for some more bread for my brothers, he gave me that, too. Then I offered to give him everything that I had to hide us somewhere underneath the ground and keep us alive. I guaranteed him more after the war if we survived. But he said, "I won't hide a Jew given the risk that I'll be killed." Now he was one of the nice guys because he didn't report me to the Germans.

🕑 🕑 🕑

WE WERE AT Gorczycki for only a few weeks. One day, an alarm sounded while we were working on a canal. The Polish overseer took us back to the camp, where German police and SS lined us up and gave us fifteen minutes to grab our belongings. We thought, *Oh, that's the end of it. They're probably going to take us on a train to kill us in Treblinka.* One guy tried to run away, and they killed him in front of our eyes. We took only what we could carry. We had to leave some of our big bundles behind.

They made a roll call, and five boys in the back row lay down on the ground and squirmed under the fence to escape. The SS noticed them outside the fence and shot all of them.

The Germans loaded us onto open trucks and drove us on Lubelski Street through the center of Kozhnitz. We saw how the Ghetto gates were locked up, and we couldn't spot a living soul inside. It was like a cemetery. We passed by the broken window of our empty house at the end of Lubelski Street, curtains blowing in the wind, and we saw our home for the last time. It was the end of our world in Kozhnitz.

Outside the Ghetto, the Polish town of Kozienice went about its business without the Jews. Poles rode by on bicycles and horse carts.

It wasn't long before we came to the street that led to the railroad station. But the trucks made a curve away from the station

and onto the highway. So, we knew they weren't taking us to
the train yet.[5]

4.) Rückleitung des Leerzuges:
Lp Kr 9231 (30.11) von Treblinka nach Szydlowiec am 24./25. Sept.

Treblinka	(11.24)/15.59	im Plan	Dg 91368 B
Siedlce	17.56/18.42	" "	Dg 91445 B
Lukow	19.36/20.37	" "	Dg 91266 B
Deblin Gbf	22.34/23.36	" "	Dg 91266 B
Radom	1.34/1.50	" "	Dg 91266 B
Szydlowiec	3.08/(21.30)		

5.) P Kr 9232 (30.9) von Szydlowiec nach Treblinka am 25./26. Sept.

Szydlowiec	(3.08)/21.50	im Plan	Dg 91249 B
Radom	22.49/0.13	" "	Dg 91255 B
Deblin Gbf	2.00/3.10	" "	Dg 91257 B
Lukow	5.17/6.08	" "	Dg 95402 B
Siedlce	6.58/8.34	" "	Dg 91365 B
Treblinka	11.24/(15.59)		

6.) Rückleitung des Leerzuges:
Lp Kr 9233 (30.11) von Treblinka nach Kozienice am 26./27. Sept.

Treblinka	(11.24)/15.59	im Plan	Dg 91368 B
Siedlce	17.56/18.42	" "	Dg 91445 B
Lukow	19.36/20.37	" "	Dg 91266 B
Deblin Gbf	22.34/23.36	" "	Dg 91266 B
Bakowiec	0.00/0.05	im Sonderplan (Kreuzung mit P
Kozienice	0.35		

7.) P Kr 9234 (30.9) von Kozienice nach Treblinka am 27./28. Sept.

Kozienice	20.00		
Bakowiec	20.30/20.43	im Plan	Dg 91237 B
Deblin	22.08/23.01	" "	Dg 91243 B
Lukow	1.08/3.11	" "	Dg 91464 B
Siedlce	4.01/5.08	" "	Dg 91359 B
Treblinka	7.20/(15.59)		

*Train schedule for the transport of the Jews of Kozienice
(Kozhnitz) to Treblinka on September 27, 1942. Contemporary
historical research indicates that around thirteen thousand
Jews from the town and surrounding areas had been assembled
in the Kozienice ghetto and evacuated on that transport.[6]
The schedule shows that the Jews of Szydlowiec (Schidlovitz)
(including Khanale Lenga and her husband Toyvia) were transported to Treblinka the day before. Treblinka was an
extermination camp built and operated by Germany in occupied Poland from the summer of 1942 until October 1943.
During this time, approximately 868,000 Jews and 2,000 Ro-
mani were transported to Treblinka in trains and murdered in
its gas chambers. More Jews were killed in Treblinka than any
other extermination camp except Auschwitz.[7]*

The Germans set up extermination camps only in Poland,
and they brought in the Jews from all over Europe. The operation was meticulously planned and decided formally by the
Germans at the Wannsee Conference, a meeting of senior government officials of Nazi Germany and the SS leaders, held in
the Berlin suburb of Wannsee on January 20, 1942. The purpose
of the conference was to secure the cooperation of administrative leaders of various government departments in the
implementation of the so-called Final Solution to the Jewish
Question, by which most of the Jews of German-occupied Europe would be transported to extermination camps located in
German-occupied Poland, where they would be killed with industrial efficiency.[8] The United States Holocaust Memorial
Museum estimates that the German SS and camp police forces
murdered 2.7 million people in these six extermination camps
by asphyxiation with poisonous gas or by shooting.[9]

CHAPTER 7

Wolanow Slave Labor Camp (October 1942– June 1943)

A ready response is a joy to a man. And how good is a word rightly timed.

—*Proverbs*, 15:23

A FEW HOURS LATER, WE reached our destination. We rode standing as the trucks entered a long field with a row of barracks surrounded by barbed wire. Ukrainian guards with rifles stood by the gate and watched us from towers. It was completely different from Gorczycki, where we could walk out whenever we wanted. Suddenly, we were in a prison. Wolanow. We hadn't imagined something like that before.

They brought us to a barrack with three levels of wooden sleeping compartments along the walls and told us to choose. Each compartment had to have three men, so the three of us shared a bed. We always tried to take the upper bunk. Mailekh learned that in the Pionki labor camp during the Kozhnitz Ghetto times. The top bunk was better for many reasons. The beds were straw sacks on top of boards that had a few inches of space between them, so dust and dirt fell into your eyes if you were on a lower bunk. Also, if somebody *pished* (urinated) on the top bed, it fell on you if you were below. It happened sometimes.

Everyone received a metal *shisel* (bowl) and cup. The bowl was how you got soup in the evening. The cup was for "coffee" in the morning. If you approached that big barrel for a ladle of soup or coffee and you didn't have something to pour it into, they told you "Get away!" And that was it. You didn't eat anything. It was like that with the bowl and cup in every German camp until the war ended.

The wakeup alarm rang at 6:00 A.M., and your first thought was to make sure you had your bowl and cup. You had to guard them as you guarded your soul. They were your lifeline. We made a hole in our belts and fastened the bowl and cup with a piece of wire. You worked with the bowl and cup on your belt, and you slept with them, too. There was also a spoon. We used to lose the spoons sometimes and make a new one from a piece of thin sheet metal.

People stole things, but that was also risky. There was a Jewish orderly in each barrack called the *blockaltester* who never left the barrack to go to work. You needed to be lucky or have some connections to get that job. His duty was to make sure that nobody stole anything and that no one came into that barrack who didn't belong there. He also swept and cleaned the barrack. Anyone who got caught stealing would be shot. If the blockaltester did not do his job properly, he would be shot. We left our watchmaking tools and parts and down comforters in the barrack when we went out to work. We worried about them all the time, but they weren't ever stolen.

When it came time to wake up, the blockaltester rang a small metal bell and everybody had to jump down. If you were still in the barrack when you were supposed to be outside, the guards came and fixed you up. Sometimes they beat you. Other times they took you away to the so-called hospital.

Outside, you lined up where they had barrels of "coffee" made from burnt turnips. When you went by the barrel, they poured some coffee into your metal cup, and you walked away. That was the end of it. That cup held about half a quart (slightly less than half a liter).

We spit it out the first time we tasted that coffee, but we had to get used to it. That was the only thing that they gave you to warm up in the morning. You didn't get any food till you came back from work in the evening.

🕰 🕰 🕰

AFTER WE DRANK our morning coffee, the Jewish foremen lined us up in groups for different types of work. Usually, you stayed with the group from the day before. Sometimes they moved you to a different work group. Each group marched out of the camp to its designated work site with a Ukrainian *Schutz* guard.[1] They were trained soldiers. Each one carried a pistol on his belt and a rifle. The Nazis supported Ukrainian independence from the Russians, and the Ukrainians had always hated Jews since I don't know when, so they enlisted to help the Germans. They shot to kill, and they enjoyed it. At the work site, a German would supervise us with help from a Jewish foreman while the Ukrainians watched over us with rifles. They didn't speak to us, and we couldn't speak to them.

The work project at Wolanow was to build barracks and other buildings for the German air force *(Luftwaffe)* soldiers who were to be stationed there. We worked on whatever needed to be done. On the first day, they took us to dig clean, brown sand to use for making lime to lay bricks for the Luftwaffe barracks. Other days, they ordered us to chop trees, cut wood, or carry lumber. Sometimes we had to carry bricks or pour cement to make a road. It was hard work all day long. Every day you prayed to God to be assigned to an easier job.

The three of us always tried to stay together in the same work group. Moishe and Mailekh were already strong because they had done a lot of hard labor during the Kozhnitz Ghetto times. I

wasn't a muscle boy like my brothers. That heavy work was difficult for me, and I wanted them to help me, but they refused
because they hardly had enough energy to do their own work.
They said I would have to get used to it and that's it. I understood.
They were right. Sometimes they helped me anyway, but I
learned how to hold a shovel and became a good worker.

There was a German boss to supervise every thirty to fifty
prisoners at a work site, and they would beat some of us every
day with police sticks. The ones who were beaten badly could
hardly work afterward. Sometimes they couldn't even walk, and
the rest of us would carry them back to the camp. As long as you
could still stand up and go to work, the Germans used you, even
if you were not such a good worker. If you couldn't work at all,
they took you to the so-called hospital. If you recovered in one
day, they took you back to work. If not, they killed you.

The German bosses hit me many times. They said I didn't
work fast enough and all kinds of different things. I always tried
to do whatever they told me because I knew that as soon as they
started to beat you with heavy blows, you could not work anymore. Before they beat you, maybe you didn't *want* to do the
work. But after a beating, when you *could not* do it, you were finished, and it didn't matter what you wanted. I was never beaten
to the point where I was disabled. We tried to protect ourselves
as much as possible.

They marched us back to the camp after work and lined us
up again for soup and a piece of bread—supper. You had to wait
your turn to hold out your bowl for soup. In Wolanow, they gave
you a nice portion of bread—I would say a quarter of a loaf—
half a pound, approximately 250 grams. If you were lucky, you
got a bigger piece, and everybody was jealous of you. If you were
not lucky, you got a smaller piece—a tragedy. Every day it was
different.

They made good thick soups with barley and sometimes with
potatoes or even meat. But they ladled only about a half quart of
soup into your bowl. It was not enough to be full or satisfied. We

lost weight, and we didn't have the kind of energy we needed to do the hard work, but we could still exist on those rations.

Sometimes on a Sunday, they gave us a piece of salami. On Christmas, the meal they gave us was a little better, too. Even in the concentration camps they did that.

Wolanow was a huge camp—about a kilometer and a half square. There were a lot of Jews there from Kozhnitz, Schidlovitz, Shelochov, and Radom, including women. A gate with a guard separated the women's camp from the men's camp to prevent us from going back and forth. But it wasn't strictly enforced; we could go over and communicate with the women.

One of the women from Schidlovitz told me about my sister Khanale's fate. Her husband, Toyvia, had had the opportunity to come to Wolanow, but Khanale couldn't work because she was four months pregnant. So, they decided to go together to the train. The Germans sent them to be gassed in Treblinka with the Jews of Schidlovitz. I hadn't known that before.

⏱ ⏱ ⏱

RIGHT AWAY, WE three brothers made a pact between us that whatever happened to one would happen to all of us. If one got taken to be killed, we all wanted to be killed. If we saw a chance to save each other, we had to try . . . and we did. It happened a few times in the camps that one faced death in order to save the others.

We didn't have to discuss it beyond that. It was a natural thing for us, and there was never a doubt.

At night, I don't think I dreamt about the past or about home. The only thing that I dreamt about was a piece of bread—a meal to fill my stomach. Each morning when you woke up and opened your eyes, there was one question: *Will I come back tonight from work?* Every day was a struggle to survive for that day.

From the beginning until the end, we knew that Hitler's Germany had to be destroyed. But the question was, would he destroy us first? And that was our struggle—to outplay him.

⏱ ⏱ ⏱

THEY BROUGHT US to Wolanow in October 1942. The work was hard, but we managed somehow. Then one day in November, they said we didn't have to go to work, and we knew something was about to happen. A group of Ukrainian SS commandos arrived at the camp. They called them Jew killers.

While we waited and watched, I noticed that Mailekh hadn't shaved for several days. I told him he had to shave immediately, but he refused at first. When I started to insist and Moishe joined in, he listened to us and shaved.

The Germans assembled us for roll call in a clearing that they called the *appel platz*, and we realized that Mailekh's jacket was all torn up. It had ripped when he carried heavy pieces of steel and other materials. He noticed, too, but he didn't have a chance to fix it. While we stood there, before they started the inspections, I told him, "Take it off fast!"

He said, "What? It's so cold, I have to have something."

I said, "I'll tell you what I'll do—we'll turn the coat inside out ... and you put it on. It won't look torn."

He took off the jacket, and we saw that the lining was not torn. We turned it inside out, and he put it back on. Moishe and I stood on each side with him in the middle, so he wouldn't draw the notice of the Germans when they walked past.

The Germans selected the prisoners who had not shaved or had torn clothes or looked beaten up or had cuts on their faces. Even strong and healthy people. They took out 117—men, women, and children—and the Ukrainians shot them.

Until then, the women still had young children hidden under straw or in all kinds of other places in their section of the camp, but the Germans raided the women's barracks in the middle of the night and during the day while the women were at work. They found almost all of the children and killed them off in that selection. There were no young children in the men's camp— only boys who were at least eleven or twelve years old.

That was our saddest day in that camp.

We saved Mailekh's life that day. They would have shot him. Thank God I was smart enough at that moment. You could trade with other prisoners in the camp, so after the selection, we bought Mailekh another coat for rations of bread or something like that.[2]

🕑 🕑 🕑

ABOUT TWO MONTHS after that first selection, they started to make those inspections and shoot prisoners every Sunday to manage the camp population. As they brought more and more people from the Ghettos that were being liquidated, I would say there were about eight to ten thousand Jews in the camp. Sometimes they would kill one hundred of us, sometimes three hundred, sometimes five hundred. It depended on their mood and how many new prisoners had arrived.

Every Sunday, we thought it would be our last day. We figured that sooner or later they would kill us, too. Most of the people in the camp were young. There were a few older people in their fifties, but none older than that. My father was fifty-five when we said goodbye to him a couple of months before. At that age, he could have been in the camp with us. But those older prisoners couldn't stand the hard work, so the Germans selected them first to be killed.

The Sunday routine was like this. The alarm rang at 7:00 A.M.—one hour later than the other days of the week. We had to prepare for a lineup outside. They called that lineup an *appel*. There was a washroom with a little running water. You put a little water on your face and your hair, that's all. We didn't wash our bodies on Sundays.[3]

Then everybody had to line up for coffee. After the coffee, you hurried to shave. That was the most important thing. During the week you didn't shave, but if you were not shaved on Sunday, you were a candidate to be shot that day. After shaving, you checked if everything was all right with your clothes. They hadn't given us any clothes. We still wore the clothes that we'd brought from Kozhnitz. If those clothes got torn, it was also a death sentence.

Then we lined up for inspection. Jewish police inside the camp arranged us and corrected us over and over so everything would be in order when the Germans came. There were five or six rows all the way from one end of the camp to the other—about one kilometer. There was room for two soldiers to walk between each row. We always faced south.

The Germans checked that we were lined up in the right way before they started the real stuff. They always found something that was not good enough. We had to rearrange this and that—like soldiers lined up at attention.

Finally, Bartman, the *Lagerführer* (camp commander), arrived. He was very tall, with a bald head and gold teeth. He dressed in civilian clothes. We had to face him as he walked down the aisle with the Jewish police captain by his side. Bartman had one artificial eye. You never knew where he was looking except when he looked into your eyes, and then a shiver would go up your spine.

He could choose anyone with a word or a wave of his finger, and the Jewish police captain would bring that prisoner to a different group by the barbed wire fence, where the prisoners faced the outside of the camp, looking away from the lines we'd formed. We knew that group was going to be shot.

Besides the unshaven and those with torn clothes, they also selected the ones whose bodies were wasting away from undernourishment. We feared that we were starting to look like that, too. My arm was like a thin stick.

We stood like that until two or three in the afternoon, when the lagerführer finished his inspection. They sent us back to the barracks, and the Ukrainian soldiers did the shooting. We could hear the shots. Sometimes the Ukrainians shot them in front of our eyes, and we saw everything.

Then they grabbed prisoners to dig graves and bury the bodies by the barbed wire fence. Whoever dug the graves would also see bones from the Russians' prisoners of war who were imprisoned and killed in Wolanow before they brought the Jews to that camp. I never had to dig those graves.

⏱ ⏱ ⏱

THE FENCE SURROUNDING the camp was a wall of barbed wire. It was difficult to climb over, but it was not impossible. Every morning, they marched us out of the camp to work sites that were quite far away, with only a few German or Ukrainian guards watching over us. Some tried to run away from the work sites, but none of them made it. The area around Wolanow was flat, empty territory for miles and miles—no buildings, no trees, no farms. You could see from one edge to the other. Even if the guards didn't shoot you, there wasn't anywhere to run. No Jews were living in the towns or countryside anymore. Your only chance, if you were lucky enough, was to reach the forest and find a group of Polish socialist partisans or Jewish partisans hiding there. But if the Polish antisemite partisans found you, then they would kill you, too. We had heard stories about this long before they took us to the camp—even before they sealed us in the Kozhnitz Ghetto.

⏱ ⏱ ⏱

I WAS WORKING at a construction site run by the Heiger Heine company, which was paid by the Germans to build barracks for the Luftwaffe. A civilian from Germany named Corbinus was in charge of the site. He was a Nazi Party guy, and they made him an SS man. They always put SS men in control of those private company work sites so they could make sure everything was done as the Nazis wanted. Corbinus was also the architect who made sure that the project was carried out according to the plans.

My job was to unload cement sacks from trains that delivered supplies. Some days, we also had to mix and pour the cement, and I came back to the camp with cement all over my skin. We didn't change our clothes. It was terrible! In the camp, you could wash with a little bit of running water, but there was no soap, and you were so tired that you didn't even want to wash. My brothers were working at a different building site, carrying bricks, so I didn't see them until the end of the day when we returned from work.

Corbinus had an office, and he would come out to inspect our work. He was such a miserable guy—a sadist. He would beat us terribly, no matter how good we did our work. I knew that if I continued working like that every day, sooner or later I would get worn out and they would kill me.

One time, as Corbinus watched us work, something inside told me to take a chance with him. I don't know why, but something . . . He was nicely dressed, sure, but he was also a good murderer, a good beater.

I walked up to him, just like that, and said, "I would like to do you a favor."

He opened his eyes wide and said, "You're going to do *me* a favor?"

I saw that I said the wrong thing and changed my tone fast. I said, "Oh, I'm sorry, I expressed myself the wrong way. I would like to fix a watch for you."

He said, "What are you talking about? Are you *farikht* (crazy)?"

I said, "No. I'm a watchmaker, and if you have a broken watch, please let me have the honor of fixing it for you."

He gave me a look of cynical curiosity and said, "What do you mean? Where are your tools?" I told him that I had watchmaking tools. I was already sorry that I had started the conversation. Then suddenly, he said, "Tomorrow I'll bring the watch." I thanked him and walked away.

In the morning, he was waiting for me when I came to the work site. He led me through his office to the back room and locked the door. Then he took a wristwatch from his pocket, handed it to me, and said, "Now, let's see if you can fix that watch for me." From the way he spoke those words, I knew something was not right.

As soon as he handed me the watch, I saw that I was in tsures, because for the size of the case, it wasn't heavy enough to have all the necessary parts inside. But I didn't say anything. I asked him for a little knife. When I opened the watch and took a look inside, I almost died. He had given me a skeleton of a watch with no parts inside other than the dial. Everything was gone! My first thought was, *Oy, I'm finished* . . . but my next thought was, *Oh, no. He won't get me.*

I didn't know what to do. I felt the intensity of his gaze piercing through me as he asked, "So, can you fix it or not?"

I said, "Yes, I can fix it," without realizing what I was saying. The words just came out of my mouth.

He said, "You mean it? You can fix that watch?"

Again, I said, "Yes sir."

He said, "Well, if you can fix that watch, I'll let you sit here. Take all the time you want, but you better know what you're saying because you know what will happen to you if you don't know how to fix a watch."

I said, "Yes sir, I'll fix it. Tomorrow I'm going to bring my tools, and I'll start to work on the watch." I told him it would take about four months to fix. When I told him yes, I didn't know if I could really fix the watch at all. But later, I had an idea. From the watch he gave me, I had the original dial and an empty case. The only thing I needed was a movement, a module containing all of the moving parts needed for a mechanical watch, that would fit the case.

The next morning, I walked over to him and said, "You told me to report to you in the morning, and here I am, the watchmaker." He nodded and asked me if I had my tools. I said yes, and he took me again to that same room. There was a table and chair, and he turned on the light. It was cold outside, the middle of winter, but inside that room there was a beautiful stove made from tiles that kept it warm.

I looked at that stove, and he said, "You'll always be warm here." Then he told me the rules that I had to obey:

1. Never look out the window so you can be seen.
2. Never leave the room.
3. You'll be locked up in the room by me in the morning. I'll see you during the day when I want to, and I'll let you out when it's time to line up to go back to the camp.

Then he said sharply, thumping his finger on the desk with each word, "But that watch has to be fixed." That was the end of the conversation.

I knew he had to be careful, too. Even though he was a big shot, he could have gotten in trouble if a higher authority had discovered that he was taking me away from the company's project and putting me to work on a watch for himself.

After work, while we ate in the camp, I told my brothers what had happened. They encouraged me to keep going with it and not to worry. They would help me find a movement. Even though we had to leave some of our bundles in the last camp, we still had tools and a lot of the movements and parts that our father had given us. We also had taken old watches from home, and I had gotten some watches there in Wolanow. Some of the Poles who worked at the camp as day laborers would bring me watches to fix. If a watch stopped working because it was dirty, I could fix it with a cleaning. If it needed a part, I said it can't be fixed anymore, and often I'd get to keep it for parts. After a few days, when I felt secure enough to bring Corbinus's watch back to the camp, we were able to find a good movement that fit in the case. That was a moment of excitement and relief. Things were going my way.

Corbinus didn't let me work outside anymore—no more sacks of cement to unload. My new job was just to look here and look there and spend the day in that nice warm room. I felt terrific. I started getting up especially early to shave every morning to look presentable for sitting inside an office. When you worked outside at hard labor, you didn't have to shave daily.

I was sitting there taking my time with that one watch, but in the meantime, I told him I had a friend who was a good tailor who could make him a beautiful suit. He didn't have a sewing machine, and Corbinus would have to give him fabric, but he could sew everything by hand. I offered to bring him to work in that room with me. Corbinus told me to bring the tailor, and he gave that tailor permission to bring in his cousin, another tailor.

Then I asked Corbinus if he would be interested if I could bring in somebody who can fix shoes. He agreed. So, now he had two tailors, one shoemaker, and me working for him. I had saved a few others for the time being.

But I was the most important guy for Corbinus because that watch was more valuable to him than anything else. Maybe he also enjoyed this little game of confidence where I was betting my life. He didn't believe that I'd fix the watch, but he remembered the due date and never failed to remind me of it. Finally, after about three months, I handed him the watch in good working order.

He didn't believe his eyes, and he said, "You are something that I have to appreciate." He spoke like he respected me. And he started to bring me watches from his friends. I fixed them, too.

Every morning, I lined up in the camp with everyone else and came to the same work site, but he pulled me away and locked me up in his office for eight or ten hours. In the evening, when he came to open the door, the four of us walked out and marched back to the camp with the group.

Corbinus didn't pay me. Sometimes he gave me bread or something else to eat. But it didn't matter. I was able to sit there, inside, and conserve my energy. That was the most important thing.

Later, he told me he had been in Paris, Berlin—many places in Europe. Nobody wanted to talk to him about that watch. They said it could not be fixed because it was an empty shell.

⏱ ⏱ ⏱

IT'S A FUNNY thing how sometimes a premonition will enter your mind. One Sunday, we were lined up for a selection, and I said to my brothers, "If God forbid, they should pick one of us to be shot, I'll step out and tell them that I am a watchmaker and the two of you are watchmakers, too, and maybe it will save us."

Just before they started to make the selection, Lagerführer Bartman, the murderer, took out a piece of paper, looked at it, and called out through his loudspeaker, "The watchmaker who works for Heiger Heine should step out."

When I heard that I almost died. Somehow, he had found out that I was fixing watches instead of doing real work. I thought they were going to shoot me. Moishe and Mailekh were ready to go out with me and die together. I said, "Wait a minute. Don't get killed because of me. Don't move. Let's see what's going to happen." I stepped out, and when I walked up to Bartman, his face did not have the murderous look that we usually saw. The dialogue went like this:

> BARTMAN: "Are you fixing watches for Herr Corbinus from Heiger Heine?"
>
> KHIL: "Yes, sir."
>
> BARTMAN: "From now on, you won't fix watches for him anymore."
>
> KHIL: "Yes, sir!"
>
> BARTMAN: "From now on, you'll fix watches for me. You'll sit here in the camp, and you'll fix all the watches that I bring to you. I have plenty watches to be fixed."
>
> KHIL: "Are you going to give me a lot of work?"
>
> BARTMAN: "Yes."
>
> KHIL: "I have two brothers, and they are watchmakers, too. Can they help me?"
>
> BARTMAN: "Yeah. Call them out."

And I called out Mailekh and Moishe. It happened in a second. Bartman gave me watches right on the spot.

Then he called the captain of the Jewish police and told him, "Take those three pieces of *dreck* (shit) to the barrack, and I'll give you instructions later. Don't send them to work outside the camp anymore and don't take them to work in the camp. They'll be my watchmakers. See to it that they have a place to fix the watches that I bring them." The captain saluted and took us out of the lineup right away. His name was Zygmunt Immerglick. He wore a special hat with a red stripe and carried a sidearm consisting of a rubber hose, which he often used.[4]

From that same lineup, that murderer Bartman singled out about seven hundred men and women to be shot. He chose each one separately with a wave of his finger. We sat in the barrack staring out the window. We saw everything.

After they finished the shooting, Immerglick came in and ordered us to bury them. He took Moishe and Mailekh, and he wanted to take me, too, but I told him, "No, I cannot do it. I have to be here to take care of the watches." Immerglick was a little bit afraid to argue with me. Suddenly, I had status.

On Sundays, they always shot people with dumdum bullets that exploded on impact and blew the victims to pieces. Some bodies were buried without heads. Moishe and Mailekh picked up arms and other body parts and threw them in the grave. It was terrible. Sickening. We were upset and disturbed about it for months after that.

The next day, I explained to Bartman that if we lived with the other prisoners in the barrack, we couldn't be responsible for the safekeeping of the watches, so it would be wise to put us in a separate room. He agreed, and they made a little private room for us to sleep and work in. I told him we needed a long workbench and three chairs, and he instructed Immerglick to set up the bench and a large bed for three boys to lie in. Everything was built perfectly with wood.

They put a straw mattress on the bed and gave us sheets. We were being treated better than everyone else in the camp. We weren't just lying on a straw sack. Now we had a straw sack with a sheet. We also had pillows and a little stove. It was terrific. And of course, we had our down comforters from home. That was worth a million dollars in the camp.

The Germans would bring us wood to put in the stove, and Bartman told the Germans in the kitchen to give me anything I needed. He didn't mention food, but they understood he meant food, too.

We worked and slept in that room. We had to get up in the morning at 6:00 A.M. like everybody. We went out to get the cup of coffee with everyone else. In the evening, we lined up to get soup and bread, but we came back to the room to eat. We didn't have to sit outside to eat like the other inmates. All the Germans and Poles who worked in the kitchen recognized us as the watchmakers. Now they gave us a full bowl of soup with two ladles. When we wanted more soup, they gave it to us.

Those guys from the kitchen also brought me watches to fix without Bartman's knowledge, and we would fix them even though we were not supposed to. Sometimes they would give me money and sometimes food. The food was more valuable for us because we couldn't spend money in the camp. The guy who delivered the bread would give us a loaf of bread once in a while. The guy who delivered vegetables let us have a little bit. We had a small storage of food in our room. Sometimes we even had an onion.

The main thing was that we didn't have to work hard outside and deplete our strength. And we didn't go out for the Sunday selections anymore, either. All of the guards and all of the Jewish police knew that they were not supposed to take us out. That alone was a very big thing. Bartman inspected us in the mornings when he came to bring watches. We watched out for him every morning so we could make sure to be busy working at the bench when he arrived. He called us the lousiest dirty names. He would say, "You *zecken* (lazy parasites, lit., ticks), you have it good!" Or he would call us *ausnutzer* (someone who tries to exploit other people). He never said good morning to us. He never smiled at us. I was the only one who spoke to him because Moishe and Mailekh were scared to talk to him.

For Bartman, it was a very good deal to have us fixing watches for him. He was making good money from it, and not only money but stature. He did favors for colonels and other leaders in the German hierarchy around him. When you fixed a watch for somebody in wartime, they appreciated it. Bartman became an important guy. It was not so easy for a German soldier to find a watchmaker during the war. He had to make the trip to a big city, and it might be difficult to take leave from his duties. And even if he went, he probably wouldn't find any watchmakers. Most of the watchmakers in Poland were Jews who had already been evacuated from the towns. There were very few Polish watchmakers.

To the other inmates, we looked like the luckiest people on this Earth.

🕛 🕛 🕛

SUDDENLY, MOISHE GOT typhus. An epidemic had broken out in the camp and many died. Thank God we were already fixing watches in that private room. He had a temperature over 41°C, which is 105.8°F. If it would have gone up one more degree, he would have died. We had a thermometer; probably, we brought it from home. I don't remember.

Typhus is a terrible sickness that is transferred by lice. First, you get chills, and then your temperature goes up real high—to the point where you can die. You lose your mind from the fever, and you can't talk straight or remember anything. If you survived the typhus for fourteen days, the fever came down and you got well.

The Germans fought the epidemic by shooting everyone who had the disease. If the doctor found out you had typhus, he was under orders to put your name on a list and hand it over to the Germans. If someone didn't get up and out of the barrack first thing in the morning and the Germans saw him lying sick when they came to inspect, the doctor put his name down and they took him to the so-called hospital. By the time you came back from work at the end of the day, he was already dead.

The "hospital" wasn't a hospital at all. It was just a doctor, who was a Jewish guy, and a nurse. The doctor supposedly helped the sick, but his real job was to prevent sick prisoners from spreading disease to the rest of the camp.[5,6]

And here was my brother. He couldn't eat. He couldn't drink. He couldn't do anything. He didn't know what he was talking about. He had hallucinations that he was seeing my father and talked to him constantly. He said, "Don't you see him? He stands in front of me." He really got it bad.

I didn't report it to the Germans. It took a lot of guts, but I went directly to the doctor instead. It was after dark, about 8:00 P.M. The conversation went like this:

KHIL: "Listen, my brother is sick."

DOCTOR: "Oh, you fool—why did you tell me?"

KHIL: "I had to tell somebody. —You're the only one left to tell, and you're the only one I have hope in."

DOCTOR: "I can't do anything."

KHIL: "I know, but you'll have to."

DOCTOR: "You shouldn't have told me because now I have to put him on the list, and you know what will happen."

KHIL: "No, you won't put him on the list. Not only will you not put him on the list, but you'll have to go and see him."

DOCTOR: "You don't know what you're talking about. I won't do it. You don't leave me any alternative. I'll have to report him."

KHIL: "Listen, you know that I have opportunities to talk to the lagerführer. And I know your sister was sick, too. Did you report that? If you don't do it, the next morning, Lagerführer Bartman will come in to us, and I will tell him about you. Maybe we will die, but you will die, too."

Oh, brother, he changed his mind in a hurry. I could see that he didn't like me when I said that. He said, "Well, I tell you, I won't come in because it will make them suspicious, but I'll give you penicillin. I'll tell the nurse to come in and give him injections, and they won't know what it's about." That's exactly what we did. I kept the penicillin in our room, and the nurse gave Moishe one shot every day for three days.

I was lucky. I had caught typhus in the Kozhnitz Ghetto, so I was immune and didn't have to fear getting sick. But it was dangerous for Mailekh, who tried to keep his distance and to not touch Moishe. I took care of Moishe, and I slept in the middle between him and Mailekh. Every morning, I would dress and feed Moishe. I put my cheek to his cheek to see how hot he was with fever. I covered him with a blanket and kept an eye on him while we sat in the barrack fixing watches. I made it so no one could see him through the window.

Two days went by without a visit from the lagerführer. We were scared to death. Then the doctor informed me that the next day they were coming for a real tough inspection of the barrack. If the lagerführer saw that I had a sick brother, he would have all three of us killed because we hadn't reported it to him right away. It wouldn't have mattered that we were fixing watches for him.

The next day, I set Moishe up to sit by the bench with a loupe, a watchmaker's magnifying glass that you hold in your eye socket, in his eye. He still had a temperature over 41°C/105.8°F and was shaking terribly from the fever. Somehow, I had to make him understand how important it was for him to be quiet during the few minutes Bartman would be there. I told him, "You don't say anything. I'll make you into a watchmaker. Keep your head down like you are working on a watch, and don't ever raise your head even if he talks to you. Please don't shake." A hairspring was lying on the bench next to him like he was working on it. He understood.

As soon as I saw Bartman coming in the door, I rose from the bench and went toward him, bowed, and handed him the watches that were ready. I wasn't going to let him close to the bench. But sure enough, he walked straight up to Moishe and said, "What is that he's doing?" I said, "Please don't disturb him. He's straightening a hairspring. It's so delicate that any little move can destroy that hairspring, and the watch won't be able to be fixed."[7]

You know something? He listened to me and moved away, and I walked him to the door, relieved.

I saved Moishe's life. It took about two weeks, but he was cured with the help of that medicine from the doctor.

🕚 🕚 🕚

AFTER THAT, BARTMAN became meaner and meaner to us. He didn't hit us. It was just evident in the way he talked. One day, when he came to pick up his watches, he suddenly said, "You zecken have wasted enough time already. I think it's good to take you out to work a little." I asked him if we should finish our watches. He said, "Yeah, I want all the watches that you have finished in one week. Then you won't be watchmakers anymore."

Immerglick, the Jewish police captain, was always with Bartman when he came to our room with the watches. He heard the way Bartman called us names and talked to us. Bartman was mean to Immerglick, too. Even though he was a captain, he was still a Jew, and Bartman didn't respect him. Immerglick respected us because we had a similar status to him. He told me, "Lenga, don't you see the way he treats you? He's trying to get something." I had thought it was enough that we fixed his watches for free and that he was a big shot because of it. I asked Immerglick what I should do, but all he said was, "I don't know. I don't know." He knew, but I guess he was scared to tell me.

Over the next few days, when Bartman arrived, I was afraid. If I did any little thing wrong, he could order for us to be shot on Sunday. That's how it was. So, I did nothing. After that week was finished, he told Immerglick to take us back to work digging outside like everyone else. Every day Bartman came to observe us—watching the way we worked and making fun of us. He never used to show up to the work sites, and suddenly he was there every day. The other prisoners were angry at us. They knew that he had come because of us, and they had to work harder when that *roshe* (evil one) was around.

Still, Bartman didn't have Immerglick remove us from our private room. We had a few watches that we hadn't finished yet, and he asked me about them all the time. I told him I was looking for parts to fix them.

Immerglick approached me again and said, "Are you so blind or so stupid? He wants something from you. He won't back down unless you do something for him, so he'll be pleased." At that moment, my eyes finally opened, and I realized he was right. Maybe Bartman had told Immerglick to speak with me. I don't know.

Anyway, we had a beautiful little lady's watch with a pearl on top of the case. It was from the materials that my father had given us when we left home. I took that watch apart, fixed it, and polished it up to look brand new. I had it ready, and when he came to see us working at the site, I walked up to him and said, "You were so nice to us. We forgot that we had a souvenir, my mother's watch, and we don't know what to do with it. I feel—we feel— that you could use it for your wife or daughter. It would be our greatest pleasure to give you this as a gift."

You should have seen how his face lit up, and he smiled. He said, "You're thinking right...." I handed him the watch. He called Immerglick over and said, "Well, it's about enough for them to be working here. Let them go back to work on the watches." We had been working outside like that for about a week.

Immerglick gave me a look as a reminder that it was *him* who helped us, and I understood.

🕐 🕐 🕐

WHEN I GAVE Bartman that watch, he melted like butter and became a completely different person to me—to all three of us. He stopped calling us names. He didn't call us pieces of dreck anymore. Sometimes he even said good morning when he came to bring us watches.

He treated me like a "friend" of his. He took me along for walks across the field in front of everyone. He wasn't ashamed. We would talk about things like watch work and the weather. Never politics, God forbid. I was afraid. . . . I had to be careful not to say the wrong thing or ask for too much. I never tried to challenge him. I tried not to push too far. In one minute, he could change his mind.

You know, I had a little power by knowing the lagerführer. But I never tried to make myself better than anyone else or use it for someone else's misfortune like others who had power. My brothers and I didn't look for trouble. We had a little extra to eat because we fixed watches. Many times, we gave other people food and helped if we could.

It was a different thing when people used to ask me to use my connection with Bartman to do favors for them. I said, "No I cannot do that because I'll be finished, too. Even though I walk with him, I'm afraid of him the same as you are."

One time, when I was walking with the lagerführer, we saw an inmate moving close to the fence like he was going to try to escape. Bartman pulled out his rifle. I was looking at this boy. So stupid. Meshuga. What was he doing in that place where you're not supposed to be? Other inmates saw what was happening and gave him a sign. He started to walk back.

Without thinking, I touched Bartman's hand gently and bent his rifle away from that guy. Bartman said, "What are you doing?" I said, "He's a little farikht. He doesn't know what he's doing. He's not going to run away. You see, he's walking back. Don't kill him." It was an impulse. I had forgotten myself at that moment and just wanted to save that life. Bartman listened to me and put his gun down. He didn't get angry at me for that. The moment passed, and that was all.

Later, my brothers said I was the one who was meshuga. Bartman could have taken out his revolver and killed me on the spot. And they were right. That would have been his normal response.

⏱ ⏱ ⏱

ON ANOTHER WALK with Bartman, I told him I was running out of watchmaking parts and asked if he could give me a permit to go to Radom to buy supplies. Radom was about sixteen kilometers from Wolanow. He agreed to let me go.

I didn't really need watch parts so much, but I wanted to see if anyone in my family from Radom was still alive. I would buy some watch parts, too. I had run out of celluloid for crystals, and I needed some balance staffs.[8] I also needed a replacement crystal for that pearl watch I had given Bartman. I figured that I could probably get that in Radom, but didn't mention anything about it to him.

He gave me a paper to travel for two days. It had signatures from Bartman and Rubbe, the top-ranking officer in the camp. He was from the Luftwaffe. I could take a bus to Radom, enter the Ghetto, leave the Ghetto, and return by bus. I went by myself—no guards. It was unusual for a Jew to be traveling at that time in Poland. I had my Star of David on my arm. The Germans stopped me everywhere, and I had to show that paper. It was very, very strict.

The Germans had liquidated the Radom Ghetto like they had in other towns, and almost all of the Jews had been taken away. Maybe a few hundred Radomer Jews remained. They didn't live in their homes anymore. They were isolated in a different place in the town that had been turned into a labor camp. I went to buy parts on the Polish side of town, but I had to sleep in that camp area.

Bartman didn't give me money to buy parts. He never gave me a penny for anything. I had my own money. We used to fix watches for the guys who worked at the camp—Germans and Poles. Ukrainians, too. We told them that they had to give us money for the parts, so we made some money from selling the parts that we had.

I was able to find a boy in the Radom camp who had been going out with my cousin, the daughter of my real mother's sister who lived in Radom. I was so moved with emotion when I met with that boy. But everyone else was gone.

WE HAD A pocket Jewish calendar, so we knew exactly when each holiday was going to happen. Just before Passover in the spring of 1943, I asked the guys from the kitchen to give me a little flour. We mixed it with water and put the dough on the top of our little iron stove to cook three *kleine matzalach* (little matzohs).

The other prisoners in the barracks could not do something like that. The only reason I could was because we lived in that private room and they knew me in the kitchen. But I didn't tell them that I wanted the flour for Passover.

We made a whole Seder from memory—just the three of us. We put up something over our window so the guards standing in the darkness outside couldn't see the light coming from our room. The Germans would have killed us if they found out what we were doing.

We made the kiddish on water instead of wine. There was no Haggadah to read from, but we remembered the text. We took turns reciting sections by heart, but quietly—in whispers. We told stories to each other about how our Seders used to be at home—to remember what it was like. We even sang the songs in whispers—like "V'he She'omdo" (והיא שעמדה).[9] It was a terrific experience.

The inmates in the barrack on the other side of our wall were making noise—talking, yelling, and fighting with each other, like always. And we were alone, like always.

When it came time for the meal, we just went to bed because we didn't have the proper food. We didn't sing the second half of the Haggadah. We weren't happy enough—God hadn't made us happy enough—to sing about those things.[10]

Instead, we asked God, "Why do you let this happen to us? Why? If you are Hashem Yisborach (God the Blessed One), why do you let this happen to the Jewish people? Your people." Many times, we asked each other this question. Many times, we were angry at God. Even the most religious people asked that question. They didn't have a good answer, either.

But we had made a Seder. One Seder. We had a big thrill doing that. We did it more out of tradition than because we were religious. There was an element of rebellion against the Germans in it, too—a declaration that we still exist and we still can do a thing like that.

But who knew for how long? We didn't know what the next day would bring us.

🕭 🕭 🕭

LATER THAT SPRING, the Germans spread rumors that a certain number of Jewish prisoners who wanted to go to Palestine could register and would be given a way to go there. People paid a lot of money and whatever possessions they had to get on that list. Of course, it was a trick, but nobody knew that. We were naïve. Even though it didn't make sense, we thought it might be true. I was really serious about it.

In the meantime, Rubbe started to give me watches to fix, too, but he didn't come to our room. I had to pick up and deliver his watches. He was a big shot, good-looking, and young—in his late twenties—with many medals on him. I figured the best thing would be to try to talk to Rubbe about the Palestine list when I delivered watches to him. He knew me, but usually he was mean. Either he didn't say anything or he called me dirty names. It was not a simple thing to talk to a German. It was forbidden even at work unless he asked you a question. If he asked me ten words, I answered him with one word. But one time, I walked into his office with two watches that belonged to his wife. I had fixed them and polished them up so beautifully that they looked brand new. He smiled and even thanked me. I thought maybe that was the right moment. I asked him, "Would it be too much if I could ask a favor if it's possible?"

He said, "What is it? Go ahead." Now he played so nice—like with silk gloves—until the moment when you had already gotten on his nerves too much.

I said, "I heard rumors that some Jews can register to be sent to Palestine, and I have an uncle who is still alive and living there. Could you do me a favor to register the three of us to go to Palestine?"

When I finished, he stood up and took a rubber stick in his hand that was used to beat people. And he started to yell at me. "What is the matter with you? You don't like it here!? It's not good enough for you!? You want to go to Palestine!?" He got so angry, and his face got all red.

I said to him, "I just thought maybe it's a good idea if it's possible, but if you cannot help me, it's okay. I like it here, and I'm glad that I can fix watches for you."

He calmed down and said, "Don't you ever say to anybody that you want to go to Palestine. Just think about it." That's how he put it. I didn't know what was going on. I sensed in his voice that he was telling me something.

I came home, and I told my brothers about the whole incident, and they didn't like my interpretation. They were disappointed that Rubbe didn't agree to register us on the Palestine list. But they didn't press further. I told some other people not to register because something was off about it.

Six weeks later, the Germans came with trucks and picked up about one hundred and fifty men who had registered to go to Palestine. The Germans drove them out to the woods and machine gunned them all to death.

How did we know? Later, the soldiers returned to the camp and took about twenty prisoners to dig ditches and bury them. Those inmates told us what had happened.

That guy Rubbe helped me. We had some money and watches that we could have used to get our names on that list. He actually saved our lives.

One time after that, Rubbe asked me who would win the war when I came up to his office. When he asked me that, I almost died from fear. It gave me a *klappen hertz* (a pounding heart). I said, "I don't know. The way I see it, Germany has the strongest army in the world. They took over everything. They are already in Russia, you know." I avoided the question, and that was all.

⏱ ⏱ ⏱

I HAD FRIENDS in Wolanow. Everybody knew us, but we brothers felt close only with each other. We were better off than anybody else at the camp, and that status created some distance between us and the other prisoners.

Khamaira Salzberg was in Wolanow, too. We were in the same barrack at the beginning, and when my brothers and I had our separate place, he would come in to talk to us. I saw him all the time, but even with him I wasn't so close anymore.

We were very respectable people in the camp and belonged to an elite group of twelve prisoners—the most educated, dignified people. The three of us and Khamaira Salzberg were from Kozhnitz. The rest were from Schidlovitz. They had to include us so they could meet in our room; we were the only ones who had a barrack to ourselves. Each of the other barracks had about two hundred inmates, and it was dangerous to have secret conversations with so many people around.

Everyone returned from work at about four or five o'clock in the afternoon. We could walk in the camp until 7:00 P.M., and then everyone had to be inside their barracks. During those couple of hours in the evening, they would come to our room and kibbitz. Everybody had a little something to tell. That helped us. They debated ideas about escape—what to do and how to do it. We also discussed politics and the war on the Russian front and whether we would survive. We were sure that the Germans would lose because they could not fight the whole world. Especially with America in the war.

We heard that kind of news from the Polish engineers working with us. They lived outside the camp and went home each day. They got paid money for their work. There were no Polish prisoners in Wolanow—only Jews. The news wasn't much. The Poles also got their news by word of mouth because the Germans had confiscated all of their radios.

At one meeting, we talked about the possibility of being moved from Wolanow. We expected that it would happen sooner or later and that they would kill us all. The guys in our meeting group wanted to dig a hole under the floor in our room big enough for twelve people to hide in. We decided it was a good idea and agreed to risk our lives to do it.

We cut out some of the floorboards in our room with a little saw, and we dug. The barrack was standing on short wooden support beams every few feet. The space underneath had enough room to lay on your belly and dig. The other men would remove the dirt from our rooms in their pockets and sprinkle it out a little bit at a time all over the yard so it wouldn't be noticeable.

We had to be very careful to keep this secret from the other Jewish prisoners. Nobody could know what we were doing. If the other prisoners found out about that hole under our barrack, everybody would want to get saved, or they might inform on us. So, we pretended that we were davening when the group visited us. When somebody came by the window, we acted as if we were rocking back and forth in the style of Jewish prayer. And we put something on our head in place of a yarmulke. But it wasn't always just for show. There were some religious people in that group, and we let them use our room to daven minkha and ma'ariv. It was the only place where that was possible. The rest of us joined in—not because we were religious, but because it was something to do. We didn't daven *hoyakh* (pray out loud with spirit). We did it very softly in whispers. We didn't even have a *siddur* (Hebrew prayer book) to read from. We did everything by heart.

We dug for about three weeks and did a terrific job. When you looked at the floors, you didn't see it. It was not a tunnel. It was just a hole deep enough for us to lie down in. We figured that if the Germans evacuated the whole camp to shoot us in the woods or take us to Treblinka, we'd hide in that hole. And when they were gone, we would run away.

One guy from the group smuggled a pistol into the camp. I don't know how he got it. I took the gun apart, wrapped it up with grease, and hid it there under our barrack. We thought that if we ended up running away, we would have something to protect ourselves. One time, the Germans took us all out and started to search each barrack to see if anybody had arms. You can imagine how nervous we felt. But they didn't find anything.

In the end, we never used that hiding place.

🕑 🕑 🕑

I HAD A girlfriend in Wolanow named Privche. She was from Schidlovitz. Officially, it was forbidden to go over to the women's section of the camp, but the guards at the gate didn't enforce this rule.

We went over there, but we didn't even think about sex. You didn't have room for that in your mind. The men who were married were able to go over there and somehow be together with their wives in secret.

Privche also came over to our barrack. She was a good-looking girl, but I didn't have anything to do sexually with her—maybe we kissed. First of all, my brothers were there, and besides that, she wouldn't allow it.

She was friends with my brothers, too. But, officially, I was the guy and she was my girlfriend. That's how it was.[11]

🕑 🕑 🕑

IT WASN'T LONG before the project to build the Luftwaffe barracks was completed. Bartman told me to fix all of his watches and get them ready. I came to him privately and asked him what was going on and if they were going to take me away. I didn't ask about the whole camp—only myself. He said they were going to dismantle the camp and move all of the prisoners to other labor camps. By this point, I felt really secure with him. I asked if he was telling me the truth. He said, "Yes, don't worry about it."

He told me they were taking the prisoners to three other camps—Skarshisc, Pionki, and Starachowice. Then he asked me, "Where would you rather go with your two brothers?" I picked the Starachowice camp because my stepmother's brother, Yirmia Wilczek, was living in the town of Starachowice. I figured that he must be in that camp, too. He was a *dreyer* (wily schemer), a makher. I thought that if he was there, maybe he could help us. Bartman told me he was doing me a favor by sending us to Starachowice.

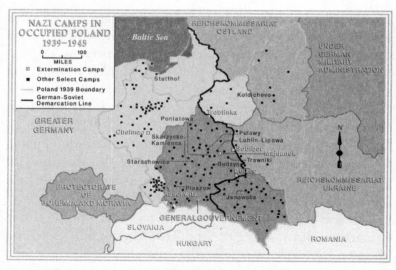

This map shows the location of Starachowice, providing some indication of the scale of slave labor utilized in occupied Poland by the German military in coordination with private industry.

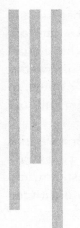

CHAPTER 8

Starachowice Slave Labor Camp (June 1943–July 1944)

W HEN WE GOT OFF THE trucks and lined up to register at the Starachowice slave labor camp, Uncle Yirmia was there in a police uniform. We called out to him, and he didn't recognize us until we told him we were his sister Malke's children from Kozhnitz. He had visited our home only once—after I had already left for Warsaw, but before the war broke out.

Right away, he took the three of us out of that line and brought us to his room with all of our stuff. As the captain of the Jewish police for that camp, he had a private barrack with a kitchen. He made us *schmaltz gribene (*crisp chicken skin cracklings with onions fried in chicken fat). It was better than the meals we had at home!

We slept in the barracks with the other prisoners, but we went to Uncle Yirmia's house to eat, and he didn't send us out to work like everyone else. He was very happy and proud to host us. Uncle Yirmia was the type of guy who could get into any place he wanted. Before the war, he owned a big, successful restaurant where they served alcohol. He was ambitious, fearless. His two sons, Adash and Avramele, and his daughter, Yitka, were also there in the camp.

For the most part, the barracks, the barbed wire, the food, and the daily routine in Starachowice were similar to those at Wolanow. The most important difference was that Starachowice did not have weekly selections to shoot prisoners. We still had our down comforters. In the summer, we slept on top of them to cushion the hard boards. In the winter, we slept under them, and the down protected us from the cold.

Uncle Yirmia's hospitality didn't last long. After a week or two, he started to ask if we had hidden money. We were afraid he would take everything from us. We couldn't trust him, and the honeymoon was over. We were sent out to work with the other prisoners.

🕑 🕑 🕑

STARACHOWICE WAS AN industrial town. Everything was on a much larger scale than in Wolanow. There was a steel mill and ammunition factories with heavy machinery.

The three of us were assigned to a smelter that we called the "high oven," where they burned coke to melt iron and make steel. Coke is refined coal that has been fired for long enough to burn away the dirt and impurities, but not to the point where the coal itself becomes ashes. It still has the substance of coal, but it's about half the size of the raw coal, and it's a little bit lighter. Coke is not black; it has a different, ash-looking color. Most importantly, coke burns hotter and keeps heat much longer than regular coal.

Our job was to unload railroad cars from Sweden filled with raw iron, coal, or coke. We stood inside the boxcar with a hand shovel and scooped chunks of cargo out of the train car and onto the platform. As we unloaded more and more, we'd be standing lower inside that boxcar and had to throw each shovel-load higher over our shoulders to clear the top. After we emptied most of the contents, they opened up the side of the boxcar so the rest would fall out a little bit. Then we cleaned out the remaining pieces and loaded everything into smaller carts, which were transported to the factory.

It was heavy, physical work, and it was burning hot. Two men were assigned to each railroad car, and they gave us two and a half hours to unload thirty tons of cargo. We had to work out our *neshome* (soul) to unload three railroad cars like that in a day— not to stop for a minute. We were beaten when they thought we weren't keeping up the right tempo of work. The foremen who beat us were mostly German Volksdeutsche. The leader in charge was a German *Reichsdeutsche,* a German who was born and raised in Germany.

Starachowice had workshops for different tradesmen. Uncle Yirmia had promised to get us into the workshop especially for watchmakers, but he sent us to the high oven instead. He had that power. If he wanted to take somebody and give him a different job, it was done. The Germans didn't care if he made changes to the work assignments, as long as he put the right number of workers in each group. He made good money from the prisoners for job placement.

🕑 🕑 🕑

BACK AT THE camp, Uncle Yirmia had about twenty-five Jewish police working for him inside the fence. They had clubs to beat the prisoners, but not guns. Uncle Yirmia abused his power to beat and take advantage of people with all kinds of lies and tricks. The prisoners hated him. They told me about it even though they knew I was family. I told them not to worry or be afraid to tell me. We became like strangers to Uncle Yirmia. We didn't bother him too much and tried to stay away, unless we needed his help in an emergency.

Ukrainian police were stationed just outside the camp, and they patrolled twenty-four hours a day with their rifles. They often came inside the camp to check everything, and the Jewish police had to obey their orders. The Germans supervised the Ukrainian police. The German commandant used to come into the camp every morning, and sometimes he came in at other times—day or night. He was in touch with everything that was going on.

The three of us were more hopeless than we were in Wolanow. This was mostly because of the Ukrainian guards. They were *farbrente* (hard-core) antisemites—worse than the Germans. They were close to us, and they saw everything. They even came inside the barracks to look and smell and hear things. We were very much afraid and had to be especially careful. I didn't even tell them that I fixed watches. Many, many times we came back and heard that someone had been shot by the Ukrainians for no reason whatsoever. It was no problem for them; no questions were asked.

⏱ ⏱ ⏱

WHILE I UNLOADED those railroad cars at the high oven, I waited for the right opportunity to repeat the watchmaking trick that had worked for me in Wolanow. It took about three months. It was the autumn of 1943.

My supervisor at that factory was an SS man from Germany—a big fat guy. I can see his face, but I can't remember his name. The factory was occupied by a German company—everything was under their control—and he was the big makher in charge.

Once, when I noticed he was in a good mood, I told him, "I'm a watchmaker. And you're such a nice guy. If you have a broken watch, bring it to me and I'll fix it." As soon as he heard that, he looked at me differently. And he talked to me differently.

One day, he finally called me aside. "I have a watch. Can you fix it for me?" He brought me into his office, and I started to fix watches with the watchmaking tools and materials we still had from home. It had worked again—just like in Wolanow. They all needed watchmakers.

From then on, I didn't unload train cars anymore. Instead, I sat with the supervisor in the weigh station. When a boxcar was loaded with the processed iron that they made in the factory, it was rolled onto the scale before they sent it out. He had to write down how many boxcars went out and record the weight for each one. Only he had the right to be inside that weigh station, but he took me in there and stashed me in a little room in the back.

I slept in the barracks of the camp with the other prisoners, and each morning I woke up with everybody and marched out to work with everybody. But when I got to the work site, I was under his control, and I went into the weigh station to fix watches. The other prisoners were jealous.

Sometimes, when some big shot German was coming to inspect, the supervisor told me, "Tomorrow don't come inside here. Go unload boxcars like everyone else." And I did.

That supervisor never gave me money or anything. I was glad to have a place to sit and fix watches. That was enough, believe me. I don't think he made money from the watch repairs, either. He just did it as a favor for his friends. He was very proud of himself for that.

The supervisor was not polite, but he was not so mean, either. —He never called me dirty names. One time, he said, "Listen, I went through plenty in the war, too. I like it better here than on the front." I could see that he was thinking differently from the other Germans. He didn't seem to hate me as a Jew. He had a better character and was more intelligent than Bartman from Wolanow.

The Polish workers at that factory received a regular salary from the Germans, and they also brought me their watches to fix. The Poles had greater responsibility. They worked at the machines, or they took liquid iron from the oven and poured it into molds. They had to be specialists for that. They paid me money for the watch repairs, and sometimes they brought me food.

MY BROTHERS WERE still unloading railroad cars. After I made some money, I set up an arrangement with Uncle Yirmia, and he put them in different jobs. This he did for us. Moishe was assigned to a factory that pressed out various sizes of round steel pieces for military equipment. His job was to work at a lathe. It wasn't too hard. I got Mailekh into the watchmakers' workshop that Uncle Yirmia had originally promised us. It required an additional payment to the supervisor of that workshop—a Jewish guy who had been there a long time.

Mailekh never got a zloty for his time at the workshop. They watched you closely, so you couldn't do work on the side. But at least he was able to sit and fix watches instead of using up all his energy unloading iron and coal from boxcars. Mailekh was able to help me with spare parts. They had everything in that workshop, and Mailekh was on good terms with his supervisor, so when I needed a part, he would let Mailekh give it to me.

There was a black market to buy things from the other prisoners if you had money or something else to trade. Mostly, it was barter. The inmates didn't have much money. The few zlotys that I made from the Poles was good money in the camp. I could buy whatever I wanted—a piece of bread, an extra soup, a cigarette, a shirt, a pair of shoes, anything. Moishe and Mailekh were both smokers. I helped them with the cost of cigarettes, but I didn't smoke, and I begged them to stop. The cigarettes were too expensive. The most valuable commodity was a pair of shoes. They didn't give you shoes if your old ones wore out or if someone stole them. You had to find a way to buy shoes from someone in the camp.

Sometimes people got into fights, but very rarely, because the police would rush in to settle it by beating both of them. If the Ukrainian guards came, they might shoot you, and that'd be the end of it. So, when there was a problem, you had to solve it quietly by yourself. The three of us never fought with anyone, and nobody fought with us. We stayed out of trouble.

🕑 🕑 🕑

STARACHOWICE WAS A more organized camp, with better facilities than Wolanow. There was a hospital with two doctors and real beds—not straw sacks like in the Wolanow "hospital." But when the typhus epidemic hit, the Germans applied the same rule that they had in Wolanow: anybody with typhus had to be reported and would be shot—the sooner, the better.

Mailekh came down with a fever during the epidemic. I was convinced it wasn't typhus, but how could we prove it? When they took him to the hospital, I ran to Uncle Yirmia. We were not on good terms with him anymore, but I came to him with tears in my eyes and said, "Listen, they took my brother, and they put him in the same hospital bed with another guy who has typhus, so he'll get typhus right away. I'm sure that he doesn't have typhus because of the way he acts. Please, help me. See to it that they give him a different bed by himself. Do me only that favor. That's all that I'm asking of you."

He said, "I cannot do that because they'll have something against me." I cried to him, and in the end, he agreed to help. He just walked into the hospital and said, "Give this one a bed for himself." And not only that, he also told them to put Mailekh in a different room with the patients who had a broken leg or some noncontagious ailment.

When they took someone to the hospital, we thought there was an 80 percent to 90 percent chance that he'd never get out. We were scared to death that we would lose Mailekh. But after three days, the doctor confirmed it wasn't typhus. He stayed in the hospital for another two days before they let him out. Mailekh was all right.

My friend Khamaira Salzberg was also in Starachowice with us, and I helped him, too. He got shot in his leg, and they took him to the hospital. I ran to Uncle Yirmia again and begged him to intervene so they wouldn't put Khamaira, my dearest friend since childhood, in a room with patients who were sick with typhus. Uncle Yirmia agreed to help. Khamaira was in the hospital for a long time. His wound was infected with pus and everything, but he got well. I visited him all the time.[1]

I never got sick in the camps.

KHAMAIRA WORKED IN a different iron smelting factory. Somehow, he found out from one of the Germans that they were going to switch all of the Jews out of that factory and when his last day would be. He felt that the German police guarding him at work were not real Nazis. Because of those two things, he thought it was the best opportunity to escape, and he did it! —He escaped from that factory the next evening and ran to the forest.

I could have gone with him. The factories where we worked weren't too far from each other. He told me that if I didn't escape then, there might not be another chance. But we couldn't have taken my brothers with us, so I didn't consider it seriously. Moishe and Mailekh were working in a different site that was too far away—they could not have gotten to us when it was time to make a run for it.[2]

WE HEARD THAT Italy had been invaded by the Allied forces and that the Russian army was pushing the Germans back. In the summer, the camp started to hire more and more Poles, and it seemed like they were preparing to replace the Jewish laborers. We were scared that something was about to happen, and some of the prisoners organized an escape. I liked the plan, but when the time came, we didn't join the others. My two brothers didn't want to go. They told me to go if I wanted, but I didn't want to leave them.

We had talked it over. My brothers argued that if the Polish villagers saw us, they would sell us out for five pounds of sugar. If we made it to the forest and came across the Polish antisemitic partisans, they would shoot us. The only chance we had was to find a Polish socialist partisan group. Except for the socialists, we could not trust the Poles.

I agreed with my brothers, but I didn't think we were better off with the Germans in the camps. We knew that their aim was to finish us off. It didn't matter if they were winning the war or losing the war. They would try to kill us.

Somehow, the Ukrainian guards found out about the escape plan. A few made it, but about 80 percent of those who tried to escape were shot. After that, the Jewish police took our shoes away and confined us to our barracks. For two days, they let the wounded lie there on the ground to suffer a slow, painful death. We saw them from the windows. We couldn't go outside at all and couldn't do anything to help them.

One day, the Germans announced they were going to evacuate Starachowice and take us to another camp. We heard rumors that all of the Jews were being liquidated from the labor camps and sent to Auschwitz. They told us not to take too much, only what we could hold in one little package. We took everything we could manage to wear on our bodies and pushed whatever we had into our pockets—watch parts, watches, and tools. We also took the down comforters. Those things had been our lifeline in all of the slave labor camps.

They loaded us onto trucks under real heavy security and drove us to the railroad platform. The camp was very close to the train lines that were used to transport iron and coal to the factories. German SS and gendarmes with machine guns were handling the whole operation. We didn't see the Ukrainians anymore.

When they took us off the trucks, we had to arrange ourselves along the length of the train so they could load us into the boxcars. There was some ability for us to choose where to line up. Our Uncle Yirmia was there, too, but he didn't have status or authority anymore. He was being evacuated just like all of the other prisoners.

Moishe and Mailekh figured that we should try to go into the same boxcar as him, in case he could help us. Somehow, I felt we shouldn't. *What will we gain to be in the same car with him?* I thought the other prisoners might take revenge on him for all of the terrible things he had done in Starachowice. He would yell for help, and we would have to take his side and protect him. So we walked away from that car and went to a different area.[3]

Then they loaded us into the cattle cars. There were two soldiers with machine guns on the roof of each train car to make sure that no one jumped out or ran away. Two SS men were standing by the entrance to each car. They pushed us in and told us we should go deeper, deeper, deeper, until finally one called, "That's enough!" And they locked up the doors from the outside.

We were packed like herring—about a hundred people in one closed railroad car—we didn't even have room to raise our arms, and we pished where we were standing. It was July, so it was hot, and we were bundled up in coats filled with all the belongings we took. It was the first time we experienced something like that.

CHAPTER 9

Auschwitz (July 1944– January 1945)

In a place where there are no men, strive to be a man.

—HILLEL, *Mishnah, Pirkei Avos*, 2:6

THE THREE OF US WERE packed together in the middle of the boxcar. One little window was built deep into the wood with crisscrossed iron bars to prevent escape. We stood there for two hours until the train took off from Starachowice in the late afternoon.

Fortunately, we had gotten into a cattle car with menschen who respected each other. One guy raised his voice to say, "If there's anybody who can do a better job than I, please let him step forward. The only thing that I want is to organize ourselves, to be able to survive this journey."

Even though we were real crowded, he ordered us to squeeze in a little closer together in order to clear one corner of the boxcar to be used for personal needs. Everybody obeyed and understood that it was the right thing to do.

Whenever someone had a reasonable suggestion, we listened to him. We didn't argue. Nobody pushed. We stood quietly, and the train rolled on. It went south, and then turned west to the setting sun—toward Germany. Some people said that we were traveling in the direction of Auschwitz. We knew for sure that they weren't taking us to Treblinka, because that was in the east.

The train stopped in the middle of the night. We heard a lot of voices talking in the distance, but nobody could make out what language those voices were speaking in. It made us confused and triggered panic. Maybe they were taking us to some kind of crazy house.[1] The smell of human flesh burning hung in the air as we stood, waiting in the crowded darkness of the boxcar. We all knew that smell and understood what it meant.

⏱ ⏱ ⏱

THE TRAIN STARTED to move again at about 7:00 A.M. It took maybe twenty minutes to get to the platform in Auschwitz. We were closed up inside the train car for another two hours at the platform, and the guys by the window saw a lot of SS men and some prisoners walking around with striped uniforms and round hats. We heard an announcement over loudspeakers that anything you had with you must be left on the train. You had to come out with empty hands. Then suddenly, the doors opened.

SS guards yelled, "Raus! Raus! Raus!" ("Out! Out! Out!"). At the same time, they shot into the crowd and over our heads with machine guns to terrorize us. We became completely disoriented; you didn't know what would happen to you in the next second. Anyone who got close to the guards was beaten. The SS beat us with rifles. The *kapos* (concentration camp foremen who were also prisoners) beat us with clubs.

We left everything we had in the boxcar, except what we could fit in our pockets.

All of the prisoners on our train were from Starachowice. They lined us up as soon as we came out. I would say we were about 1,500 people in ten long lines. A group of prisoners were assigned to remove everything from the boxcars. We saw them carrying dead people out from some of the cars. Later, we heard what happened. One prisoner tried to give orders, and other ones didn't want to obey. They couldn't control their anger and frustration and started to push and fight. People fell down and got stomped to death by the others. Uncle Yirmia and his younger son, Avrumale, were also beaten to death by other Jewish inmates in the train car. That was no accident. If we had gotten into that same boxcar, they would have killed us, too. Uncle Yirmia got what was coming to him. He was a son of a bitch to the other prisoners in Starachowice. I hated him for it, even though he helped us.[2]

When we were all lined up, a high-ranking SS officer came to inspect us with two other big shots. They looked in your eyes. They looked at your face. They didn't say anything. The head guy had a little stick in his hand, and he gave you a touch on the shoulder. If he hit you on the right shoulder, you went to the right. If he hit you on the left shoulder, you went to the left. Other SS men pulled you out with force if you didn't want to go. It must have been Dr. Mengele, the German doctor who was responsible for selections and the cruel, inhuman medical experiments they performed on prisoners. I didn't know his name at the time. We heard it later in the camp.

About 80 percent of the transport was taken to the right side. That group included older people and those who didn't look so strong. There were little kids as young as ten or twelve years old. Mothers had their children dragged away from them. The Germans marched that group away with the help of Jewish kapos who spoke Yiddish and Polish to control the crowd and hit them to keep everyone frightened and obedient.

The other 20 percent who went to the left side were young and strong people, like me and my brothers. Everyone on our side was between the ages of about seventeen to twenty-five.

WE WERE STILL standing in lines after the selection was completed, and somehow a woman who was with us in our group was holding a baby that was two or three months old.[3] I don't know how she hid it from the Germans until then.

A plain, low-ranking SS man saw the baby and walked up to the woman. With cool nerves like nothing happened, he pushed the bayonet of his rifle into the baby's body, plucked it out of her arms, and threw it up in the air. He caught the falling baby on the bayonet and flung him to the ground. He did it with pleasure—like it was sport for him.

In a split second, the mother jumped at that SS man, pushed her fingers straight into his eyes, and popped his eyeballs like two little eggs. We didn't see his eyes anymore, only blood running out of the sockets.

It happened so fast. All of us were filled with shock and pleasure that she had the courage to do something like that—without fear or hesitation.

They shot her full of bullets from three directions. She was done. The SS man started to scream from the pain. That was important for us, too. Before, they seemed different from us, but here we saw that the SS were not so superior. That guy had the same body with the same weak spots, and he screamed just like us.

Other guards came and took the SS man away. They probably shipped him back to a hospital in Germany. I'm sure he was blind for the rest of his life. The last thing he ever saw was her hands coming toward his eyes.

⏱ ⏱ ⏱

THEY SEPARATED THE men and the women into two columns and ordered our group to march. Jewish kapos walked with us and told us in Yiddish that we were the lucky ones and were going to live for a while yet. We asked one of them what was going to happen to the others who were selected to the right side and taken away. His answer was, "Don't ask. Just look at the chimney. They won't live till tonight."

I was holding a picture of my father and stepmother. I hid it in the cupped palm of my hand while I was marching. That Jewish kapo gave me a hit on my hand and said, "You son of a whore, do you want to die!?"

I said, "That's my father and mother."

He said, "Brother, don't worry about them. You'll see them later when you're dead, so don't rush. If an SS man had seen it, you would be dead already."

We marched for about twenty minutes, until we came to a big building where we were supposed to take a shower. Some in our group knew prisoners working there from before the war who told us, "Don't be afraid. You're not going to die. You were selected to work." We felt a little bit relieved that we were not going to be gassed, but we couldn't allow ourselves to trust what they were telling us. Maybe they had to tell us that, or maybe they just didn't want us to know the truth.

Finally, the Germans called over the loudspeakers, "Undress! Completely naked. Take everything out of your pockets and throw it down. Keep your shoes, but don't take anything else with you. Everyone will be searched. If we find hidden gold or diamonds in your mouth or in your behind, or anywhere else, you'll be shot immediately, so don't take a chance."

We had watch parts and watches in our pockets, but we undressed and went in without anything except a few pictures that we'd hidden in our shoes. We didn't know if we were walking to our deaths.

At the first station, they shaved all the hair off our heads, armpits, and pubic area. Then we came to a place where they had buckets filled with some kind of liquid disinfectant. They dipped a big sponge with a handle into the pail and gave you a *shmir* (wipe) in your shaved underarms and private areas. It burned so bad—like acid on your skin. It felt like we were going to die. And we could hardly stand the smell.

After that, they lined us up and when they called, we had to leave with our left hands stretched out. We were still naked, and from the line, we could see several guys and a few nurses working. We didn't know what they were doing. When it was my turn, I watched as they stuck my arm with a needle. After about five minutes, they sent me away, and the number A19367 was now tattooed on my arm. They gave Mailekh 66, and Moishe had 68.

They hadn't given us anything to drink or eat since the day before, when they evacuated us from Starachowice. Even so, I didn't feel the thirst. You don't feel that physical desire under such circumstances. My only thought was that these were the last moments of our lives.

They checked each one of us with a flashlight to see if we had diamonds or gold pieces or some other valuables hidden in our bodies. They told me to open my mouth and raise my tongue. They looked in my ears. They told me to bend down and put a pipe deep into my *tukhes* (bottom) and shined a flashlight to see inside. Oh, it hurt terribly.

At the next station, they checked if we had anything inside our shoes. The guy who checked my shoes was a Jewish prisoner. He saw the pictures I had hidden there and threw them away. I said, "That's all I have left of my family. Can I keep them?"

He said, "Be glad that they let you keep your shoes." He was doing me a favor. I could have been shot.

They gave everyone a piece of soap and marched us into the shower room with our shoes in our hands. We were very suspicious of the shower; we had heard how they gassed people in the shower room at Treblinka. Immediately, we raised our eyes to the ceiling and saw water dripping from the shower fixtures. It gave us hope and relief that we were going to live a little longer. We still didn't know for sure. Maybe it was a trick. But when the whole group moved into that huge shower room, the water sprayed down over us.

After we washed ourselves, they moved us out through the other side of the room with no towels. We walked dripping wet to the next station, where they threw each of us a package of clothes.

I didn't see my brothers while we were dressing, and when I walked outside, I couldn't find them there, either. Suddenly, I realized they were already standing very close by. I knew their faces, but we could barely recognize each other. I started laughing, and then they were laughing . . . looking at me.

Why were we laughing? Mailekh was a tall guy, and they had given him a pair of pants that reached to his knees. I was short, and they gave me a pair of pants that were dragging on the ground, covering my shoes. My shirt and jacket were real big on me, with sleeves that were too long. On my head was a round hat. Everything had blue and white stripes. They had changed us. Now we looked like crazy people.

We hugged each other and started to cry because we recognized that we were still alive and we were together. Every minute through that whole procedure, from the train to the showers, we thought they were going to kill us. We had survived the first ordeal in Auschwitz. We stood there for quite a while . . . just laughing and crying and even more surprised that we were able to laugh in such a moment—that we still had some kind of joy in our hearts.

Other people around us were alone. They didn't even know how they looked.

The SS lined us up again and told us, "From now on forget your name. Your name means nothing. You have to remember your number." They made an example of a few prisoners by asking, "What is your number!?" And if you didn't remember, the kapos hit you. We learned that number right away.

The SS marched us to the barracks. We stopped at one barrack, and it filled up with prisoners, and then we moved to the next, and so on. They told us again, "Learn your number, because this is your name from now on."

In our barrack, the blockaltester read out the ordinances that we had to obey, and they gave each one of us a metal shisel and cup. Some were old and rusted.

The disinfectant burned our skin terribly for hours after. And we still had pain in our behinds from when they pushed that pipe inside. But we didn't care because we saw that they were not handling us like they were going to kill us.

Everybody had to be on his bunk bed by 8:00 P.M. curfew. That was it for the day.

🕐 🕐 🕐

AUSCHWITZ-BIRKENAU WAS A huge place—a death factory. The Germans lived right outside the fence, so if something happened in the middle of the night, they could react immediately. They had cut down all of the trees in the area so they could easily see what was going on, and they evacuated a lot of Polish people who lived in the vicinity of the camp.

Within the camp, each group of maybe fifty barracks was surrounded by another fence with concrete posts. They called that a field. On the other side of that fence was another field. There were many fields—for men and for women—and we had to remember the number of our field. One road went down the middle of the field, a row of barracks standing on each side—almost like a town. It was a long way just to walk from the gate to the end of the field.

Every couple of hundred feet, there was a tower with a guard on the top pointing his machine gun at the prisoners below. At night, they shined searchlights to monitor us. There was another guard on the ground about every fifty feet. The guards worked in shifts all day and all night.

You could not leave your field unless a German took you out, and you could only move within your field if the Germans instructed you to. Otherwise, you had to stick close to your barrack. If you entered someone else's barrack without permission, you were finished.

Our barrack was in Birkenau (Auschwitz II).[4] Five men slept in one compartment. The three of us were on a top bunk with another two guys. We were lying on straw—like cattle. There wasn't much room, so each of us had to lie down on our side. A long oven ran lengthwise down the middle of the floor, with rows of three-story bunks along both sides against the wall. Each three-tier bunk had fifteen men. There were maybe a thousand people sleeping in our barrack.

We slept with everything we owned so it wouldn't be stolen. We had to be especially careful to guard our shoes. My shoes were the same ones I'd had on my feet when I left home in Kozhnitz. We put any clothes we didn't wear under our heads to sleep on, like a pillow.

When we woke up in the morning, we went to a latrine in one long room outside the barrack. It was the same length as the barrack. You had to rush to take care of your needs and to wash your face and hands. There were faucets with cold water running constantly when we got up in the morning. Once a week, on Sunday, they took us to the shower building where we had showers with warm water.

If you needed to go to the bathroom in the nighttime, you had to use a wooden barrel that was inside the barrack.

In our barrack, the prisoners who had been in Auschwitz the longest were non-Jewish Poles. They had probably committed political crimes, like saying something against the Germans. The Poles had been sent to Auschwitz when the Jews were still living in the Ghettos—before the Germans started emptying towns and sending masses of Jews to the camps. If a Pole committed a more substantial crime, the Germans would shoot him right there in the town. If he did something less offensive, they sent him to Auschwitz.

The blockaltester in charge of our barrack was a Pole. He didn't have to go out to work. I don't know what he ate, but we never saw him standing in line with the shisel for his ration of food.

There was a group of about ten men, usually Poles like him, who also didn't go out to work. Their job was to take care of the barrack. They looked better than us because they had more food rations and their striped camp uniforms were washed and pressed. They kept order in the barrack, which was important for us, too. Sometimes they helped us, but they also did the dirty work for the Germans.

Those barrack attendants advised us not to get close to the fence. The only reason to go close was to kill yourself by touching the electrified wires. I never saw that happen, but we heard that suicides had been much more common before we'd come to

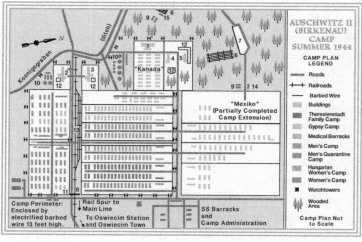

An estimated 1.3 million people were deported to Auschwitz between 1940 and 1945, including Jews from all over Europe; 1.1 million of these people were murdered, of which 1 million were Jews. This map shows that each "field" in the mens' section of the camp contained approximately thirty-eight barracks constructed in two rows. Each one was originally intended to house approximately 550 prisoners, but the Germans crammed as many as eight hundred to a thousand in each barrack by adding a third level to the bunks and increasing the number of inmates sharing a bed. If each barrack shown on the map housed eight hundred prisoners, the prisoner population capacity at Birkenau would have been 134,000 without the partially completed "Mexiko" section. Construction was carried out in stages and the goal was to achieve housing capacity of two hundred thousand inmates.[5]

Auschwitz. Many of the Jews who had been brought to Auschwitz in the early transports were loaded onto trains from various cities in Europe and brought directly there. It was so hard and such a shock that some decided it was better to die quickly than to experience such a life. Over time, these suicides occurred less and less because the people they were bringing to Auschwitz were already used to tsures from the Germans in Ghettos and other camps.

Aside from those few Poles, our barrack was filled only with Jews who had come on the train with us from Starachowice. There were all different nationalities together at Auschwitz, but not in our barrack.

🕑 🕑 🕑

OUR FIRST MORNING, everyone had to get up at 4:00 A.M. and line up for "coffee" made from burnt turnips. We knew that smell from Wolanow. It tasted terrible. We missed the *ersatz* coffee from Starachowice that was made from burnt corn.

Then we had to line up for an appel and wait quietly; we didn't know what was going to happen. That same guy, Mengele, came with other SS men. We had to stand at attention and remain still when they walked by to inspect us. They took out a few who didn't look young enough or strong enough for work. Maybe they were too short or unshaved—any little thing that they missed when they looked us over the first time on the train platform.

They finished the morning inspection at about 10:00 or 11:00 A.M. and sent away the group of prisoners who were selected. We never saw them again. Afterward, they ordered us back to the barrack. They didn't take us out to work yet. We had time to watch the smoke and fire reaching out from the five chimneys in the distance. We sat waiting in the barrack and talked about how long it would be until they finished us off.

For several days, we were subject to those selections, and they didn't send us to work. All together, they chose about a hundred men from our barrack and took them away. During the day, they came to check us again and again and called our numbers to make sure everyone on their list was accounted for.

After about four days of selections and lying around in the barrack, they told us that we were going to work. The alarm sounded at 4:00 A.M., and we had to jump down from our bunk and hurry to wash our hands, drink our coffee, and line up outside for inspection. Then for the first time, they marched us about two to three hundred yards to the gate at the end of the field and lined us up again to stand and wait.

There was a small clearing by the gate to the right of us where an orchestra sat and played the most beautiful music. We had heard that music before in the distance, but we hadn't known where it was coming from.

Starting at 5:00 A.M., we were lined up at attention as the SS counted us again and again, and the orchestra played symphonies and marches—Mozart and Beethoven—only German composers. Close to where the orchestra played was a guardhouse where German guards stood watching us. They had telephones to manage the field and call for help in case something happened. Other guards were stationed at the gate.

The musicians continued playing until the gate was opened at about 7:30 A.M. and we were marched out to work. On the way, we passed farms and saw Polish people working their fields. They looked at us, too, but the road wasn't close enough for us to have contact with them. It was the same strange routine at the gate every day. We called those musicians lucky because their job was just to play for a couple of hours in the morning. They were privileged—the best Jewish musicians from Europe.

That first day, they took us to a place with heavy rocks, and a Jewish kapo ordered us to pick them up, carry them to a certain place, and throw them down. If you didn't do it, he beat you up with his wooden club. The SS didn't stay and watch, but once in a while, they came to check on us.

The next morning, we had to pick up the rocks from the place where we put them the day before and carry them back to the first place. That's how it was every single day. Probably, this work was meant to teach us obedience and to see who was strong and suitable for slave labor. Some people thought they took us to do that stupid labor because they had too many prisoners and didn't have enough work for us. We thought that they wanted to wear us out. That our faces would get more and more *mager* (thin, emaciated) and we would lose weight until they would finally take us to the gas chamber. We could see it happening. After about a week of moving rocks back and forth, they took us to the second job, digging irrigation ditches in sandy fields.

Not only did you have to do hard labor, but you also had to watch constantly for the kapo coming at you with his club. The kapos had two jobs to accomplish each day—to see that everyone worked and to see that everyone was beaten. Only men who showed an ability to beat and kill were chosen for that job. Sometimes the SS would watch while the kapos beat us. If they were not beating us, they were not good kapos. So, they always tried to demonstrate that they were performing their job with enthusiasm.

No matter how good you worked—or didn't work—the kapos beat the hell out of you. You didn't move fast enough. You didn't work hard enough. They always found some excuse. They would beat you on the back and shoulders or on your hands. Sometimes they aimed at your head to kill you. You had to bend your head down to protect it as much as possible.

All three of us tried to blend in and not be noticed. We were very careful never to say something that could give them a reason to hit us. If you asked, "Why are you doing this to me?" they hit you again and harder. It was best not to say anything.

God forbid that someone should put his hands up to protect himself from the blows. Then they would throw him to the ground, and the other kapos would help beat him to the point where he couldn't walk anymore. They also beat prisoners to death right there at the work site. It was a terrible thing to see. The kapos didn't give a damn. They assigned two men to carry the dead body five kilometers back to the camp on a stretcher.

That was also a hard job because we were weak after a full day of work and beatings with no food until the evening.

Some of the kapos were Jews. Most of them were Poles and other nationalities—criminals, antisemites. We heard rumors that the SS didn't use Jewish kapos for the most brutal jobs because incidents had occurred where a Jewish kapo snapped and attacked his German supervisors. I never witnessed something like that. Those things happened before we arrived at Auschwitz.

⏱ ⏱ ⏱

WE KNEW THAT our hair would grow back and that the numbers were tattooed on our arms, not in our minds. But losing our watchmaking tools left us completely naked. Right away, I made a screwdriver by grinding the end of a nail. Then I made a tweezer from an old pair of earmuffs that I found. I broke off a piece from the spring that goes around your head, ground it down on a stone to make points, and bent the spring to function like a tweezer. I also found a little toothbrush I could use to clean watch parts.

There were so many watches in Auschwitz. Every day, trainloads of Jews came with their watches and other possessions. They had to strip naked and leave everything they had before they were pushed into the gas chambers or marched through the shower procedure to live a little longer. The Germans would trade those watches with each other inside the camp.

One day, an SS guard at the work site gave me a watch and had me hide in a deep ditch while I tried to fix it. He was scared to death, too. It meant a lot that I didn't have to give away my *koy-akh* (strength) digging that day.

The blockaltester in our barrack also got a hold of broken watches somehow, and we fixed them in his office after work. With those few tools, I could take apart a watch to clean it and put it back together. Of course, I couldn't fix a watch that needed a new part. When that happened, I told him the watch could not be fixed and asked if he would let me have it for the parts. He agreed, and soon we had watches for ourselves in Auschwitz.

Now we had to worry about our watches getting stolen. Moishe had the idea to hide a watch in a bar of soap so one of us could carry it and no one could see that it was a watch. He would work the soap in his hands until it was soft. Then he would put the watch inside and re-form the soap around it into the shape of a regular bar of soap. He did this with a few watches that we accumulated.

When the Germans needed a certain number of skilled workers, they lined us up and asked what trade we had learned at home before the war. The first time my brothers and I said we were watchmakers, they were not interested. They needed metal workers. The next time, we told them we were metal workers, and they took Moishe and Mailekh away to another barrack. But they didn't take me. I was afraid and worried what would happen if we did not stay together. They always tried to divide brothers. We had been at Auschwitz for about five weeks. Their new barrack was still in the same field, so I could see them after work—we had about an hour before dinner. Sometimes we managed to eat together.

Their new work consisted of taking apart shot-down airplanes and chopping the metal to pieces so it could be melted for reuse. It was lighter work. When my brothers told the guards they were also watchmakers, they were assigned to unscrew and take apart the compasses and other instruments. For that kind of precision work, you didn't get beaten. Not only that, the SS were not overseeing them. The regular Luftwaffe were in charge there. The SS were trained to hate and beat and kill the Jews, but the Luftwaffe were often not so mean.

Mailekh found the opportunity to tell the division supervisor that he was a watchmaker and could fix a watch for him. From then on, every morning, Mailekh came to his office and fixed watches there until the end of the day. On the days when the SS came to inspect, Mailekh worked with the other guys in the factory.

Meanwhile, I was completely alone—digging ditches in the rain with the kapos over me.

⏱ ⏱ ⏱

ONE MORNING, A week after they sent my brothers to a different barrack, they gathered us out for a roll call to select men for a special kind of job. That's all we knew. The SS man in charge came up to me, asked for my number, and wrote it down.

When the selection was over, the young Polish guy who assisted the blockaltester in charge of our barrack told me, "I saw your number on the list. You're going to be sent to the *Sonderkommando*."

When I heard that, I almost died from fear. The Jews who were selected to be killed in the gas chambers were processed by the Sonderkommando. They had to make sure that the Jews undressed, then they pushed them into the gas chambers, took out the dead bodies, and moved them into the flames of the crematoriums. That was their job. Can you imagine?

I hadn't been at Auschwitz long, but I had already heard what was going on. A Sonderkommando assignment meant certain death. Every six months, they took a group of the Sonderkommandos and gassed them, too, so there would be no witnesses left alive. That was why they constantly selected new men for the job. Usually, they took real powerful guys. I don't know why they chose me. It was just my mazel.

I talked it over with my brothers in the evenings. I knew I couldn't go through with that kind of work. But nobody had any ideas. Finally, Moishe said, "Listen, we have watches. Why don't you walk over to the block commandant and offer him a watch? Maybe he'll agree to take you off the list and put somebody else. For him, it won't make a difference."

I didn't know the block commandant. He was not from our barrack, but he sat in the building at the end of the field where my barrack was located. He was a French guy—a prisoner, not a

Jew—who worked for the general secretary in the Auschwitz concentration camps. I was able to find out that he administered the work assignments for the prisoners in our field. Everything was in his hands, including the Sonderkommando list. He was considered a dignitary.

I decided to try. What was there to lose? I reasoned that I was dead either way. It was better to get shot trying to bribe that guy than to be sent to the Sonderkommando.

Soldiers were usually hanging around the entrance to the block commandant's building, and I didn't know who would be sitting with him in his room. Somehow, I managed to sneak my way into his office when the soldiers were gone. You should have seen his eyes when he saw me. He could have pressed his alarm, and I would have been dead. Our dialogue went like this:

BLOCK COMMANDANT: "What are you doing here?"

KHIL: "I need your help."

BLOCK COMMANDANT: "What is it?"

KHIL: "I know I'm on the list to be taken to the Sonderkommando. I am not a killer, and as long as I live, I don't want to kill anybody else. I won't be able to do it. Please take me off the list."

Tears started to come down from my eyes.

BLOCK COMMANDANT: "Who told you that?"

KHIL: "Nobody told me, but somehow I found out. I have a watch. It's not with me, but I can get it from somebody, and I can give it to you. I only ask this one favor, if you would be kind enough, just take me off the list for that special commando work."

BLOCK COMMANDANT: "I don't think I'll be able to do it, but I'll try. And that is only between me and you. Are you sure you can give me the watch?"

He wrote down my number, but he didn't promise anything.

KHIL: "As soon as my number is taken off the list, I'll give you the watch."
BLOCK COMMANDANT: "All right, it's done."

I didn't want to accuse him of being a liar, but I couldn't leave anything to chance.

KHIL: "How will I know that you won't forget? Why don't you do it right now? Let me see you take me off the list."

He found the list and scratched my number off and then looked up a number from another list to replace me. It bothered me that someone would have to take my place, but I'll be honest, I didn't worry about that too much. As long as I was off that list.

BLOCK COMMANDANT: "Listen, I did everything that you asked, so you better be sure to bring me that watch, because if that watch does not come to this room, in my hand, I'll see to it that you'll be inside the Sonderkommando."

Only then had he actually confirmed that it was the Sonderkommando list.

KHIL: "You don't have to worry. It'll be a couple of days, but you'll have it. Thank you very much. Please let God take care of you, too."

I ran out carefully and made sure the guards wouldn't see me. Two days later, I cut the watch out of Moishe's bar of soap and cleaned it up nicely. I brought it to that Frenchman and placed it down on his table. He didn't pick it up. He didn't even look at the watch. It seemed like he was being careful, too. He said to me, "You know, I didn't believe that you could bring me a watch. You were so brave. I admired your courage to offer such a proposition."

I had seen him change the list, but I still felt no assurance. I went over it in my head over the next few days. I thought his actions meant a lot. He could have easily sounded the alarm and told the SS, "Take that guy, he doesn't belong here." They would have given me a bullet right away. But he hadn't done that.

After another few days, they called out the numbers, and my number was not on the list. Right away, they removed those men from our barrack and put them in the Sonderkommando.

That French guy lived up to his promise. I still remember him. He was tall, aristocratic, and good-looking, with white hair. I don't know why he did that for me. I guess he just admired my guts to try something like that.

That young assistant to the blockaltester saved my life by telling me that my number was on the Sonderkommando list. I would say good morning to him, but we didn't have any kind of a relationship beyond that.

It was only much, much later, after the war, that I remembered who he was. His father had worked in the city hall in Kozhnitz. I think I'd even gone to school with him; he was a little older, not in my class. He was an intelligent boy from a nice home. I knew him as a kid, but I hadn't recognized him as a grown man in the camp. When I talked to my brothers about it, they remembered him, too.

🕰 🕰 🕰

GETTING OFF THE Sonderkommando list gave me the confidence to take more risks. Now I had to figure out how to reunite with my brothers. We knew we had to stay together to survive, but it was more than that. Being together was more important to us than survival. It was what we lived for. When I thought, I thought for all of us. Mailekh and Moishe did the same, but in their own way.

I had the heavy burden of being a leader because my brothers were not capable, and they knew it, too. Not everybody's made the same way. They didn't take big risks, and I didn't want them to because I worried they might slip up, and it would be a disaster. They knew that in my *kop* (head), I was a little different. I had more confidence. I had a feeling for when to push and when not to push. Sometimes I would act on impulse, without thinking about it first. My mind worked faster and better, and I examined things from every angle. From the beginning, I tried to engrave everything that happened into my brain—to remember in case I survived. Mailekh and Moishe didn't think this way.

I was still digging ditches, so the first step was to get my assignment changed to the airplane dismantling factory where Moishe and Mailekh worked. The blockaltester of our barrack had the authority to decide where to send you for work. If someone got killed or sick, it was his job to fill up the work groups each day with replacements. He agreed to switch me in exchange for a watch. He was a Pole—an antisemite—but I had been fixing watches in his office and giving him things. I had built up the relationship to the point where I could trust him to ask for a favor.

About two weeks later, after I was already working in the same place as my brothers, we heard rumors that all the men in the barrack where my brothers were now sleeping were going to be taken away to some other camp.

The blockaltester did not have the authority to send me to another barrack, and I found out that the only guy who could help was that same Frenchman who took my name off the Sonderkommando list. It was a life or death situation for us, so I went to him again and gave him a watch before I started talking. Then I said, "You did me one favor which I appreciated very much. I would like you to do me another."

He looked at me with a curious and cynical smile. "What is it now?" he asked.

I told him, "My brothers are in a different block, and rumors are going around that they are going to be sent away. Nobody envies them. They'll probably have it much worse than here, because this is a good place to be! But I just want to be with them, so I don't mind. Actually, you'll be doing somebody else a favor if you put me with my brothers, where I'll have it worse."

He gave me a warmer smile and said, "I'll do that for you."

He switched me as I'd requested. We didn't know what was going to happen to us, but at least we were together. What actually happened later was the opposite of the rumors. They kept my new barrack in Auschwitz to work on the planes and cleared out my old barrack and eleven others, taking those prisoners away to different camps in Germany. The Russian front was moving closer to Auschwitz, so they had started to move people out. It was around September 1944.

Our workplace was called the Tzileger Batreeb Factory. It was run only by the Luftwaffe, with no SS overseeing the work. The factory was a huge hangar set up to bring in airplanes that were shot down or were no longer fixable for some other reason. They had about a hundred slave laborers working there. There were Poles and Germans, too—engineers and other skilled workers.

Moishe and I sat at workbenches—with a bowl, cup, and spoon tied around our waists—and took apart the compasses, meters, and other instruments from the plane cockpits. We sorted each type of part into a separate box so they could be shipped out for reuse in other factories. It was lighter, more delicate work, so we were able to conserve some energy. And they didn't beat us. That was the best part. Maybe I received a hit once in a while, but never a beating.

Meanwhile, Mailekh sat in the supervisor's office fixing watches.

Mailekh had told his supervisor that I was also a watchmaker, and one time he took me into a private home to fix a watch. Sometimes the Luftwaffe officers used us as free labor for odd jobs in their gardens and homes. The supervisor locked the door behind us and introduced me to the guy who lived there with his wife. While I worked, she walked by the table where I was sitting and left a piece of bread next to me, as if by accident. Even inside her home, she was afraid someone might see her give it to me. Of course, I hadn't asked her for the bread. We weren't supposed to ask for anything.

She gave me a signal to eat it and said, "Fres schnell!" ("Eat fast!"). It was not a nice expression. *Fres* is the German word for "eat" that applies to animals. The horses they give to *fres*. You would use a different word—*es*—to describe giving food to humans.

Well, I didn't give a damn what she said. I wished I could have gone there every day for a piece of bread.

$$\textcircled{8} \quad \textcircled{8} \quad \textcircled{8}$$

CONDITIONS AT OUR work site were better, but the daily routine in the camp didn't change. Every morning, we had to line up for roll call. The SS were already there to discipline us. "Stay here! Go there! Line up straight! You're not standing at attention! You don't have four men in your row! You have only three!" There were a lot of SS guys moving around, and they did whatever they wanted to us until they counted us and marched us out of the field to the work sites.

Except for the smelly coffee in the morning, we didn't eat anything the whole day. After the SS marched us back to the camp in the evening, we untied the shisels from our waists and lined up by the kitchen. When it was your turn, the guy at the barrel poured a ladle full of soup in your bowl and gave you a piece of bread, and you moved on.

If you didn't have a bowl, you couldn't get soup. Sometimes people stole bowls from others. You remembered every little scratch and dent and spot on your bowl so you could identify it if someone took it. When we went to sleep, we tied it around our body so that if somebody tried to steal it, we would wake up. We didn't have belts with our camp uniforms, so we used cords. Losing your bowl meant death unless you had something to trade for another one. It was an expensive item and not so easy to get. One time, Moishe's bowl was stolen, and we had to buy him another one from a Jewish fellow who had different tricks to get everything. I think we paid three cigarettes.

The soup in Auschwitz wasn't bad. Most of the time it was thick with barley, beans, and potatoes or noodles. Sometimes I saw meat in the pot, but I never found a piece of meat in my bowl. They cut a loaf of bread into six pieces, and you got one piece. And that's all. It was heavy, dark bread that filled you up. We became mager, but we could exist on those rations for twenty-four hours until the next time we ate. Of course, it helped that we were not doing heavy work and taking beatings.

In Starachowice, the food had been better, and you could buy more food if you had money or something to trade. That option didn't exist in Auschwitz.

The big fear in Auschwitz came from the selections. In the morning lineup for work, an SS would tap someone on the shoulder who had bruises or some injury from the day before. They took him away, and we never saw him again. The rest of us would march out to work.

Every Sunday, they made a more formal selection in each field. We used to rub each other's cheeks so they would look red and healthy. The SS inspector walked by. Then he came back and inspected us again. With a wave of his finger, he'd select all of the muselmänner along with the ones that didn't shave, didn't fix the rips in their clothes, didn't care anymore.

"Muselmänner" was German slang (lit., a Muslim) for a man who was oyshgeshpielt (spent, used up). Someone with big eyes, hollow cheeks, and big teeth—no face. The body was already completely worn out from starvation and hard labor and didn't have any life in it anymore. We didn't have a razor to shave. There were a few barbers in the barrack who were appointed to that. We would line up and wait for the barber to give us a shave. That shave could be the difference between life and death the next day.[6]

The inspector could also tap healthy, strong men for no reason whatsoever; maybe he didn't like the way you looked. Sometimes he took out more people, and sometimes he took fewer people. We observed everything closely to learn the details that separated our lives from death. Eventually, we found out they had to fill a quota of people to destroy.

The SS took their selected group of prisoners away in trucks with quiet military efficiency—no talk of where they were going. It was simple and routine. But we knew those men were going to be killed in the gas chamber and burned in the furnace.

We had been through the selections in Wolanow, where they'd line up Jews and shoot them on Sundays. The violence had been immediate, dramatic, bloody. In Auschwitz, the murder was routine, systematic, industrial—engineered for a large scale. The ovens were burning twenty-four hours per day.

Many evenings, they made surprise inspections of your clothes. They were afraid of lice, which carried typhus. If they found a louse on your shirt, they took you immediately to the gas chamber. The three of us inspected each other's clothes all the time. After work, we would kill any lice with a nail. The prisoners who didn't have a brother or a close friend helped each other the same way. Maybe not so intensively as we did, but everyone was willing to help. In our first barrack, it was mostly Polish Jews from Starachowice. Now we were together with other national-ities from all over Europe—Russians, Czechs, Hungarians, Romanians, French, Dutch, Belgians—not only Jews. Sometimes I would ask a stranger to check if my collar was straight or if my coat was torn in the back.

Clothes got torn to pieces as well, usually at work, but they didn't give us replacements. So, we would fix the rips by our-selves as much as possible. Sometimes we would use pins that we bought with pieces of bread or a few spoons of soup: that was the currency in Auschwitz. We didn't try to take clothes from people who died. We felt that wasn't the respectable, humane thing to do, even in those conditions.

⏱ ⏱ ⏱

FIGURING OUT THE dates of Jewish holidays was complicated, but we kept it up. The Jewish holidays follow the ancient Hebrew lunar calendar, and most holidays coincide with the full moon. We knew that the *Shavues* holiday occurs either in late May or at the beginning of June on the Gregorian calendar. Also, we knew that from Passover to Shavues was fifty days.

If we could figure out the date of one of those holidays, we could calculate the number of months and the days in each month on the Hebrew calendar to determine the dates for Rosh Hashanah, Yom Kippur, and the other holidays. We did the calculations for the approximate dates and checked with other prisoners who were doing the same thing. Also, new transports of Jews arrived all the time from other places in Europe, and they could tell us the actual dates. Most of the time, we were right.

We couldn't celebrate the holidays in Auschwitz, and we didn't talk about it much. But at least we knew that today was Rosh Hashanah or today was Yom Kippur. After we came back from work on Yom Kippur (September 27, 1944), one guy in the group said, "Who would like to commemorate Yom Kippur? I remember a few prayers by heart." So about eighteen men lay down on our bunk beds and listened to him recite the "Unisaneh Tokef"[7] and some other *piyutim* (liturgical poetry from the Yom Kippur service). He had to do it quietly so nobody from the other areas in the barrack could hear. We didn't know if we could trust them.

🕐 🕐 🕐

ONE AUTUMN DAY in October 1944, they ordered us to stop all work and line up for a roll call. Suddenly, we were surrounded by SS with machine guns. They marched us to a place where a lot of prisoners were already lined up from other factories. We thought they were going to kill us, but they just kept us standing there for hours.

We didn't find out what was going on until they took us back to the camp. There were rumors that the Sonderkommando had exploded a bomb in a crematorium and made a daring escape. We didn't know how much of the story was true. Only after the war did we learn that it really did happen.

The Sonderkommando had access to all of the possessions that people brought with them on the trains to Auschwitz. Sometimes they found ammunition, dynamite, and other explosive materials, and they had organized themselves to hide and accumulate those items. The SS didn't suspect a thing.

On that day, in a surprise attack, the Sonderkommando hit their SS guards from behind, killed them, and threw them into the crematorium. Then they set fire to a part of the crematorium and ran. They had everything prepared to turn off the electric current from the portion of the fence where they cut the barbed wire to escape.

The landscape was completely barren outside the camp. The Germans could see everything. Not a single tree was left to grow in that area. The Sonderkommando threw smoke bombs while they ran so the guards on the towers couldn't see where to shoot. That's how they made it.[8]

The guards managed to kill many of them, but a few escaped to the mountains, where it was possible to hide. The Germans also caught some alive and brought them back to the camp, where they made a big ceremony of announcing their crime and hang them in front of our eyes. Whenever they had a hanging, they took us all out and forced us to watch.

We were glad that some had escaped. At the same time, we hated the Sonderkommando. They were the killers, and we felt that they deserved to die, anyway. They killed so many, and yet we understood that they were forced to do that job. I myself could have become one of those killers if that French guy didn't take me off the Sonderkommando list.

The Sonderkommandos had succeeded setting fire to a part of one crematorium, but the Germans had it rebuilt, and the other four crematoriums had continued to work around the clock.

In November, there was a big change. Rumors were going around that they had stopped gassing people and had demolished the gas chambers. We couldn't know for sure because we were confined to our field and the gas chambers were far away.

⏱ ⏱ ⏱

THE SS IN the camps were enthusiastic in their work. They had been chosen because they possessed the required personality traits and believed in the Nazi ideology. If they weren't 100 percent committed, they were well-trained and became accustomed to it.

Some had cameras and took pictures of us to show their superiority and probably to report on what was going on to their commanders. Big shots from the SS and Gestapo often came to visit Auschwitz. After one of these visits, we heard that Heinrich Himmler had been one of the visitors. I didn't yet know who he was at that point.[9]

The SS thought we were shit. They treated us like shit. They called us shit. They tried to dehumanize us, but we never viewed ourselves that way. We knew that they were murderers who didn't have any humane qualities left in them. We thought they would pay very dearly for their crimes when the war ended.

In Auschwitz, we were already more dead than alive. Nothing about our situation indicated that we had a chance of surviving. Our struggle and our resistance was simply to hope for a better tomorrow. We would say that a miracle could happen a minute from now. Everything could turn around in a day or a week or a month, so it was worth it to push yourself through one more day.

We worked hard to keep hope in our minds and not to become meshuga. And the more you talked yourself into it, the more you believed in that hope. If a hungry person believes that he'll find something to eat later, he can last longer. If he thinks, *It's pointless, and I won't survive,* he dies faster. I saw it happen many times. Pessimism is a terrible sickness. You destroy yourself. You have to have optimism all the time.

But the mind turns. Sometimes we fell into despair—better to die than to be put through the torture. Many times, I prayed to God for death. We never talked about suicide. Still, it passed through our minds. Any day you could grab the fence wire and electrocute yourself. We left it to the German murderers to finish us off. According to Jewish law, if you kill yourself, you are a murderer, too.[10] We were not murderers.

But our episodes of despair were temporary. One gave support and encouragement when another brother was down. Our minds were still in good shape. We wanted to live. We would tell each other stories that were not true. One would come back to the barracks and say, "I heard a German say it won't be long till the war is over," or "A Pole told me about something he saw in the newspaper." The rest of us knew it probably wasn't the truth, but it was nice to hear something that could give us hope.

We did know that the Germans had retreated from Stalingrad. That was a big deal. And we heard that the Russians had taken most of Poland and were advancing toward us. But we didn't know details.

We had a few sources for this information. The Polish engineers who worked in the factory were not prisoners; they got a salary and went home after work. Some of them hated us and told us that we deserved what we were getting. But others were not antisemites and had rakhmunes. They told us what was going on with the war and tried to encourage us not to give up. It meant a lot. Otherwise, we wouldn't have known anything.

There were also German prisoners who worked in the factory. They had authority over us but were not kapos—they didn't beat us—and sometimes they shared a bit of news. Even some German soldiers in the Luftwaffe would tell us, "It won't be long."

There was a special patch on the uniform for each type of prisoner according to his nationality and crime. For example, murderers and common criminals had a green insignia. A political prisoner, like a communist, had a red insignia.[11] We didn't talk politics with non-Jewish German or Polish prisoners. We only listened. We were afraid that they might be trying to trick us or that we would make them angry and they could use something we said to get us shot. Even though they were prisoners like us, we were very careful.

The Jew had the lowest status of all the nationalities in the camp. It didn't matter if he was from Germany or Hungary or Poland or France. Wherever he was from, he was just a Jew, and he wore a star on his uniform. Being a Jew was your crime. Everyone else had privileges over the Jew and could do anything to a Jew.

The second worst status was the Gypsy. They were kept in a separate field. The Germans gassed them and burned them like they did to us, but they still had more privileges at work than we did. A Gypsy kapo was respected a little more than a Jew.

The Russians and Poles had the third worst status level. Then in ascending order came the French, the Dutch, and the Czechs. The Germans respected the Czechs. It was bad for anyone to be in a concentration camp, but if you were a Reichsdeutsche prisoner—a real iron German—you had the highest status and the most privileges of all the nationalities in the camp. The Nazis always gave the easiest work to the Germans.

AFTER WORK, WE would sit on the bunk beds and talk. Everybody told his story—where he lived and how he lived before the war. Sometimes we sang songs. Mostly, we talked about when death would catch us. We were fortunate to be close with boys we knew from Starachowice or Kozhnitz. There was a joke about the ARBEIT MACHT FREI ("Work Makes You Free") sign on the gate to the Auschwitz I camp. We would point to the smoke and the fire coming up from the crematoriums and say, "Probably tomorrow that will be our ticket to freedom."

They turned the lights out in the barrack at 9:00 P.M. From that moment on, we had to be quiet; not even whispering was permitted.

It was now winter, and the stove that ran down the middle of the barrack gave enough warmth to sleep. It wasn't warm enough to be comfortable, but we didn't freeze. They gave us a blanket to sleep with and a "jacket" to wear outside that was really just a long shirt made of thin striped material, like the rest of our uniform.

The normal temperature during a Polish winter was about 15°F/–10°C, and sometimes it got down to 0°F/–17.8°C. Every morning, we lined up and stood at attention for hours in the freezing cold while the musicians played symphonies by the gate. We now felt sorry for them as they sat holding a trumpet or a violin without gloves and maneuvered the instruments with their frozen hands. A lot of them lost fingers from frostbite and were taken away to the gas chambers.

Then we marched forty-five minutes in the snow to the factory. Once we got there, we worked inside, where it was warm. We were lucky. A lot of prisoners worked outside, and many died from the cold.

In January 1945, we saw that something was changing. Rumors circulated that the whole camp would be evacuated soon because the Russian forces were very close. They started to give us bigger portions of food and even gave us soup in the morning instead of coffee.

The Germans knew that they were going to lose the war. But the daily routine of persecution didn't stop.

⏱ ⏱ ⏱

ONE LATE JANUARY morning, Moishe woke up with a start: "Where are my shoes!? I don't have my shoes!" We searched through everything. They were gone—stolen in the night.

That was a tragedy. Without shoes, you had to walk barefoot on rocks and snow in the freezing cold. It didn't take long before your feet were bleeding and frozen. You fell down and couldn't walk. You were finished. They would give you a pair of wooden

Holland shoes, but those hurt your feet worse than anything else and didn't protect your feet from the cold.

At night, you tied your shoes together and slept holding a shoe in each hand, with the laces knotted together behind your neck. You tried to hold them tightly so you would feel any little touch and wake up right away if someone tried to grab them. But in the middle of sleep, you could unintentionally let go and move your hands away. We were on the top bunk, so it was more difficult for someone to steal from us. But somehow it had happened. We were so angry at Moishe for not guarding his shoes.

Stealing shoes was a terrible, dirty thing to do. We didn't know who had done it. Many things had been stolen from other people that same night.

A lot of people found out about Moishe's situation right away. Some prisoners in the barrack always had shoes to sell. I don't know how. Maybe they worked in a place where shoes from dead people were sorted. Maybe they stole shoes or bought stolen shoes from somebody else. One guy came to ask Moishe's shoe size and returned with a pair that fit him perfectly. That was mazel. I'm telling you. We had only half an hour from the time we woke up to go to the washroom, get our coffee, buy the shoes, and line up outside for the roll call.

The bargaining was not a big to-do. The guy saw three brothers, so he asked for three rations of bread. We told him, "We cannot all three of us die. We will give you two rations, and one ration we'll divide between ourselves." He agreed. He was under pressure, too. If he walked out to the roll call with an extra pair of shoes, he would be shot. If he left shoes in the barrack, somebody else would steal them.

We didn't have any bread in the morning, so payment for the shoes would have to wait until we got our evening rations. Everybody bought on credit like this. You had to. But if you didn't pay what you promised, you could be stabbed by the other prisoner in your sleep, and they would find you dead in the morning. Even if your creditor didn't take revenge, everybody in the barrack would know that you tried to cheat him, and you wouldn't be able to get credit the next time.

We avoided that kind of danger. In the evening, we gave the guy two rations of bread, as promised, and divided the third ration between ourselves. It was a big sacrifice, but we made sure Moishe got shoes.

If we hadn't been together with him and he had been alone in that situation, it would have been a dangerous thing for him to promise two rations of bread. If he couldn't control himself and ate his bread rations, all he could have done was steal from somebody else. If he was caught stealing, the guards would have killed him, and if he couldn't pay the ration that he owed to another inmate, that guy could have stabbed him.

You can't imagine what it felt like when you're so hungry, and you have a piece of bread in your hands that you feel could prevent you from dying that day. It's a terrible, terrible thing.

The Germans would shoot you for stealing from another prisoner, but they didn't involve themselves in our life tragedies if we killed each other. For them, we were nothing, like ashes from a cigarette that you flick away.

CHAPTER 10

Death March, Mauthausen, and Melk (Late January 1945–April 1945)

A DAY OR TWO AFTER we bought the shoes for Moishe, we woke up to an emergency siren at 4:00 A.M. That meant you had to dress immediately and run out for a roll call as fast as you could. Outside, we saw that the Germans were rushing around and disorganized. We could have hidden ourselves in the camp, but we didn't understand what was happening and didn't think quickly enough to take advantage of the situation. We had a couple of watches in our pockets and the two tools that I'd made.

They gave each of us about a quarter loaf of bread and a can of meat! We never saw that before in the camps. The can had a key to open it, like a sardine can. They didn't give us any coffee that morning or any water to take with us, and they told us that the food would have to last us until the next destination. Of course, we ate up the meat and bread right away. We were always hungry, and a single thought was always on our minds: *If you have food, eat it now while you're alive, because you don't know what will happen to you the next minute.*

They didn't line us up. They didn't count us. No time for that. They just opened the gates and yelled at us to run! We ran, and they ran with us. We were six in a row. SS men ran on each side of the column with machine guns in their hands, ready to fire. There were several inches of snow on the ground.

The continuing pace was almost a run because they thought the Russians were chasing us. The SS marching with us shot anyone who tried to break away. They also had a platoon driving in vehicles behind us, and if somebody was able to get away from the column, that group would give chase and kill them instead.

People marched at different speeds. As long as you stayed in the column, they let you march. Weak people and older people got slower and slower, until finally they fell and couldn't get up anymore. The SS platoon in the cars shot them and left them dead on the road. We were afraid we would run out of koyakh, too.

Later, in the dark of night, we couldn't make out what was going on. A lot of people fell down. Suddenly, we were stepping on other humans as we ran. Some were trampled to death. In the middle of the second night, we passed through a town, and a few prisoners tried to run away in the dark. It was the Russians, mostly; they had guts. The Germans went after them.

They terrorized us like that for three days and two nights without rest, without food, without water. No stop whatsoever. "Schnell, schnell!" they would yell. You grabbed dirty snow from the ground and pushed it into your mouth to wet your throat and your tongue. We couldn't run out to the side and get clean snow.

The SS who marched with us were probably miserable, too. Of course, they drank from their canteens and ate constantly. Even though they were running from the Russians, they stuck to their mission to drive us forward.

We didn't know where they were taking us. The column was moving south toward Czechoslovakia. We couldn't talk. We had to concentrate on running. We had to go on.

⏱ ⏱ ⏱

THE THIRD DAY of the Death March ended at a huge farm surrounded by barbed wire. We were maybe four thousand people, and they herded us toward a barn to stay there overnight. Within five minutes, that barn was filled to standing capacity, and fewer than half of the prisoners were able to get inside.

The rest of us were left outside with nowhere to go. We'd been hot the whole day while we were running. Now that we'd stopped, the freezing cold hit us. Snow was still on the ground. The temperature must have been about 5°F/-15°C—something like that. Who had a thermometer?

We were completely worn out. It took a lot of energy just to pull up your leg to take another step. The Germans had disappeared. They needed rest, too. But it didn't matter. We were too tired to try anything. Many people surrendered to exhaustion and fell to the ground. Mailekh said to us, "Brothers, we don't have to suffer anymore. We're tired. Let's lie down and fall asleep. It's the easiest thing. We'll have no pain. We'll freeze, and that will be the end of our lives. It's over."

I got so angry at him. I said, "You're going to help those lousy, dirty Germans save some gas or a few bullets!? You're going to destroy yourself for them!? We have to try to stay alive as long as we can. If we have to die, we die. But so long as we have our life in us, we have to fight."

It was a good speech, but I didn't have another idea to propose. I didn't want to talk to him anymore, so I walked away, leaving Mailekh and Moishe standing there in the crowd.

While walking, I saw a big building at the distant end of the farm with lights on the upper floors. It was the size of a small apartment building. As I drew closer, I heard soldiers singing German songs high up on the second floor. They sounded like they were drunk already. The first floor was dark. Then I noticed little basement windows, and they were completely dark.

I went back to my brothers and called them away from the crowd. I told them what I'd found and said that if we could get into that basement real quietly, we'd be able to survive the night. "We'll have time to die later. Let's see now what we can do with this."

We walked together. The other prisoners didn't have the koy-akh to pay attention to each other or where we were going. No guards were watching us. They were probably all upstairs in that building, resting. Don't forget, they ran with us for three days and two nights. They were not supermen.

At the building, I took off my striped Auschwitz jacket, tied it around my foot, and kicked the window in gently so it didn't make noise. Then I put my hand inside to release the latch at the top of the window, and it opened the entire window frame with enough room for a person to climb through.

My brothers held my arms and lowered me through the window. When my feet hit the dry floor, I told them to let me loose. I couldn't see anything, so I started to feel around the walls to find a light switch—up and down, slowly, slowly, slowly.

I found the switch and turned on the light. I couldn't believe my own eyes. There were huge piles of fresh vegetables lying in the corners—potatoes, onions, beets, turnips, carrots, celery, cabbage. Plenty! I grabbed three potatoes—they were the closest to me. I put one potato to my mouth. When I sunk my teeth in, the best wine in the world wouldn't have tasted so good. It was the biggest treasure. I hadn't eaten a fresh carrot or potato since before Auschwitz—probably a year or more.

I ran over to the window and handed each brother a potato. I said, "Now this is a start. We have plenty to eat here. It's not heated, but we won't freeze. The only thing is, we can save some more lives. I think between 250 to 300 boys will be able to fit if we just stand here overnight. Go back. I'll stay here and turn off the light. Go to each person very quietly. Don't think too much. When you think you've reached enough people, stop. Send them in this direction one by one, and tell them how to get in the window. Nobody should speak. The most important thing is not to bring too many people. Don't let the ones you tell talk to others. Because if they all come, they won't get in, and we will be discovered. We'll all be finished."

They agreed and brought back a bunch of people. In the end, everyone came all at once, but they didn't say a word, and no one saw them. It was a dark night with no moon, and I'm sure that many prisoners were already asleep outside in the snow.

As they entered the basement, they took vegetables. Later, when the room was filled to standing capacity, we were handing vegetables around. Everyone had enough potatoes or carrots to eat and enough to load their pockets, too.

We turned off the light so no one would spot us. We could still hear the Germans upstairs singing. We closed the windows so it wouldn't be cold. Everybody stood there chewing and behaved themselves according to our instructions. We were angels to them.

We couldn't eat much. After two or three raw vegetables, you were full. It didn't take us long to fall asleep standing. We were close together, and the walls of the basement held us up. You didn't sleep like you would be lying down, but you were so tired and a little satisfied in your stomach, so you started to *drimmel and drimmel* (doze and doze).

I don't think I stood next to Moishe and Mailekh that night because they had been waiting outside by the windows to make sure everyone was entering quietly and nobody was running away. They came in last.

The early risers woke everybody up, and each of us climbed outside before the morning light. The three of us were the last to leave, and we filled our pockets again with potatoes and carrots. They were the best to eat while marching. Even with all those people eating and loading their pockets with food, we couldn't take everything. There was still a lot left.

Outside was terrible. Lifeless people were lying all over the farm. They'd frozen to death in the night. I don't know how many, but it was more than hundreds. There were maybe two thousand bodies.

The Germans organized us, and we started to march again. They didn't give us anything to eat or drink. Thank God we had found that food in the basement.

🕑 🕑 🕑

WE MARCHED ABOUT half a day to a train station, where they loaded us into cattle cars that were open on top. The train was going through Czechoslovakia, and we could feel the cold wind. At one point, our train was diverted to a sidetrack in a station to let a more important train pass us. The Czech employees who worked at the station started to talk to us through the windows. They spoke in Czech, and we told them in Polish that we were prisoners from the concentration camps. Czech and Polish are both Slavic languages, so we could understand each other.

At the same time, Czech peasants—men and women—ran toward the train and started to throw packages to us over the top of the open cattle cars: bread, candies, bottles of milk! We reached up our hands to catch what we could and grabbed every little thing off the floor. The SS shot over their heads to scare them away. But those Czechs didn't give a damn. I would never have believed that free people on the outside would risk their lives to help us. I'd never seen something like that before.

The train took off again. It was hard to be crowded like that. If you had an itch and wanted to scratch, you tried to push a little in order to pull out your arm. If the guy next to you pushed back with a little aggression, other people would lose their balance, so they started to push. If a fight broke out, everybody could go after you. If you fell down, they could step on you and kill you.

Well, one guy gave Moishe a push, and he pushed back. Moishe was anxious and couldn't control himself. He started to yell at the guy. I grabbed him away and said, "Don't you ever open your mouth like that again, or *I'll* kill you. Stay quiet and don't react. Hopefully, nobody will bother you. And if you get a hit, be glad it's only one." He backed down after that.

🕑 🕑 🕑

THE TRAIN STOPPED at around 4:00 in the afternoon, and they marched us. It was night by the time we arrived at the Mauthausen concentration camp. They assembled us in a closed-up area in front of a bathhouse. We wandered around that area until they ordered us to line up. It was ice cold and windy. We were exhausted and thirsty and hungry, and we had to stand in place, freezing.

Every twenty minutes or so, two German gendarmes came out and took about fifty prisoners into the bathhouse. We waited until midnight, when they grabbed me and another guy to carry out the clothes left by the prisoners who had undressed themselves before they entered the shower. We were working inside, close to the shower room, and they were going to let us into the shower once we were finished carrying the clothes. My brothers were still outside freezing.

Finally, Moishe and Mailekh came in, too, but not because it was their turn. We still had two watches that we'd held onto through the Death March, and I gave one of those watches to the attendant inside the room to take my brothers into the shower room sooner.

Inside, they gave each prisoner a piece of soap and told us, "Take off your clothes and leave everything except the shoes."

The other watch we had was hidden in a piece of soap. Moishe had done that one in Auschwitz, too. Now he took a chance and carried it into the shower at Mauthausen. It looked like an ordinary piece of soap, but had they taken that soap out of his hand, they would have felt right away that it was too heavy. Luckily, they didn't think to check it.

After a hot shower, they brought us outside with no towels. We were wet and completely naked, except for the shoes on our feet. Moishe was still holding the bar of soap with a watch in it. I touched my shaved head, and it was covered with ice. We stood there shivering. We didn't know what they were waiting for. *What?* I thought. *They didn't have any room? They were looking for a place for us in the barracks?*

People couldn't withstand it. They started to spit blood and fall down dead. Moishe had an idea: "Let's huddle our bodies together. We can hypnotize ourselves." I would never have thought of it. We pressed our bodies together real tight and started to chant, "Only a bullet or the gas chamber will kill us." We repeated that over and over and over. And do you know something? We stopped feeling the cold. We stood naked and chanting for three hours and saw people falling down around us, but we didn't feel any cold whatsoever. We didn't spit. We didn't even cough. The togetherness—the will to live—was so strong.

We knew that if they wanted to finish us off, they could have killed us in Auschwitz or at any point in the Death March. But they still needed our labor. They set up this cruel game, and we gambled with them for our lives. If we gave up for a moment, we would be finished. Eventually, they took us down into a basement and gave each one a package of clothes—a pair of pants, a shirt, and a thin jacket—all with the usual concentration camp stripes.

⏱ ⏱ ⏱

THEN THEY BROUGHT us into a barrack. It was warm. We thought, finally, after three days marching and going through that naked, frozen hell after the shower, we'll have a chance to stretch out our legs—to warm up and rest. Utopia.

The reality was something else. There were no bunk beds, just straw sacks about fifteen feet long lined up on the floor. We had to sit on them to sleep, with a leg on each side of the sack, like you would sit on a horse. Another guy sat down between your legs in front of you, and so on, until prisoners sat along the full length of each straw sack.

I had a Russian guy in front of me and a Russian guy behind me. I don't remember how I got separated from my brothers. The one in front leaned back and rested his whole weight on my chest. When I tried to do the same thing to the guy behind me, he started to hit me and said that I shouldn't lie on him. So I tried to push that front guy off me. I punched him and said, "Sit on your own! Don't lie on me!" He turned around and hit me, too. I was so dehydrated and weak that I couldn't fight with either one.

The Russian prisoners were still fat and strong. The Germans started to treat them with more respect once it was clear that the Russians would be the victors. Everything was different in 1945 except for one thing: the Jew was still the lowest class. The Ger-

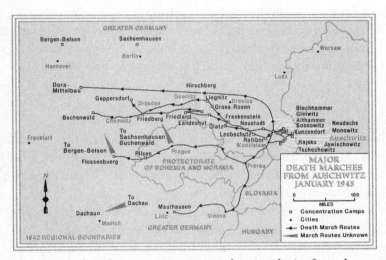

Nine days before the Soviet army arrived at Auschwitz from the east, the Germans forced some sixty thousand prisoners—mostly Jews—on death marches from the Auschwitz camp system. More than fifteen thousand were shot or died from exhaustion, exposure, starvation, and other causes., before reaching a destination. Tens of thousands (which probably included the Lenga brothers) were marched southwest to the city of Wodzisław at the border of Poland and Bohemia-Moravia (formerly Czechoslovakia).[1] In the days when Auschwitz prisoners arrived at Wodzisław, temperatures of −4 °F/ −20 °C and lower were recorded.[2] "In Wodzisław, the prisoners [were] put on unheated freight trains and deported to concentration camps in Germany [and Austria], particularly to Flossenbuerg, Sachsenhausen, Gross-Rosen, Buchenwald, Dachau, and Mauthausen," which is where the Lenga brothers were sent before being taken to Melk the next day.[3]

mans made sure we were always the weakest. And the other classes of prisoners were allowed to mistreat or kill a Jew.

In the barrack, the SS ordered us to be quiet. Kapos walked around with clubs in their hands, and whoever made a noise was hit over the head with deadly force. It was terrible.

So, I had to concentrate all my strength on holding that front guy on my chest for hours, until the morning finally came and they ordered us to get up. I couldn't stand up by myself for a while after. Again, they didn't give us anything to eat that morning. The Germans marched us for about six hours to a railroad station, where they loaded us into train cars and took us to another a concentration camp in Melk, which was very close to Vienna.

MELK WAS A tougher camp than Auschwitz. The food routine was the same. In the morning you got burnt turnip coffee, and after work you got soup with a piece of bread. But the work conditions were much worse.

We dug corridors in the hills for the Germans to build underground factories that would be hidden from the Allied planes and protected from aerial bombing. Some of the underground factories had been finished before we got there and were operating to manufacture airplane parts.[4]

The work was so hard and dangerous. There were electric lights in the tunnel, and SS supervised us along with the kapos. You had to stand there with an electric jackhammer pointed up above your head and dig into the rock and sandy earth. You didn't have any protection—no hard hats, no glasses. Many times, rocks fell down on you. Not only did you have to operate that jackhammer, which was so heavy, but you also had to keep an eagle eye on each piece of rock that might come loose so you would have enough time to jump away if it fell. Then we filled up little wagons with the sand and rocks. Other prisoners pushed those wagons in and out of the tunnel to clear the rubble.

A lot of prisoners got killed by heavy rocks falling on their heads. There were also cave-ins when a tunnel collapsed, and twenty, fifty, or sometimes even a hundred people got killed. Any prisoners who were killed at the work site had to be carried back to the crematorium in the camp. They assigned two people to carry each dead body. A corpse is heavy, even when it looks skinny and starved, and sometimes those who carried the bodies couldn't go on and fell down themselves. The kapos and the SS would beat them until they had to be carried home, too. I always prayed to God I wouldn't get assigned to that commando.

⏱ ⏱ ⏱

IT WAS so cold. We would rip paper from the cement sacks and put it under our shirts to protect our bodies from the cold with a little insulation. The Germans didn't allow that. You had to throw away the paper when the guards weren't paying attention as we got closer to the camp. If they found it while you were marching back to the camp, they beat you. The guards also would come in to search our barracks. If they found a piece of paper on you or behind your bed, they gave you twenty-five lashes with a whip.

One time, an SS man caught me wearing an extra jacket. He told me to take it off and wrote down my number. I pleaded with him, "You know how cold it is, and look, it's so thin . . . nothing . . . and I work really hard. . . . I found it lying somewhere just today, and I put it on."

He said, "I'll have to report you."

But he was talking to me. That was a good sign. Another SS guy would have beaten me up right there on the spot. This one preferred to give the dirty work to another unit that punished inmates who didn't obey the rules.

The punishment would be fifty lashes or maybe seventy-five. It didn't matter which. After fifty lashes, you were finished, anyway. I was really worried. Mailekh said, "I bet he won't report you. Nothing will happen . . . you'll see." I didn't hear anything for three days. On the fourth day, they removed all the prisoners who'd been caught with a piece of a paper sack or did some other small thing that was against their rules. They didn't call my number. I don't know why he didn't report me. I was lucky.

🕐 🕐 🕐

I HAD MADE up my mind and persuaded my brothers that if we had to do the job, we'd do the job. It was better than getting beaten. If you were beaten up to the point that you couldn't work, they beat you more until you couldn't get up anymore. If that didn't kill you, they just put you to the side until the end of the day, when the other prisoners carried you back to the camp. If you were still unable to walk on your own, the Germans brought you to the "hospital," where they finished you off. So, I was always trying to be more active and diligent at work—to do exactly what the guards wanted me to.

One time, I was assigned to carry the long, steel rails that they were using to build railroad tracks so that carts could travel into the tunnels. That was the worst job of all. I prayed to God, *Please let me come out of this alive.* One of the older SS men was supervising our work. The younger SS men who'd previously guarded us were no longer at the work site. The SS man took me with one other guy to pick up a rail and take it underground to another destination. The rail lay right on my shoulder with no padding. It was three or four meters long, and the cold steel pushed into my flesh and bones. Our bodies sagged under the crushing weight.

I was in the back. I figured out that I should always try to be in the back, so I could observe the guy in the front. I saw the guy in front of me starting to sink down deep and wobble back and forth. I knew it wouldn't be long. Either his legs would break down under him or he'd jump away. I had seen this happen before with other people carrying those rails. I kept my eyes only on him. That's all I focused on. Sure enough, a few seconds later, he collapsed. Right at that moment, I jumped away, so the rail

wouldn't hit me when it dropped. Those rails bounced when they
hit the ground. The falling rail killed the guy in front on the spot.
It came down on his head, I think.

The SS man who was leading us saw the whole scene. Right
away, he called someone to take the dead guy and bring a new
prisoner to be my partner. We lifted the rail and carried it farther
down into the tunnel.

While I was walking, that same SS man passed by and
touched me in the area of my pocket. I felt it, but I didn't dare
look. The light was dim—the tunnel was almost dark—and I
knew that I had to stay focused on the guy in front of me in order
to live. Finally, we came to the destination and put down the rail.
I reached into my pocket, and what did I find? A piece of bread.
That SS man saw how I was maneuvering to survive and re-
warded me for it. I took a look at him, and he gave me a sign with
his eyes and looked away, as if to say, *Don't make anything of it.* I
understood. In another minute, that same guy could shoot me
without hesitation. That was the norm. But in that moment,
he'd shown a spark of kindness. I appreciated that very much; it
gave me encouragement. That couldn't have been an easy thing
for him to do. He would have been punished if he was caught
giving bread to a prisoner. Sometimes things like that happened,
but it was very, very rare to see any sign of conscience in the SS
men. I felt so lucky that I got a thick piece of bread. Of course, I
didn't eat it while he was watching me. I waited until I was alone.
That piece of bread, especially in Melk, meant more than a million dollars.

⏱ ⏱ ⏱

A KAPO WHO supervised Moishe at work flew into a rage and beat
him up terribly with a club. The guy was a common criminal from
Germany—a Reichsdeutsche. Instead of being sentenced to
prison in Germany, he had been sent to Melk. Everyone knew that
he was the worst sadist in the camp. Moishe came back from work

bleeding from his eyes, from his face, from his head. His back was all swollen. He said, "I'm giving up. I don't want to live anymore."

Mailekh and I grabbed him and took him to the washroom. He resisted us. He didn't want it. But we washed his bloody wounds. We tried to talk to him. "Are you going to give them what they want? They want us to be killed. You have a chance to survive. When we survive a day, that means we are one day closer to our liberation . . . to our redemption. So, you are fighting back. That's what you have to do. Fight back."

He didn't even want to go to the kitchen for his meal. He insisted he wanted to die. So, we dragged him with us into the kitchen, forced him to stand up, and persuaded him to get in line for soup. We told him, "Don't take it for yourself. You'll take it, and we'll eat it. Otherwise, none of us will have that soup." That convinced him, and in the end, we made sure that he got his portion and ate it, too.

We told him, "We heard rumors that the American forces are really close to the borders of Germany and it won't be long until they come here to liberate us." We manufactured those stories, and they helped, even if they weren't true. In this case, it turned out that the story was true, but we didn't know that at the time.

The next morning, Moishe didn't want to leave, and we pulled him down from the bunk. If he didn't line up for work in the morning, they would have beaten the hell out of him and dragged him to the hospital. That would have been the end of it. By the second day, he settled down and came back to his senses.

I was never beaten as badly as Moishe was that time, but sometimes I got beaten up, too. And I also felt like it was not worth it and wanted to give up. Every minute and every second, you had to fight and say to yourself, "You have to survive. You will survive." Mentally, I was stronger and had more guts than my brothers. And I had hope, too. We knew that it wouldn't be long until the war ended. I really believed that if we tried hard, we might survive for long enough to be liberated. There was a beautiful castle in the town of Melk that we could see from the concentration camp. I used to promise myself that I would visit that castle as a free man when I got liberated.[5]

Many times, we prayed to God. Who else did we have to pray to? It was automatic for me to say, "Oy, God help me." I didn't think about whether God existed or didn't exist. It wasn't something religious. I was just glad I had a word to say that might help ease my mind. When you pray, you feel like you're accomplishing something. I imagine that everyone feels that way.

🕰 🕰 🕰

LUCKILY, WE GOT selected to sleep in the best prisoner barrack when we arrived at Melk. It was a two-story brick building with strong walls and solid windows, and it was warm inside. The rest of the barracks were shacks built out of lumber, without windows or any protection from the cold.

After about three weeks, the blockaltester for our barrack started to call out numbers. Our three numbers were on his list, so we stepped out. When the group was assembled, he gave a speech that it was too crowded in that barrack and he couldn't manage so many prisoners, so we were going to be transferred to the wooden barracks.

When we heard that, we knew it would be certain death. Prisoners would lie down in those barracks after a day of heavy work, and within a few nights they would die in their sleep from the cold.

We decided that we had to try to bribe that blockaltester. We still had the one good watch that Moishe had hidden in a piece of soap in Auschwitz and carried through the showers at Mauthausen. It was an Omega. It wasn't an easy decision to tell him that we still had something valuable. When we first arrived at our barrack in Melk, that same guy had announced that anybody who had any possessions—watches, gold, or anything else—had one last chance to surrender it voluntarily, right then, because if anything would be found on anyone later, they'd be shot to death by the SS.

We discussed who should approach the blockaltester, and my brothers told me, "You are the best one to go. You have ways..." I am so bashful now; I wouldn't have the guts do those things anymore. But at that time, something was driving me to take big, calculated risks. I didn't prepare what I was going to say. I just walked up to that blockaltester, and it felt like some divine power was putting the words in my mouth. The conversation went like this:

> KHIL: "I'd like you to do me a favor."
> BLOCKALTESTER: "Who are you?"

He gave me a surprised look.

> KHIL: "I'm the one that you called to go into the other barrack."
> BLOCKALTESTER: "You mean to tell me you don't want to go?"
> KHIL: "No, I'll go."
> BLOCKALTESTER: "What then? What is it that you want?"
> KHIL: "I'd like to give you a gift."

I didn't mention anything about my brothers, so in case something happened, I would be the only one who got shot.

> BLOCKALTESTER: "What do you mean?"
> KHIL: "I'd like to give you a gift."
> BLOCKALTESTER: "For what?"

I didn't say anything for a moment.

> BLOCKALTESTER: "Come on, come on, tell me what it is."
> KHIL: "It's a beautiful watch. It has been in my family for generations, and my grandmother gave it to me. It's the most precious thing in my life, but I'd like to give it to you."

I didn't show it to him yet, and of course the story wasn't true. We had managed to get that watch in Auschwitz.

BLOCKALTESTER: "Okay, I like the watch. I know it's precious to you. What do you want for it?"

KHIL: "I don't want to go to those barracks over there."

BLOCKALTESTER: "Why? How did you find out that those barracks are not so good?"

KHIL: "I heard rumors that it's very cold there."

BLOCKALTESTER: "That's all you want?"

KHIL: "No."

BLOCKALTESTER: "What else do you want?"

KHIL: "I have two brothers."

BLOCKALTESTER: "Are you crazy by any chance?"

When I heard that, I knew that I already had him on my side. He could have hit me or told me he's going to turn me over to the SS. But he wasn't talking like that, so I got more *chutzpah* (assertive confidence).

KHIL: "I want my two brothers to stay here in this barrack, too, with me."

BLOCKALTESTER: "Do you know their numbers?"

So I gave him the numbers—A19366, A19367, and A19368—and he wrote them down.

BLOCKALTESTER: "You know what will happen to you if you don't give me that watch?"

KHIL: "You can be sure that you'll get it."

A group of prisoners were removed from our barrack to those wooden shacks the next morning. Our three numbers weren't called. When we returned from work that day, I went in and gave him the watch. He liked it.

After that, he didn't mistreat us like he did the other inmates in his barrack. Several weeks later, he approached me. "You know the watch that you gave me is not running." I told him not to worry, that either I or my brother would fix it whenever he wants. I still had the two tools that I carried from Auschwitz. When the time came, he called Mailekh into his office to fix the watch.

That blockaltester was a Reichsdeutsche. The red patch on his uniform meant that his crime was political. He was aristocratic, educated—not a common criminal. Probably, he was a socialist or a communist. They treated him well and gave him privileges in the camp—better food, better work, better clothes. He was always dressed up nicely. Later, he would save our lives.

⏱ ⏱ ⏱

ONE TIME, THAT same blockaltester was giving out the soup when I returned to the camp after working the night shift. It was early in the morning. He smiled when I got my ration and whispered, "If you want a little more, come back right away." I worried that his big pot might be empty when I returned, so I ate up my regular soup ration in a hurry. When I looked at him, he waved me over and filled up my bowl. Usually, they filled it halfway, which was about a quart. But he gave me almost two quarts of soup. I was ready to eat it immediately because the first portion had just built up my appetite for more.

But I wanted to share with my brothers, who worked the day shift. They wouldn't be back until late afternoon. Waiting for them to return was my biggest struggle. I hid the soup under my wooden bunk bed so nobody would see it and steal it away from me. But I was constantly thinking about it. Every few minutes, my mind pushed me. *I can eat it up. They won't have to know.* But my heart didn't let me. That bond between us was so strong . . . I couldn't do it. Many times, I went over to that soup and said to myself, *Maybe I could take just one spoonful. What if he had given me only half? I could eat half now and share the rest with my brothers.*

But I kept telling myself, *No, the guard gave me a full bowl, and I'm going to share all of it.*

You should never feel in your life what real hunger means. It's the worst thing that a human being can experience.

I didn't touch that soup until they came back from work. Not one drop. They were astonished to see an extra soup, and they understood what it meant for me to save it for them. I was proud of myself for that. We sat down and took turns—one spoonful at a time—until we finished it. We had such a feeling of togetherness, I'm telling you.

Sometimes my brothers did things like that for me, too. This was unusual in the camps. Brothers from other families were fighting and stealing pieces of bread from one another. Terrible things were going on. But that didn't happen to us. There was complete trust. No betrayal. I'm sure it had to do with what we went through as children, right from the beginning when our mother died. We all felt responsible to care for each other.

🕰 🕰 🕰

ONE MORNING IN April, they lined all of us up for a selection. The Russian front was moving closer to Melk, and we heard rumors that they were going to evacuate the camp.

We were a big group of people—maybe ten thousand prisoners. They told us that the ones who they take to one side will remain in the camp, and the others will be taken to a different camp. We didn't know which side was better. We were only interested in staying together. As it happened, all three of us were sent to the side that was supposed to be removed from the camp. Almost all of the prisoners were on our side.

That same blockaltester who was in charge of our barrack was helping the SS men. He stood in front with them. After we were selected, he noticed Mailekh, grabbed him by the collar, and pulled him over to the other side with the small group of prisoners. He remembered that Mailekh had fixed a watch for him in his office, but he didn't notice me or Moishe, and we were left with the majority.

Like I told you before, we'd made a pact between us: Where one goes, all of us go, even if it means death. So, Mailekh managed to run back to us. We were glad to be standing all together. A miracle.

Well, that blockaltester walked by again and saw Mailekh back with the majority group! He went up to him and said, "You *verflukhte hund* (cursed dog)! Are you farikht? I risked my life to get you out of here, and now you're going back!?"

Mailekh said, "I can't. You know I have two brothers. I want to be with them."

The blockaltester replied, "Oh. Yeah, that's right," and he moved all three of us from that group.

An SS man saw and asked, "What are you doing here? Why are you moving prisoners to the other side?"

The blockaltester said, "You told me to help you—to show you which ones are good workers. Those three are the best workers in my barrack, and I think we can use them here." The SS man waved him on.

We didn't know what would happen, but so long as the three of us were together, it was good for us. Our group was only about five hundred prisoners. The thousands of prisoners in the other group were loaded onto riverboats and sent down the Danube.

We remained in the camp for another week or so. Our work was the same as before, but we didn't work as hard. And they gave us a lot to eat that week because so much food had accumulated in their warehouses. It was the best time in the camps.

At this point, everyone knew that the end was coming. We saw Russian and American planes flying around at low altitudes all the time. The Russians bombed the military installations around the camp. One time, they dropped a few bombs in the camp and machine-gunned the guards in the towers. A barrack was completely destroyed, and some prisoners were killed. When the Russian planes did air raids, the Germans hid in their houses, but they told us to get out of the barracks and lie down on the ground outside.

We were happy to see with our own eyes that it was really happening. We didn't even mind getting killed so long as the Germans got what was coming to them. But we had to be careful to conceal our joy, or the Germans would shoot us right away.

The day before they removed us from the camp, I spoke with the blockaltester. He said, "They think in another day or a day and a half, the Russians will be here." The Germans evacuated the camp in a rush and loaded us into cattle cars, their machine guns pointed at us the whole time. They weren't watching everything else so carefully, but they guarded us with perfect intensity—like we were the most valuable things to them. A treasure to kill. Isn't that a funny thing?

The SS men who were guarding us then were the older ones and not as violent against us. You could tell from their behavior that they were not so confident anymore, but they still obeyed their orders to the letter. The Germans blew up everything in the camp. We heard the explosions while we stood in the train waiting to leave.

CHAPTER 11

Ebensee and Liberation (April 1945–October 1945)

You are not obligated to complete the work, but
neither are you free to desist from it.
—RABBI TARFON, *Mishnah, Pirkei Avos,* 2:21

NESTLED IN AN ALPINE VALLEY with a beautiful lake surrounded by high mountains, Ebensee was the worst concentration camp of all. We arrived at the train station at around 4:00 P.M., and they marched us a few kilometers to the camp. They gave each of us a piece of bread that was so thin—about half a centimeter thick. You could see the sun shining through it. We also got a half quart of soup. It was supposed to be potato-peeling soup, but there were no peelings. It was only water that was cooked with peelings. It stank, and I vomited when I ate the soup that first day.[1]

Mailekh refused to eat it. I said, "I'll bet you that tomorrow, not only will you eat it, but you'll lick your shisel to get every last drop." He didn't back down, and I told him, "You better eat it now because otherwise you won't live until tomorrow, and I want you to live another day so I can prove it to you." He ate it.

The next day, they took us underground to dig corridors in the mountains. It's amazing what they did. They built factories in those tunnels and were preparing for the war to go on for years.[2] Our job was to hammer into solid rock with electric jack-hammers. Then we would fill carts with the broken rocks and push them outside along the rails that ran the length of the tunnel. The prisoners who had come to Ebensee before us were weak from the hard work and starvation rations. We called them the "old ones." Many of them died at the work site throughout the day. We saw that we would not be able to survive for long in this place.

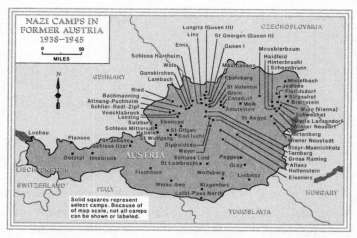

As World War II came to an end, mass evacuations from other concentration camps put tremendous pressure on the Mauthausen complex (which included Melk and Ebensee), the last remaining concentration camps in the area still controlled by the Nazis. The twenty-five Ebensee barracks had been designed to hold 100 prisoners each, but they eventually held as many as 750 each. Additional prisoners were ordered to sleep in the tunnels or outdoors under the open sky. The crematorium was unable to keep pace with the deaths, and naked bodies were stacked outside the barrack blocks and the crematorium itself. In the closing weeks of the war, the death rate exceeded 350 per day. During this period, the inmate population reached a high of eighteen thousand.[3]

It was April 1945. The Americans were pushing through Germany from the west, and the Russian front was moving toward us from the east. The Germans were evacuating more and more concentration camp prisoners from all over German-occupied Europe and sending them to Ebensee. They didn't have enough food for so many people.

We met some of the prisoners there who had been sent away from Melk before us in riverboats. They'd been in transit for almost the whole week that we stayed in Melk. The Germans hardly gave them any food or water. Some were put on damaged ships and drowned in the Danube River. Others died from hunger and thirst. More than half died on the way to Ebensee. The ones who survived were close to death and the crematorium, anyway. They didn't have gas chambers in Ebensee, but they did have a crematorium.

The guards never talked to us, and when they watched us, they were careful not to talk to each other, either. But one time, we overheard some German engineers talking about a new bomb they were waiting for. The engineers were from a private company that was supervising the construction. We did the manual labor for them. They didn't do anything to help us, but sometimes they talked to us if they had a chance. We had to be careful with them. We couldn't go up and ask them when the Americans are coming. We would say something like, "How long do you think until the war will be over? Then Germany will be free."

We wound them up, and they started to talk: "Germany? Forget about it. Germany is *kaput* (finished)." That's how we found out little bits of information. If one of us heard some news, we told the others, to give them hope for that day. If there was no news, we made up stories. "They said the Americans are only fifty kilometers away. Now, they're only thirty kilometers away . . ."

We never saw the sun in Ebensee. It was always cloudy. We were starving to death. Moishe and I became really thin. Mailekh's body looked like he was getting fat, and his legs started to swell. We thought it was because he was filling his stomach with water as a substitute for food.[4] He would hold his mouth under the faucet in the washroom, and we'd have to fight with him to stop drinking so much.

Moishe started to chew dirt to satisfy his hunger. Many other prisoners did the same. It was dangerous because when you chewed the dirt, you couldn't help yourself from swallowing it. When you swallowed it, your intestines became enlarged and you got sick with dysentery, which was a fatal illness in the camp. Many times, I saw him chewing dirt, and I would push my hand into his mouth to make him spit it out.[5]

I stopped myself from doing those things. I didn't want to die.

One time, a Russian prisoner brought a piece of human flesh into the barrack and roasted it for himself on the stove. It was smoking. We couldn't stand the smell. We didn't say anything. What was there to say? We were standing and praying that the Germans didn't finish us off right there. Even later, that smell lingered in the barrack.

Some of the Russian guys would cut off the flesh from the tukhes of a dead person. It was the only place on our bodies where you could find a little piece of muscle. Those things happened in Ebensee. I saw it with my own eyes. We couldn't do that. No Jews were doing that.

⏱ ⏱ ⏱

WE GOT WEAKER and weaker, and we saw other men give up. It was very easy to finish yourself off. All you had to do was remain in your bed in the morning. When they came in to inspect, they didn't ask you anything. They just grabbed you and said, "We're going to take you to the hospital," which meant they were going to kill you.

There was a French Jew who slept in the same bunk bed as me. He told me that he was a famous neurosurgeon from Paris, that he was one of three doctors in the world who knew how to do certain types of brain surgery. Patients would come to him from all over the world. Nowadays, every city has brain surgeons, but at that time it was a novelty.

The brain surgeon believed that the war wouldn't end for at least another year, and he'd lost hope that he could live through it. I tried to argue with him and give him encouragement. "Keep going. You've made it this long. Fight for your life." I begged him not to give up, but he didn't want to listen. They took him down from his bunk in the morning and finished him off just like that. He could have survived. His body wasn't yet completely spent.

We were hoping and praying to God that if we were going to be liberated, please have it be soon. We were not angry, anymore. We just continued to push ourselves. Each day, you had to fight with yourself, to harness your will to something you wanted to live for. That was the most important thing. Otherwise, you wouldn't survive the day.

On Friday afternoon, May 4, 1945, we came back from work completely worn out. In the previous few days, it had taken all of our energy and concentration just to stand on our feet. It felt like I'd completely lost my mental willpower. Mailekh was in especially bad shape. He had swollen eyes, and puss was oozing out of his swollen feet. That was a sure sign that it wouldn't be long until he died.

We were lying in our bunks and decided together that we weren't going back to work. We would stay in our bunks the next morning, and the guards would take us away. We didn't want to live anymore.

But on Saturday, they didn't take us out to work. We heard rumors that the Americans were very close to Ebensee—that it wouldn't be long. When we heard that news, we changed our minds. We held on with everything we had.

Everybody had to step out from the barracks that morning and assemble in the appel platz. Thousands of prisoners from all the German-occupied countries in Europe—Russians, French, Dutch, Belgians, Hungarians, Romanians, Greeks, and Yugoslavians. Everybody. I don't remember all the nationalities.

The lagerführer came out and made a speech in German: "The war won't last long. The enemies are close, and they're going to drop bombs all over the camp. They'll probably kill all of you, and I want to spare your lives. I want you to go in the corridors that you were digging in the mountains, and there you'll be protected from the air raids."

His secretary translated the speech into all of the different languages. That secretary was a Frenchman—not a Jew—and had been a prisoner in Auschwitz with us, but he still had his hair and looked fat.

When the lagerführer said, "I want to spare your lives," the translator changed it into a question: "Do our lives have to be protected?" From that little change, we got the hint that it was a trick and that they were planning to destroy us in the tunnels. It was especially clear to people like us who also understood the German. A week earlier, the Germans had us put ten pounds of dynamite every twenty-five meters in each corridor. We'd heard them say that when the enemy came close, they would blow up all of the tunnels.

Thousands of prisoners yelled, "No, we're not going anywhere! We want to die here from the air raids!"

While that was going on, the lagerführer gave his deputy an order to kill us all and went to get in a Mercedes Benz that was waiting for him. In front of our eyes, the deputy said, "You're going to leave me here for the Americans? And *I'll* pay with *my* life for what *you* did!?" At that same moment, he took out his pistol and shot the lagerführer dead.

He could have had the guards shoot us right there, but he didn't. He was afraid. Things were happening too fast. Not only that, all the young SS men had already withdrawn from the camp, and the *alte kockers* (old farts) were standing guard over us. They walked like we walked. But we were young, and they were around sixty-five years old.

After that, we went back to the barrack. We had to force ourselves to live for another few hours or another day.

Mikhoel Lenga, 36, with sons Mailekh (left), 10, and Itshele (right), 11, in 1924, when the boys were leaving their home in Kozhnitz to go to yeshiva in Shedlitz, 127 kilometers away.

Hirsh Leib, a water carrier in Kozhnitz, circa 1938. According to other Kozhnitzer townspeople, Hirsh Leib toiled and suffered and joked with everyone.

Friends seeing off Tsvi Mada before he made aliya to Er Yisroel, 1933. Mailekh Le is at the far left in the back r and Izak Lenga is fourth fr the right in the back r

The large dots on this watch movement are jewels that serve as bearings for the high-wear moving parts. A small hole woul be drilled into the jewel to house each end of a shaft that would pivot back and forth inside the hole with minimal friction.

A Jew being abused by Germans who are cutting his hair and sidelocks, circa 1939. This photo is reported by some to have been taken in Kozhnitz, Poland.

Moishe Lenga (left) and Mikhoel Lenga with his daughter Khana Lenga (below) in Kozhnitz, circa 1940. These photos were among a collection of negatives found in Kozhnitz in the early 2000s. This is the only existing photo of Khana.

3

Jewish men in Kozhnitz taking off their hats when they pass German soldiers, as required by law, circa 1940. Note the sign on the top left with the photo of a clock (and the blow-up of that section below). The left side says WATCHMAKER in Polish, and the right says JEWELER. Across the bottom it says MICHAL LENGA. This was the family store at 35 Radomska Street, where the Lenga family worked and lived in Kozhnitz.

Khil Lenga (left) with his best friend Khamaira Salzberg (right)
during the summer of 1941 in the Kozhnitz Ghetto.

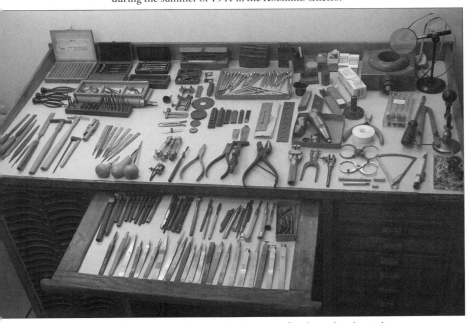

Typical watchmaker's workbench with the array of tools used in the trade.

Jews from the Kozhnitz Ghetto at forced labor digging a canal in the nearby village of Wolka, circa 1942. They are working for the Gorczycki company, which was building the canal.

Watch hairspring—the beating heart of a mechanical watch. It pulsates in a horizontal circle and serves the same function as the pendulum in a clock.

Stock photo of a watchmaker wearing a magnification loupe in his eye socket and holding a hairspring in his tweezers.

6

Jews from Hungary arrive by train and undergo a selection on the ramp at Auschwitz-Birkenau, May 1944.

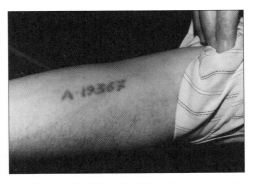

Larry Lenga, in 1993, shows the number tattoo — 19367 — that he received in Auschwitz-Birkenau upon arrival in July 1944.

Watchmaker's screwdriver and tweezers made in Auschwitz from materials available in the camp by Chaim Shtatler, a Jewish prisoner.

De Intérieur d'un block
(The interior of a
concentration camp barrack).

Travaux d'avanceme
(Work in progres
This drawing depicts prison
digging a tunnel with elect
jackhammers at the M
concentration can

Traveux extérieurs en hiver (Outside work in winter). This drawing depicts prisoners carrying steel rails in winter outside a tunnel at the Melk concentration camp.

Stift Melk, 2012, the "castle" that was visible to the prisoners at the Melk concentration camp.

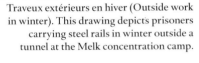

Site of the Melk concentration camp, 1948.

Scott Lenga viewing the town of Melk from the terrace of the "castle" (Stift Melk), 2015.
It is located on a prominent hill, so anyone strolling on the terrace enjoys a 360-degree view of the Danube River, the entire town of Melk, and the now indiscernible site of the Melk concentration camp.

Travaux dans une galerie (Work in a tunnel). This drawing depicts one of the tunnels that housed underground armaments factories.

View of the Ebensee concentration camp, May 194

U.S. Army Sergeant Dick Pomante (left) and Platoon Sergeant Robert Persinger (right), Germany, 1945. They were the commanders of the two tanks that liberated the Ebensee concentration camp.

A crowd of survivors gathers in the main square of the Ebensee concentration camp May 7, 1945, one day after liberation.

Survivors of Ebensee concentration camp pose undressed for a U.S. Army photographer to show the effects of malnutrition, May 8, 1945 — two days after liberation. Khil Lenga is the marked person closer to the right. Moishe Lenga is the marked person closer to the center.
At liberation, Khil weighed seventy-five pounds, and Moishe weighed seventy.

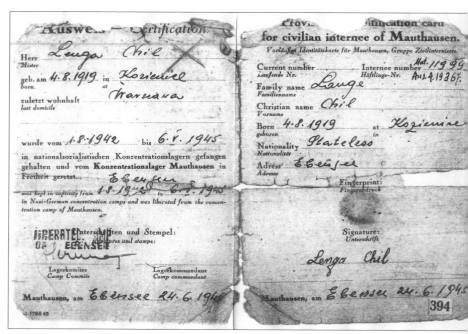

UNRRA identification card confirming Khil Lenga's internment in the Ebensee concentration camp. Note the entry "Nationality: Stateless."

Uniform patch for the Palestine Jewish Brigade soldiers of the British Army in World War

FROM THE LEFT:
Moishe, Mailekh, and Khil Lenga after the war in either Rome or Stuttgart, circa 1945.

12

WORLD ORT UNION
U. S. Zone Centr. Office
MÜNCHEN 27
Möhlstraße 10

MAIL ADRESS:
World ORT Union
PC IRO ADMIN. SUB-UNIT
APO 407 US Army

TELEPHONE:
Civ. line 45 83 88
43 79 6
Mil. line 23 80

368

Munich, 26th of May, 1948

CERTIFICATE

Mr. Mxx LENGA Chil   born on 4th of Aug., 1919

in Kozienice/Poland   reported on 13th of May, 1948

to ORT Vocational School in Schwäbisch Hall   for a survey

test of his pxxx professional knowledge in the trade of watch repairing

After an examination it was found that the above named person has a working knowledge of this trade. This certificate has been issued for submission to the proper emigration authorities.

For the Director of US. Zone

Place for Photo

ORGANIZATION FOR REHABILITATION THROUGH TRAINING

Certificate of Professional Competence in Watchmaking issued to Khil Lenga, May 26, 1948. This was required for his emigration application to the United States.

FROM THE LEFT:
Moishe, Khil, and Izak Lenga in Stuttgart, circa 1947, during the period when all four of the Lenga brothers were reunited after the war.

FROM THE LEFT IN THE CAR:
Izak, Khil, and Moishe Lenga in Stuttgart, circa 1947.

13

Wedding of Harry and Dorothy Lenga,
St. Louis, Missouri, 1950.

Wedding of Morris and Ann Len
St. Louis, Missouri, 19

FROM THE LEFT:
Dorothy, Scott, Michael,
Harry, and Mark Lenga
at Michael's bar mitzvah,
St. Louis, Missouri, 1964.

FROM THE LEFT:
Margi, Morris, and Bobbie Lenga,
St. Louis, Missouri, 1966.

e four Lenga brothers reunited for the
wedding of Morris and Ann Lenga's
daughter, Margi, to Michael Kahn,
St. Louis, Missouri, 1975.
FRONT ROW: Morris, Ann, Margi,
Bobbie, Dorothy, and Harry Lenga;
SECOND ROW: Marcel, Violet,
Yitzkhak, and Riva Lenga;
BACK ROW: Monique, Mark,
Patricia, and Scott Lenga.

The four Lenga brothers at the wedding of Margi Lenga and Michael Kahn, St. Louis, Missouri, 1975.
FROM THE LEFT:
Morris, Marcel, Harry, and Yitzkhak Lenga. This was their first and only reunion after they said their goodbyes in Stuttgart around 1948.

Harry Lenga, St. L(
Missouri, circa 1(

Harry Lenga and his son Scott Lenga in San Francisco, California, 1993, during the week of intensive interviews that formed the basis of this book.

HARRY LENGA
יחיאל בן ציון

בן מיכאל ומלכה רייזלה

August 4, 1919
to January 2, 2000

נולד ט' אב תרע"ט
נפטר כ"ד טבת תש"ס

One of three brothers
who survived
the concentration camps
by keeping a promise
to stay together

In memoriam. Gravestone of
Harry Lenga, Raanana, Israel.

16

That same Saturday afternoon, the Germans told the prisoners, "Go take whatever food you want from the storage magazines." Everyone started to run. The chaos was hard for us because we were too weak to run and couldn't move so well, anymore. We managed to get ourselves a few potatoes and burned them on a fire.

We knew that it was the end.

⏱ ⏱ ⏱

WE HEARD YELLING Sunday morning. "The Americans are marching in!" In our excitement, we climbed down from the bunk beds—in slow motion from our weakened condition—and made our way outside. Everyone was running to the American tanks driving into the camp. We cried tears of joy. The lead tank stopped in the middle of the appel platz, and a soldier climbed out. He said a few words that were translated into many languages. His unit had come from Salzburg, and their orders had been to travel in a different direction. But on the way, they heard about the camp at Ebensee and took it upon themselves to liberate us.[6]

All the nationalities fabricated little flags, and each group sang their national anthem in turn. When they all finished, we Jews, the weak Jews who had been tortured for so long, started to sing "The Hatikva" real softly.[7] We didn't have a flag. We hardly had the strength to sing. For the other national anthems, all of the groups had listened quietly, but when the Jews started to sing, the others started to make noise, to mock us: "Quiet! Don't sing! Who are you!?" That American captain stood up on his tank, pulled out his revolver, and fired into the air. Then he yelled into the loudspeaker, "I want it to be quiet! I don't want to hear a sound! Don't you hear that a nation is singing their national anthem!?" I'm telling you, it got so quiet that you could hear a fly buzzing in the background. After we finished singing, we ran to kiss the tank. I came over, too, and saw the captain up close. He climbed down from the tank with tears in his eyes and embraced us. We were stinking dirty. It was no pleasure to be close to us.

He was a generous, beautiful personality. He didn't say "the Jews" when he yelled for everyone to be quiet. You know what I mean? We figured that he must be Jewish because of that. We never met him again. We never found out his name or anything about him. But I'll never forget his face.

The Americans didn't even need to search for the SS and the other guilty people. The German alte kockers surrendered right away. They came in uniform and gave up their arms. The deputy SS man who shot the lagerführer also surrendered to the Americans. He didn't run away. The Germans themselves were glad that the Americans had arrived instead of the Russians. The Russians were much tougher on the Germans when they came to liberate a camp.

We were finally liberated. We'd been in Ebensee three or four weeks. If it had taken a little longer, all three of us would surely have died.

⏱ ⏱ ⏱

AROUND THE TIME that the Germans were starting to surrender, some prisoners, mostly the Russians, managed to get clubs and knives and took revenge on some of the guards and kapos. Eventually, the Germans would run to the Americans for protection, which stopped the Russians. But before that, the Russians caught the Reichsdeutsche kapo who had beaten up Moishe in Melk and had come to Ebensee with our transport. He had beaten so many people to death . . . for nothing.

The Russians beat him and kicked him, and when they finally knocked him down, he fell right at my feet. I said, "Moishe, look who it is. Your murderer is here." The kapo was lying helpless with blood pouring out of him. Quickly, I raised my foot to step on his head. My mind dictated that I should do it. But there was a struggle going on inside me, and my heart wouldn't let my foot react. It became paralyzed.

I hated that guy so much. In those times he hit me, I probably could have killed him, but in that moment, when I saw that he was defeated, I couldn't do it. Instead, the Russians came around and finished him off. I saw his brains coming out of his shattered skull.[8] I wasn't sorry for him, but I was glad that I didn't take part in the revenge killing.

BEFORE LIBERATION, WE would dream about going out to the fields, finding a few potatoes to cook, and eating them until we were full. That was our biggest dream.

Right away, that same morning, the American G.I.s gave us packages of food with bread, some sausage or sardines, I think, and jam. It was delicious for us—the first taste of freedom.

The American unit that came to liberate us didn't have supplies to feed the prisoners beyond that. So, they took food supplies from the German storehouses. That first evening, they made us a delicious, fatty, Hungarian goulash, and you could eat as much as you wanted. It was the second taste of freedom. And that was our problem. Our *kishkes* (intestines, guts) were not able to digest something so fatty. The three of us vomited and got sick with diarrhea. I didn't overeat, and recovered quickly. Moishe had it especially bad; he got dysentery. It was terrible. A lot of people died from that meal.

The Americans had made a big mistake. They didn't have the medical understanding to handle people in our condition. The next day, they realized what they'd done and started to feed us bread with milk and other food that was not so fatty. That helped. They didn't give us any clothes yet. They were very careful not to get close to us. We looked like a disease to them.

SUDDENLY, WE WERE liberated. But I looked around, and we were still sitting in that same camp. We didn't see Germans anymore. Yet, we were still hungry, and we still had to wait in line for someone to give us food. The Americans let us move around in the camp, but they were still guarding us.

I heard that they let people leave the camp, but they couldn't take anything with them and they had to come back. I said to my brothers, "You know what? I just want to see if I can go through the gate—to see if I'm really free." The liberation was Sunday, so it must have been Monday or Tuesday.

Two American G.I.s were standing guard at the gate with their rifles. I walked up to them slowly. When I came real close, they said something I couldn't understand and motioned for me to go back. I didn't speak a word of English. I said in German with hand gestures, "I'm just going out, and I'll be back right away." One of the guards said "go" in German and waved me through. He didn't understand German. He just knew how to say simple words like "go" or "stay."

I started to play a little game, where I stepped inside the gate and then outside the gate a few times to test my freedom.

The G.I. and I exchanged a few words and gestures, and I saw that he was wearing two watches on his wrists. One watch showed the correct time, which was around 8:00 A.M. The other watch showed about 1:00, so I figured it wasn't running.

I tried with gestures to show him that I was a watchmaker, pointing to his broken watch to tell him that I would like to fix it. He didn't understand me, and I couldn't understand what he said. He probably thought I wanted him to give me the watch! But he seemed to appreciate the way I tried to communicate with him. This went on for quite a while.

Finally, I told him, "German, German, German." He went away with a nod and returned with an American G.I. who spoke a little German. This man asked me what I wanted. I said, "You liberated us. What can I do to thank you? I see that your comrade has a watch that is not running, and I am a watchmaker. I would like to fix it to show my appreciation for setting us free."

He translated, and the first guy said, "Aw, it's all right. Don't worry."

I said, "No, I insist."

You know, they were treating me with respect. Another guy could have given me a kick in my tukhes and said, "Get back!" and that would have been the end of it. They didn't do that!

They were talking back and forth between themselves, and the interpreter said to me, "You don't even have tools. How can you fix a watch?"

I said, "Yes, I have tools." I reached into my pocket and showed them the tools that I'd made for myself in Auschwitz—the pair of tweezers I'd made from an earmuff spring and the screwdriver I'd made from a nail.

They started to laugh. "Those are the tools?"

I said to them, "Don't laugh. Let me take a look at the watch. If something is broken and it needs a part, I cannot fix it. But if it's just dirty inside and needs to be cleaned, I'll be able to fix it for you with these tools of mine, if you bring me a toothbrush and a little benzene."

They looked at each other like they thought I was crazy. Finally, the interpreter said, "Oh, what can you lose? Do it."

So, they let me sit at a table in the little booth at the gate. One guy left and came back with a toothbrush and a whole bottle of benzene. He put the broken watch down on the table and said, "Okay. You don't have to, but if you want to, fix it." I asked him for a knife. He gave it to me, and I opened the watch.

I could see that something had gotten stuck between the gears and the only thing that watch needed was a cleaning. I washed it out with the toothbrush and let it dry. When I started to put it back together, they were shaking their heads.

My hands were trembling from excitement and fear. I prayed to God that there wouldn't be any complications, because if I broke something, there was nothing I could do to fix it. When I put everything back in place, the movement started to tick. I put the watch in the case and said, "Here it is! Your watch is running now." The G.I. put it up to his ear to listen. He got a big kick out of it and showed it to the other guys.

The G.I. took out his wallet to pay me. I said no and gestured for him to put back the wallet. I knew what a dollar was, but what could I buy with money in the camp?

The guy who spoke German said, "What's the matter? Why don't you want money?"

I said, "You don't owe me anything. You did so much. You already paid me by liberating me and my two brothers."

He said, "Oh, no, no," and we argued back and forth.

So, the interpreter must have said something like, "Look at him. Why don't you give him something to eat or something to smoke?" because right away, all three of them took out cigarettes.

I said, "A cigarette I'll take, but not because I want to get paid."

Then the guy with the watch said something to the other two in English and walked away. He came back with a loaf of American white bread under his arm. I had never seen white bread before. In the other hand, he held a carton of American cigarettes. You don't know what that meant. It was a fortune for me.

American cigarettes were traded one at a time in the camp. For one cigarette, you could get an extra soup from the kitchen. For one pack of cigarettes, you could have bought up the whole camp. And here he hands me a carton, ten packs of American cigarettes, with twenty of them in each pack. I said, "Oh, no, this is too much!" He insisted, so I took it and thanked him.

Suddenly, I was the richest man in the camp. I went back to my brothers to show them. I said, "Listen, we don't have to go to the field and find potatoes. We are already rich!" They wanted to smoke, and I said, "Oh, no! These cigarettes will give us more than that." And how true it was. We hid the bread and the cigarettes under the straw sack in the bunk so nobody would see, and I told them to stay there and guard them like our lives depended on it.

I took one pack of cigarettes to the kitchen and walked up to the supervisor. He was a Russian inmate, a kapo who was the chief cook at Ebensee during the war. The Americans kept him in the same job. Now I wasn't scared of him anymore. I asked, "Do you smoke? What will you give me for a pack of American cigarettes?"

He looked surprised and said, "You have American cigarettes already? The Americans just got here." He almost went crazy! He was ready to give me all kinds of things.

I said, "No. You don't have to give me that much. I just want you to promise me that every single day you'll give an extra soup to me and my two brothers."

He said, "Yeah, I'll do it. Give me the cigarettes."

I said, "Oh, no. I'll give you the cigarettes *after* you give us the extra soups a few times. If you keep your word, I'll give you the cigarettes."

He said, "Don't worry, I'll do it. Do you have the cigarettes with you?"

I told him no. He was a strong guy. If I had told him the truth, he would have just grabbed them away from me then and there.

I went back, and the three of us ate that white bread—something we had never tasted before.

The cook lived up to his end of the bargain and gave us extra soups every day. After the third or fourth day of our arrangement, I gave him the cigarettes.

The food setup was still exactly like before in the camp, but now the Americans were supplying the food. It wasn't that dirty potato-peeling water anymore. It was a terrific barley and bean soup with pieces of meat and a quarter of a loaf of bread. You got one bowl and that was it. It was enough to eat, but we still wanted double.

You don't understand how we were. We thought we could eat up the whole world. I was a muselmänner. You could see each bone in my body and my face. I weighed seventy-five pounds. Moishe was seventy pounds. We lost all that weight in Ebensee. I don't know how much Mailekh weighed. He was all swollen.

⏱ ⏱ ⏱

PILES AND PILES of dead bodies were stacked up around the camp. The Americans brought the local Austrian population into the camp and made them bury the corpses.

In the first couple of days after we were liberated, a lot of prisoners ran out of the camp, and we could hear shooting in the distance. We talked about going out to see what was happening. I told my brothers, "We've been through so much. Let's be careful and preserve our lives."

We decided to stay in the camp until the U.S. Army got everything under control in the surrounding area. We had enough bread, and we had enough soup. The U.S. Army management made sure they brought food supplies for their soldiers and for us. They were humane. They had rakhmunes.

Some of the inmates who walked off in the beginning got killed by German snipers. The Americans had ordered the German soldiers, the Gestapo, and the civilian population to surrender their arms, but it took time for the Americans to enforce that law and make sure they had all complied.

The inmates were doing a lot of shooting, too. The German camp guards had laid down their rifles and handguns in big piles when the Americans entered. Some of the inmates had grabbed a gun and started to shoot in the air. Others put handguns in their pockets and went out to terrorize the town.

There were all kinds of prisoners in Ebensee, from Russia and all over Europe—and not only Jews. There were also political prisoners and criminals who had been sent to the concentration camps for killing, or raping, or other violent crimes. They had crowded us all together in the same barracks.

That didn't change with liberation. I had to sleep in the same bed as a Russian guy who drove me nuts by putting his feet on me to get warmth from my body. His feet were completely cold—like a corpse. I would pinch them to get his attention, but he didn't even feel it.

The Americans wanted us to stay in the camp. They believed that we were not yet ready to face society. We were free, but not free enough to have a normal life.

On the third or fourth day, the administrative army platoons came in with supplies and equipment, and the tank unit that had liberated us left. There was a new rule that if you wanted to leave, you had to give them a reason—any reason—even something simple like you wanted to buy something or go see something. They gave you a pass and let you out, but you had to report back at the camp before nightfall.

We didn't hear shooting anymore, so Mailekh and I decided to go out. It felt terrific. We didn't look like normal people, though. Anyone could see on our faces that we were from the concentration camp. Our hair was real short, and we were still dressed in the striped camp uniforms.

Suddenly, the Austrians were bidding us good morning. They called us *herr* (sir). Some of them even invited prisoners into their homes and gave them clothes.

One Austrian guy came over to me and said, "My gosh! We didn't know that you people were tortured so much. We didn't know what was going on." He told me that he lived not too far away.

I got so angry at him. "You *verflukhte Deutsche* (cursed German)![9] You are still a *Hitlerovietz* (Hitlerite). You're telling me that you didn't know? If you live here, you saw us leaving every morning, and you saw us coming back every evening with dead people. How could you miss that!?" I spat in his face, and he left.

For us, the Austrians were the same as the Germans. Before, Hitler was their *yeshua* (savior). They were happy to follow him. Now that the war was over, they tried to pretend that they weren't responsible and that only Germany was to blame. It was a lie.

There were prisoners who tried to steal clothes and other things from the Austrians in town. They felt that they were entitled to take what they needed after all the suffering they'd endured. We didn't feel that way. The crimes that had been committed against us did not turn us into criminals.

⏱ ⏱ ⏱

MAILEKH AND I recovered quickly from that first meal, and Mailekh's swelling went down as he got nourishment in his body, but Moishe's dysentery grew worse and worse every day. His digestive system was bleeding. He'd lost his strength completely and couldn't get down from bed anymore. He couldn't eat any of the food that they were giving us. His life was in danger. We needed to find a way to help him.

A lot of inmates got sick after liberation and just lay in their bunks without proper medical care. Many died like that. The U.S. Army didn't have the facilities to treat so many sick people. This was before the Red Cross came in with a dedicated medical staff, field hospitals, and civilian administration.

I said to Mailekh, "Listen, why don't we go out to the camp where the Americans are staying? We'll tell them we are watchmakers and make some connections." He agreed.

When we arrived at the U.S. Army camp, we asked the guard to bring someone who spoke German, and I told him, "I'd be glad to work fixing watches for you here. I'm not asking for much. I'll be happy with whatever you'll give me."

Just like that, he asked, "Will you fix my watch?"

I said, "Sure, we're going to fix everything. Just give us a chance."

The soldiers went inside and came back out with several broken watches. I fixed them with the tweezers and screwdriver that I had made in Auschwitz. I had the toothbrush that I'd gotten from the guard at the Ebensee gate a few days before, and they gave us benzene to clean the parts. They watched as we worked, and when they saw that the watches were running perfectly, they went to tell the officer in charge. He gave us permission to do it officially.

This was about a week after I fixed the first watch for the American guard at the Ebensee gate. I never saw him again, but he had told me, "Go to our boys. A lot of them have broken watches." Maybe he told the other American soldiers, because many had already heard about me. For them, it was something interesting to talk about.

They took us to a shower and gave us U.S. Army fatigue uniforms to wear. We threw away all of our *shmates* (rags) from the concentration camp. Suddenly, Mailekh and I looked like Americans—at least in our eyes.

One G.I. who spoke German to us was a tall, blond Texan named Harvey. He wanted to help us. His German was not so good, but it was enough to communicate. He must have been of German ancestry. Harvey went around to all the G.I.s and told them that we could fix their watches.

We were in business. Everything worked out so quickly and better than we had hoped—like it was our destiny. They had so many watches that needed to be fixed, and that same day we were already sitting outside in the yard and fixing them. They saw that we only had those two tools and right away brought us real watchmaking tools—enough for both of us to work. I don't know how they did it.

They offered me money, but I didn't want to take money. I asked for cigarettes. Some soldiers gave me a few cigarettes, others gave a pack or a carton. We also got chocolates and all kinds of different things. The American G.I.s got cigarettes from the Army for nothing, so they would give us a lot without thinking about it. For us, a pack of cigarettes was better than money. At that time, you couldn't spend U.S. dollars in the town.

When we returned the next day, I approached Harvey and said, "I have another brother who is very sick, and we don't know what's wrong with him. He's going to die if he doesn't get the right food and medication." Tears came to my eyes.

He told me to wait a minute, then he came back in a jeep with a doctor. They said, "Come, the doctor will check your brother."

Mailekh went with him to the concentration camp, where the doctor examined Moishe and gave him two shots of antibiotics.

I stayed in the U.S. Army camp, where a doctor gave me medicine and food for Moishe—milk, cocoa, and a whole bag of really good crackers. They drove me back to the concentration camp that afternoon because all that stuff was so heavy. Moishe couldn't eat anything—only drink milk and cocoa. We nurtured him back to health. After three or four more days, he started to get better.

Mailekh and I went to work each day. Everyone in the American camp knew us. They treated us like we were G.I.s. We ate their food. They knew we had a sick brother, and whenever they gave us something, they gave extra to bring to Moishe. They even gave us army fatigue pants for him.

That was really because of Harvey. He did everything to take care of us. Oh, he was a terrific guy. A good-hearted fellow. I don't know why he got so attached to us. When we fixed a watch for him, he paid us more than anybody else.

All of the Americans treated us very nicely, except one Jewish wise guy who spoke Yiddish. He made fun of us. I couldn't understand why. He was just a jerk. He must have been a spoiled brat at home. He didn't understand what Judaism was or what life was all about.

We had boils on our skin. Little pimples that itched a lot. I guess it was part of the recovery process after living so long on starvation rations and being completely exhausted from hard labor. The doctor gave us medicine to apply on our bodies. He told us to walk around with our shirts off in the sun. After three days, our skin was cleared up. We still looked like skeletons, though. It took about two weeks after the liberation until we could walk normally and started to look a little better.

Every evening, we returned to the barrack in the concentration camp. The other inmates saw that we were bringing back a lot of cigarettes and chocolate, and they started to steal from us. In the morning, we left Moishe to guard our newfound wealth.

Everything moved fast. All of this had happened within days. At that time in May, 1945, I was twenty-five years old. Moishe was twenty-three, and Mailekh was thirty.

🕰 🕰 🕰

WE DIDN'T KNOW so many people in the Ebensee concentration camp. But while Moishe was recovering, we became close friends with a couple of boys whom we knew from Kozhnitz and a few others. We gave them chocolate and cigarettes without any trading—just to help them out. One of those guys was walking outside of the concentration camp, and he saw that the barracks where the SS used to live stood empty. So he gave us an idea: *Why do we have to stay in this camp? Why don't we get out? Maybe we could move into one of those empty barracks.* He asked if I would be willing to check with the Americans.

We were careful not to create problems for ourselves, but I felt like I could talk with Harvey. The next day at work, I told him the story. "It's so uncomfortable in the camp. Why should we live in a camp now that we are free? There are so many empty barracks here. Would it be all right if we take a barrack? Will anybody interfere?"

He discussed it with the ranking officer and came back with an answer. "We can't give you official permission, but nobody will bother you. If something happens, just tell them that we said it's okay." That's all the permission we needed. The Americans liked the idea, too. If we were working for them, they wanted us to be clean and living away from the diseased people in the concentration camp.

So, we just moved in. It was about three weeks after liberation. We didn't have anything to move except our cigarettes and chocolates. And the watchmaking tools.

We didn't have any necessities like soap or towels. The soldiers who brought me watches gave me whatever I asked them for as payment for my work. When I finished a watch and a G.I.

gave me a pack of cigarettes, I asked if he could give me some soap. He wouldn't give me just one piece of soap; he'd give me a whole box of it. It was the same thing with towels and anything else they could get from the U.S. Army supplies. Nothing was official, but it was all open, and everyone seemed okay with it.

That SS barrack was beautiful inside, with furniture and bedding. We were eleven all together. We had taken those eight friends of ours, too. They didn't have work, so we would bring home all the food and share what we had with them. We knew those guys and trusted them.

That SS barrack was about three kilometers away from the camp. When Moishe started to regain his strength, we took him to work so he could enjoy the good meals with us in the U.S. Army camp. We would go in the food line, and we ate breakfast and lunch with the soldiers.

We loaded our room with cigarettes and chocolate and all the goodies. We could trade cigarettes for bread, for meat, for whatever we needed. We had a kitchen. We cooked for ourselves, and most of the time, we all ate dinner together.

About six weeks later, they moved all of the survivors out of the concentration camp and into a separate refugee camp that they built near the town of Ebensee. It was supervised by the American civilian administration—not the U.S. Army. It didn't have barbed wire fences or guard towers, but everyone still had to stay in that camp. The United Nations Relief and Rehabilitation Administration (UNRRA) brought in food, medicine, clothing, and all kinds of different things. The U.S. Army now used the concentration camp facility as a temporary prison for the SS men who they'd arrested instead.

We stayed in our SS barrack. We could get meals in the refugee camp if we wanted, but we didn't have to go there for any of our daily needs. We actually didn't mix with them very much.

Our barrack was by a highway, and there were trees and grass around it, like a park. We lived beautifully there with our windows open—like kings compared to everybody else. We were lucky, I'm telling you.

⏱ ⏱ ⏱

THE CONCENTRATION CAMP survivors called each other *katzet* or *katzetnik*, a slang term from the camps. The United Nations named us Displaced Persons, or DPs for short. That was our legal status.

Everything about our situation was temporary, but we had confidence and hope. During the war, we manipulated and maneuvered any little thing we could in the concentration camps to fix a watch or to take care of each other. We did the right things, thank God. We didn't believe any of us would make it out alive. It was mostly luck, but we felt like we'd accomplished something. Now we figured that we'd be able to go to Palestine. That's what we talked about all the time. At that time, Israel wasn't yet established.

We wondered what the Americans planned to do with us. Rumors were circulating that they were going to send us back to Poland. We'd never felt like Poland was our home, and the Poles had persecuted us our whole lives. We decided that if they tried to take us to Poland by force, we would resist. We were 100 percent sure of this. Most of the Polish Jews who'd survived the war felt the same way. We read stories in the newspapers that the United Nations was trying to pass a law not to force the Jews back to Poland or other European countries.

When the UNRRA registered me for an ID certificate, they asked, "What nationality are you?"

I told them to write "Stateless" because I didn't want anything to do with Poland again. They rejected my response and asked where I was born. I said, "I don't know. I don't have a country. The country I came from is not my country." It wasn't only me. My brothers and a lot of the other Jewish DPs did the same thing. The UNRRA administrators didn't know how to handle this situation and told us to come back again in a few days.

In the end, they put Kozienice as my birthplace and wrote "Stateless" as my nationality.

ⓞ ⓞ ⓞ

WE WERE SITTING and fixing watches at that U.S. Army camp for about two months. Then the platoon stationed there received orders to leave Ebensee, and I lost Harvey. He said goodbye. We watched as the trucks moved out, and he waved.

Harvey was the first person who showed me how freely the Americans lived and how open they were. You could feel the freeness in them—all over them. In the way they talked—no fear. That made a big impression on me. I really felt free with them.

And how rich they lived . . . We could live for a year just on what they were wasting. They took a meal and threw half of it in the garbage. I looked at the meat and thought, *Oh gosh, what are they doing?* After we endured starvation in the German concentration camps and saw how a piece of bread could be the difference between life and death that day, it was a shock to see people wasting food like it was nothing.

I wore a U.S. insignia. Harvey pinned it up on my fatigue uniform, and I was so proud of it. Harvey had one stripe on his arm. He must have been a private first class. One time, a colonel in his dress uniform walked up to me and saw that pin on my shirt. He started to ask me questions in German: "You're not American, are you? Why do you wear this? Where did you get it? Who gave it to you?"

I was scared, and I didn't want to get Harvey in trouble. I answered, "I'm working here. Nobody gave it to me. They gave me something to wear, and that pin was on it. I didn't want to take it off."

He said, "You can't." Then he became suddenly soft. He said, "You can't wear that. Only Americans . . . real Americans can wear it." He spoke beautiful German. I asked him if I should take it off. He said, "I'll take it off." I understood. I had heard a few remarks before that I shouldn't wear it, but I didn't listen.

That was the end of it. That colonel didn't do anything to punish me because of that pin. In fact, before Harvey's platoon left, that same colonel gave me a letter of recommendation. It said that I was a good watchmaker who worked for them, and I was an honest person who can be recommended to do service for the Americans. Everybody told me, if you've got that, you can go anywhere.

So, we lost our jobs, but we didn't worry so much. There were still American soldiers in the area, and we found another U.S. Army camp. I showed them that letter of recommendation, and we got permission to fix watches for the G.I.s in that camp. It was a long walk to go there every day, but we didn't mind. It was good for us to walk.

🕑 🕑 🕑

OUR STAY IN the SS barrack together with those eight other boys was a good time for us. I didn't look back and cry about the bad things that had happened. I only focused on the good things and the future. My cigarette fortune was growing every day. I had real money, too.

There was a curfew that applied to us and the entire civilian population in the area. Nobody could be out on the street after 7:00 P.M. In early July, about eight weeks after liberation, we were sitting together singing Hebrew songs around midnight. Our windows were open to the highway, and we sang in a loud voice. We felt free.

Suddenly, we heard a knock. When I opened the door, two soldiers were standing there. I could not make out their uniforms. They weren't American or British. Then I saw a Jewish star on their hats, and one of them asked me in Hebrew, "Yehudi ata?" ("Are you a Jew?"). I said, "Ken, mi atem?" ("Yes, who are you?").

He answered, "Shalom, we are Jews from Eretz Yisroel, khayalim (soldiers)," and he shook my hand. I couldn't believe my eyes.

I invited them in. They had seen the lights from our barrack from their truck and stopped for directions. When they heard us singing in Hebrew, they knew that we must be Jews.

Inside, we could see the patch on their uniforms with the word *khayal* (military force) written in Hebrew and a Star of David. We were so touched by that. It was the first time we had seen a Jewish soldier from Palestine. He had a machine gun on him and everything.

The soldiers were from the Jewish Brigade from Palestine that had fought with the Allies in Italy as part of the British army, and they'd been stationed in Italy after the war, too. We hadn't heard anything about them before. They spoke Yiddish and told us the whole history of their unit. The Arabs didn't want to fight in the British Army, but the Jews did it because they wanted to defeat Hitler.

The soldiers had heard there were Jews from all over Europe in the Ebensee refugee camp, and their mission was to organize Jewish DPs to go to Palestine. They told us that the Americans were cooperating with them, unofficially.

One of the soldiers asked me to take them to the Ebensee camp. I told him about the curfew, but he dismissed it with a wave of his hand. "Don't worry," he said. "There's no curfew for us. We can go wherever we want." I replied that it was no use going so late at night while everybody was asleep in the camp and invited them to stay with us for the night.

They accepted with a smile and called in another three soldiers from the truck. We gave them coffee and chocolates and made some food. They said, "Don't worry about us. We have plenty to eat." Then they brought in all kinds of different cans of food from the truck. They wanted to feed us . . . we wanted to feed them. It was terrific.

They told us they were organizing an illegal *aliyah* (immigration). We asked them a lot of questions about how they would be able to smuggle people into Palestine without the cooperation of the British Mandate. But we didn't have to think much. All eleven of us registered right there in our barrack. We'd all been Zionists way before the war when we were kids. We felt like a miracle had happened to us.

In the morning, they took me and Mailekh to the camp and appointed us as assistants. I never saw such guys in my life. They were so determined, and everything they wanted to do, they accomplished. They went right to the American administration and talked to the captain in charge of the DP camp. The Americans allowed the soldiers into the camp, but officially, they couldn't support illegal emigration to Palestine because Britain was very much against it. The British Army controlled Italy and Palestine, and they were not allowing Jewish refugees to travel to Palestine. But Ebensee was in Austria, which was controlled by the Americans. The official line was that the Jewish Brigade came to the camp to encourage and lift the morale of the Jewish refugees.

With permission from the captain, the Jewish Brigade soldiers called a meeting for the Jews in the camp over the loudspeaker: "We bring greetings from your brothers and your family." Everybody came running. They gave a warm speech and invited people to register for emigration to Palestine. The journey there and life in Palestine would be difficult, so the soldiers only wanted young men and women who were healthy and strong. They told everyone that emigration was against the current laws of the British Mandate. Still, people signed up left and right. They registered over six hundred Jews. We were proud that our names were at the top of the list.

They told us, "This is no monkey business. We are leaving tonight. We'll come back for you in a week with more soldiers and trucks. Be ready to leave."

⏱ ⏱ ⏱

THE JEWISH BRIGADE soldiers returned as planned. I don't know how they got American trucks, but it didn't take much time for them to load everyone up and drive away. We didn't have much to take. I had fifty or sixty cartons of cigarettes and some other goodies. I was a little makher already because I knew them.

It was mid-July. After the excitement of liberation had faded, we started to get discouraged. For the time being, we'd been well situated in our barrack with plenty to eat and cigarettes and money. But we worried that the Americans would try to send us back to Poland. That transport was the biggest thing for us.

Now suddenly, we were on our way to Palestine. It was something we never believed was possible. More than a dream. Everybody clung to it like salvation had come for us. We were ordered around by the Jewish soldiers, and we saw how fast and efficiently they worked. We loved that! For us, it meant that after everything we went through, we were really going someplace where we'd belong.

American soldiers were stationed at checkpoints to control the highways in Austria. I don't know how those Jewish Brigade soldiers arranged it, but the guards let us through. Along the way, we were transferred to a column of small trucks that transported us to a train station close to the Italian border in Innsbruck, Austria.

Russia had released all of its Italian prisoners of war, and trains filled with those Italian soldiers were passing through Innsbruck on their way to Italy. Somehow, those guys from the Jewish Brigade had made arrangements with the Americans to allow us to board those trains and mix ourselves in with the Italian POWs.

The Jewish Brigade soldiers took off their uniforms and joined us on the train. They were terrific. I *shepped* so much *nakhes* (took so much joy) from the way they handled things. They said, "If the British ask you something at the border, act like you are sick. If they ask you again, say that you are Italiano. Whoever knows a few words of Italian should say something if it comes up, and whoever doesn't should stay quiet." Our train crossed the border at Brenner Pass into British-occupied Italy without any problems. That train was taking us to Rome and then to Naples, where there was a port. From there, they would put us on a ship to Palestine. It was easier to leave for Palestine through that port because the British didn't patrol there too much and the Italians were cooperative (unofficially).

On the way, the train stopped in Bologna. A Jewish Brigade soldier came over and said, "Sit quiet. We have trouble now, but don't worry. Everything will be all right. We're going to bring trucks. As soon as they come, move off the train and into the trucks. Be ready. We don't have much time."

Within an hour, the trucks had arrived. Then the Jewish Brigade soldiers moved among us on the train, announcing in an undertone, "Alle Yiden aroys. Alle Yiden aroys" ("All Jews get out. All Jews get out."). They loaded us in the trucks with quiet efficiency and took off.

When we were several kilometers from Bologna, they told us what had happened. The British had found out about our illegal transport to Palestine and were coming to arrest us. Those Jewish Brigade soldiers had caught wind of it and got us out of there before the British reached the train. I don't know how they did it. They said they were working with Jewish soldiers in the transport division of the British Army; those soldiers supplied the Jewish Brigade with the trucks to pick us up. If we'd been caught, the British would have sent us back to the American zone in Germany or Austria.

🕐 🕐 🕐

THEY DROVE US to a big Displaced Persons camp in Modena, Italy, which is about fifty kilometers away from Bologna. That camp was located in the British occupation zone, but it wasn't run by the British. It was controlled by the UNRRA. If we could get into that DP camp, the British army wouldn't have the right to arrest us or kick us out of the camp because we would be DPs under UNRRA administration.

To get us in, our Jewish Brigade soldiers told the UNRRA that we were prisoners in the concentration camps located in Italy and that they'd found us in the mountains. They instructed us, "If they ask you questions, play dumb like you don't know anything. Even if you speak English or other languages, just say, 'Shema Yisroel.'[10] That's all."

The UNRRA registered us in the DP camp in July 1945 and gave us official papers confirming our status as DPs in their camp. The papers didn't indicate which concentration camp we were liberated from or where it was located.

There were all different nationalities staying in that DP camp. It was crowded, and they didn't have any beds for us. We were lying on the floors, but we were treated well. They gave us three good meals a day. There were guards standing at the gate of the camp. We could go out during the day and visit the town of Modena to shop or do anything we wanted, but we had to return in the evening. Also, they didn't let you leave the camp with a suitcase or any parcel that looked like you were intending to move away. To leave the camp with your belongings, you had to get a permit from the UNRRA big shots, and they didn't want to issue those permits because they wanted to keep us concentrated and under their control while they figured out a long-term plan for the postwar refugee population.

The Italian people were very friendly to us and told us where to buy what we needed. We could go into a shop with a carton of cigarettes and trade for goods or sell it for money. But it was against the law for DPs to live in the city with the Italian population, and I understood why. It would have caused terrible problems. We were nice people, but a lot of the concentration camp inmates and prisoners of war had allowed themselves to become *ganuvim* (thieves) and *hefker* (lawless) people.

Even though they gave us plenty to eat and we had some money, it was a little depressing. We thought we would be taken to Palestine. But the British had thwarted our dream, and we were stuck in that camp. The soldiers who had taken us out of Ebensee were gone. We didn't see them anymore. A different group of Jewish Brigade soldiers would visit and tell us, "We're working at it, it won't be long, it's still happening. Right now, we cannot do anything. We have to be quiet and look for the right moment to get you out of here."

The British knew that the Jewish Brigade soldiers had organized a transport for us, so they were watching the camp very closely to prevent our group from leaving. Even after the British had witnessed what had happened to the Jews while they'd closed their doors before and during the war and had left us to our fate with the Germans, they still didn't let the Jews escape from Europe.

In the meantime, Mailekh and I fixed watches for the UNRRA staff and British soldiers. The idea was that we didn't pay for our room and board, so they shouldn't pay for our work. We could work only in the camp. They didn't allow us to work in Modena. If somebody gave us a tip, we could take it, but we couldn't ask for money. The British soldiers also gave us nice things, but they were not as rich and generous as the American G.I.s in Ebensee.

After three or four weeks, Moishe had had enough. He wanted to go to Rome and be independent. We were all tired of that life. We were free people, and we didn't want to be constantly watched by the UNRRA. Moishe was the organizer. He was ready to leave on his own, and that pushed us to join. Most of the other boys who had lived in the SS barrack with us in Ebensee decided to come to Rome with us, too.

So what did we do? There was a building whose back wall formed the boundary of the camp. There wasn't a fence around it, and the wall had windows we could open. We watched and learned that the area outside that wall was not patrolled so much by the British. One morning, we all left and went to the spot outside the camp that the windows overlooked. Moishe was inside the building with all of our luggage, and he threw it to us out the windows. Then Moishe walked out of the camp alone and met us. It was early October. We were a group of ten boys. We couldn't go to the Modena central train station because the British would notice us and send us back to the UNRRA camp. So, we walked to the railroad tracks that headed away from the station in the direction of Rome.

We saw a freight train standing on the track and jumped into an open car. The train took off. We thought we were traveling toward Rome, but we didn't know for sure. After about three hours, the train stopped, and we sent one guy outside to check

The United Nations Relief and Rehabilitation Administration (UNRRA) was an international relief agency, dominated by the United States and representing forty-four nations. Founded in 1943, it became part of the United Nations in 1945, but it largely shut down operations in 1947. Its purpose was to "plan, co-ordinate, administer or arrange for the administration of measures for the relief of victims of war in any area under the control of any of the United Nations through the provision of food, fuel, clothing, shelter and other basic necessities, medical and other essential services."[11]

it out. He found a railroad man who told him the train was going to Rome. A miracle.

We waited hours and hours for that train to take off again. Finally, we started moving. After traveling for another ten or fifteen hours, it stopped at a station. We all disembarked and got on a regular passenger train to Rome. We split up, two in each compartment, so we wouldn't attract attention.

One guy we met in the UNRRA camp had some experience traveling in postwar Italy. He told us that on the Italian trains, they were letting Jewish survivors ride without tickets, the only thing that you need to do is show the conductor something with Hebrew writing. If you show a page from a siddur, it's enough. Eventually, the conductor came. He took one look at us and knew we were from the concentration camps. He said, "Katzet, katzet." We showed him a piece of paper with Hebrew writing and said, "Roma, Roma." He didn't bother us, and we arrived in Rome. It was September 1945.

CHAPTER 12

Postwar Europe (October 1945–March 1949)

W E WERE TEN BOYS WALKING the late afternoon streets of Rome. No one had a room for us. We had dollars. We had liras. We were well-dressed. We could even speak a few words of Italian. At 9:00 P.M., we were still searching for a place to stay. A priest walked toward us with his black hat and long cotton robe, and I asked him for help. He spoke German. I told him that every hotel had turned us away after seeing that we were foreigners. I also told him we had been in the concentration camps, but we didn't need to tell him that. He knew just by looking at us.

He walked with us for hours, but still we had no success. On the way, we talked about the concentration camps and the war. He was a German priest, and he told us that he was also angry at Hitler. I didn't know whether that was true, but we appreciated that he was so kind to us.

Around midnight, he approached some Italians for advice, and they sent us to a woman who rented out rooms in her private home. After discussing it alone with the priest, she spoke with us a bit in German, and then with hesitation in her voice and gestures, she agreed to let us stay for three nights. We thanked the priest, and he went on his way.

⏱ ⏱ ⏱

MAILEKH GOT A job as a watchmaker the next morning. I also got a watchmaking job in Rome, but I quit soon afterward to work as a peddler in the outdoor market at the Piazza Venezia. Moishe came along with me, and we started selling the American cigarettes and chocolates that we had brought to Rome. It was easy work. We were able to pay our landlady whatever she asked. The other guys who came with us left that guest house after the first few days, but we continued living there.

Later, we started to trade other products. We bought pairs of pants or cigarette papers from one refugee and sold them to another refugee or to the Italians. We made a little money.

We also registered with the local UNRRA office as DPs. Every month, the UNRRA gave us a package of clothing and food rations from the United States. They also gave us some pocket money. In the market, we spoke with other Jewish refugees who came from Germany with merchandise. We could see that they were making more money than we were.

Then we ran into Mortra Kaufman and his brother Meyer, who had been with us in the Starachowice slave labor camp. They had also been in Auschwitz, but we hadn't seen each other there. Mortra told me that he bought gold in Munich and sold it for a higher price in Rome. We decided to form a smuggling partnership. Mortra had a good head for figures. He could look at the daily price of gold and the currency exchange rates that were published in the newspaper and calculate the prices for our buying or selling transactions in one second. And I knew how to find buyers and sellers and how to take a risk. It was terrific the way we worked together.

The German army, which included the Austrians, had plundered a lot of gold from the Jews and others in the countries they had occupied during the war. It had been an official policy of the conquering German army to plunder homes and stores. The soldiers often put some of the stolen items in their own pockets. After the war, individual Germans and Austrians were selling their gold jewelry and coins on the streets to get some spendable cash to pay basic living expenses. We bought most of our gold in Austria because it was closer to Italy and more convenient to cross the border.

Sometimes we bought directly from the Germans and Austrians, but mostly we bought from Jewish boys from the refugee camps; many of them also went into that same gold and currency trading business. If they wanted cash, we paid them in whatever currency they wanted. If they wanted cigarettes, we paid them with cigarettes. We knew how to test the gold to see if it was real or not.[1]

In the beginning, we crossed the Austria-Italy border by train. Later, the police started searching people on trains, so we had to cross the border by hiking over the Brenner Pass in the Tyrol mountains. There were no border patrols in the mountains.

Back in Italy, the Italians were willing to pay a high, black-market price for gold because the Italian lira was not stable. The Italians paid us in liras or dollars or American cigarettes. We got so rich smuggling gold that we didn't know what to do with all the money. At one point, my rucksack was filled with enough Italian liras to buy an entire apartment building in Rome.

The economy was chaotic in postwar Europe. It wasn't like normal times. Although smuggling was against the law, we didn't feel we were doing anything wrong. Everything had been taken away from us in the war, and we had to try to make back some of what we'd lost. The authorities could have stopped the smuggling, but they turned a blind eye—probably because they felt some kind of guilt for what they had done to us.

Then the authorities suddenly started to put stricter patrols on the borders. If we had been smart, we would have quit immediately, but we thought we could get away with one last smuggling run.

The Austrian bicycle patrol caught us at the border when we were crossing the mountains from Italy to Austria. Our rucksacks were filled with U.S. dollars that were wrapped inside bedsheets. They didn't know that we were carrying bags full of money. They thought we were smuggling sheets. We tried to bribe the policeman, but it didn't work. He seemed afraid and brought us to the border police station in Austria. They didn't arrest us for smuggling; that privilege they let us have because we had been in the concentration camps. But they confiscated our rucksacks and made us cross the border back to Italy.

We didn't give up. We traveled back to the closest town to where we got caught in Austria, and asked the local Jewish community organization to help us. They set up a meeting with the police at the border patrol station where they were holding our rucksacks. While they sat and discussed our case in one room, I sat in the room where they had left our rucksacks. The police had stationed a woman there to watch me, and she allowed me to open one of the bags, take out one package of sheets and put it in my coat. She didn't let me take more. The police gave us a receipt for our confiscated sheets and sent us on our way. I'm sure they found the money later and took it for themselves. There were a few thousand U.S. dollars in that package of sheets. I don't remember exactly. But we lost all the rest of the money we'd made. We had been carrying everything with us each time we traveled—we hadn't saved anything back in Italy as a cautionary measure—because there was no safe place to store our valuables. It was a mistake. We could have figured out some arrangement.

That was the end of it. Our smuggling days were over.

BACK IN ROME, we reevaluated our situation and decided to move to Stuttgart, Germany. It was the spring of 1946. In Italy at that time, you didn't get much support from the UNRRA if you were living independently. That hadn't mattered to us when we were rich from smuggling, but now we looked at things differently. If we wanted real assistance from the UNRRA in Italy, we would have to live in a DP camp with all kinds of restrictions.

In Germany, however, the UNRRA rules were more flexible. You could register as a DP and get regular meals and other benefits for free, even if you were renting a private room outside of the DP camp. Also, the food at the Stuttgart DP camp was good and they housed the DPs in apartments, not in tents like in Italy. We got a place to live in the camp, but only Mailekh actually lived there. Moishe and I rented a room in another neighborhood in Stuttgart from a nice German family who needed the money.

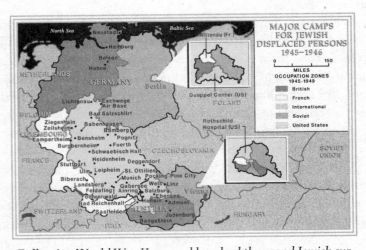

Following World War II, several hundred thousand Jewish survivors were unable to return to their home countries and remained in Germany, Austria, or Italy. The Allies established camps for displaced persons (DPs) for the refugees. The report issued by US special envoy Earl Harrison in August 1945 chronicled the plight of Jewish DPs and led to improved conditions in the camps. Many Jewish DPs preferred to emigrate to Palestine, though many also sought entry into the United States and Canada. They remained in the DP camps until they could leave Europe. At the end of 1946, the number of Jewish DPs was estimated at 250,000.[2]

Sometimes the three of us slept together in the DP camp, and sometimes Mailekh slept with us in the rented room.

WE FIGURED THAT our fourth brother Izak was probably alive and that somehow we would find him. The DP camp in Stuttgart was well-organized to help refugees find their relatives. That was one of the reasons we decided to move there. You registered your name, your hometown, and the names of your immediate family members. There was a book published by the UNRRA listing the survivors for each town.

When I was living in the Warsaw Ghetto, I knew that Izak had crossed over into the Russian-occupied part of Poland and had arrived at the town of Mestlik. A guy who was in Mestlik at the time told us that he saw my brother get arrested by the Russian police for smuggling food and that they were sending a lot of the Jewish refugees to Siberia. Izak was a strong young man who could withstand hard labor. Even in the camps, we figured that if we were killed, at least Izak would survive.

My friend Benny was also living in Stuttgart at that time, and he would travel back and forth to Poland. He came from a prosperous Kozhnitz family who had buried valuables in the buildings they owned during the war. After the war, Benny took trips to recover those hidden assets and take them out of Poland, little by little. He had to be careful. Officially, he claimed that he was going to look for his family. If the Poles had found out what he was really doing, they would have confiscated his property. Whenever he came back to Stuttgart, he returned with news of whatever was going on in Kozhnitz and Warsaw.

On one of his visits, he was walking in Warsaw, and by chance, he passed my brother Izak on the street. They embraced and kissed each other. I can't tell you how much it meant in those times to find somebody from your town or someone you knew from the camps who was still alive.

My brother cried to Benny, "Look, I'm the only one left. Why did I survive? I came to Kozhnitz. Nothing is there, nobody. No one can tell me anything."

Benny cut him off. "What are you talking about? Your three brothers are alive in Stuttgart. They survived! They are healthy. I just talked to them a few days ago."

Oh, you can imagine . . . Izak's tears of grief turned into tears of joy. Benny put a new soul into Izak's body.

Izak gave Benny a letter to deliver to us. He wrote that he was living in Warsaw with his wife, Riva, and their two children—Rosa, who was born in Russia, and Moni, a six-month-old baby who was born on the train ride from Russia to Poland. Right away, we mailed a letter back to Izak saying, "Don't stay another day in Poland. Don't wait even a minute. As soon as you receive this letter, cross the border to Czechoslovakia. From there it is easy to cross the border into Germany and come to Stuttgart. We have everything for you here." We were afraid that the Russians would close the borders to western Europe and that Izak would get trapped in Poland. Russia controlled Poland after the war, and a lot of Jewish refugees were starting to come over from the Russian side. There were rumors that the Russians didn't want them to leave.

When Izak and his family crossed the Czech border into Germany, he showed their Polish DP passports and told the authorities that he had brothers in Stuttgart. That entitled them to free train tickets in Germany.

🕐 🕐 🕐

OUR TEARFUL REUNION in Stuttgart was an indescribable moment that quickly faded into the practical matters of getting Izak's family settled. They registered with the UNRRA, and we made sure they got a nice private apartment in the Stuttgart DP Camp. It was around January 1947.

At first, Riva would cook for all of us and we ate together, but taking care of her two little children and cooking for another three hungry men became too much for her. We told Izak and Riva that we didn't want to cause problems for them: "We survived on our own until now, and we will continue to survive." So, it was decided we would come only on Friday nights.

Riva was Izak's second wife. No one knew what happened to his first wife, whom he had married during the war in Warsaw. We asked him how he could be certain that his first wife wasn't alive and what would happen if she came back. But nobody ever heard from her after she'd tried to escape from the Warsaw Ghetto, and no one else from her family survived the war, so there was no one to ask.

Riva was from Bessarabia, Romania, which was under Russian occupation early in the war. At that time, it was easy to cross over the border into Russia. When the Germans invaded Russia, Riva's family fled deep into Russia. She had been separated from them, but they also survived.

The Russians sent Izak to a slave labor camp in Siberia, close to the Chinese border. He did hard labor on the railroad. When Russia was still on good terms with Hitler at the beginning of the war, Russia treated the Polish Jews like enemies. The Russians put them in slave camps and didn't give them much to eat. Some died from hunger in the Russian camps, but the Russians didn't have a program to exterminate the Jews like the Germans did.

When Germany invaded Russia in June 1941, they became enemies, and the Russians became allied with Great Britain. Suddenly, the Poles were no longer enemies of Russia, and Izak was released from the slave labor camp. The Russians allowed the Poles to live in Russia as resident aliens and even gave them the option of becoming Russian citizens. Izak got a job and started a family there during the war, but he kept his Polish citizenship. That was lucky. If he were a Russian citizen, he might not have been able to leave Russia when the war ended.

After the war, the Russians released all the Polish refugees who had survived and sent them back to Poland. The train took them to Warsaw, and Izak went immediately to Kozhnitz. Everything having to do with Jewish life in Kozhnitz had been destroyed. Nothing was left of our home. All he found was the desecrated Jewish cemetery. During the war, rumors had spread that the Jews had hidden their gold and money in the graves before the Germans took them away. So, the Poles unearthed all the graves and left bones lying all over the cemetery. My mother was buried there. Can you imagine? There had been a brick wall surrounding the Jewish cemetery. The local people took it apart and used the bricks and tombstones to build their houses. Izak didn't stay for long. That was the end of Kozhnitz for him.[3]

Izak went back to Warsaw. He had no idea of what was happening on the western side of Europe, which was controlled by the United States and Britain. The Russians didn't allow much information about the West to get through to Poland. Izak had heard that some of the Polish Jews had survived, but he never thought he would see us again.

Izak and Riva lived in Stuttgart for about a year. Riva didn't like it there and insisted on going to Israel to reunite with her parents and sisters. I told them that we might try to emigrate to the United States and tried to persuade them to wait and come with us. They finally left Stuttgart for Israel in 1948 after the State of Israel was established.

🕰 🕰 🕰

WE GOT USED to living in Germany after the war. Surprisingly, it didn't feel strange. Most of the Jewish DPs were waiting to emigrate to Israel, the United States, Canada, and other places. Some blended themselves into the German life and economy. I could have done that, too. I made a lot of contacts in the jewelry business and the watchmaker community who wanted to create opportunities for me to stay there. But I never seriously considered it.

Whenever a German met a Jew after the war, he would say that he wasn't a Nazi and that he didn't have anything to do with

their terrible crimes. Every German you met told you that he was
a saver of Jews. They praised us and did what they could to help
us. Although we appreciated the help, we assumed those words
were lies. They didn't express any hatred toward us in those postwar days, but you can't see into someone's heart, and inside, a lot
of them were probably still Jew-haters who missed the good old
days under Hitler when they were conquering Europe.

🕑 🕑 🕑

MY BROTHERS AND I were not so religious after the war. In the
camps, I never stopped believing in God. I think maybe that
helped me survive. We saw miracles with our own eyes. Many,
many times, we faced certain death. Each time, we were saved
and managed to stay together. You couldn't explain it as coincidence. Maybe it was a sign from God that He exists and wanted
some of us to live. Who knows?

As we settled into a more normal life in Stuttgart, we thought
more about these things and discussed them among ourselves.
We began to question God. At one point, I vowed that I would
not circumcise my sons, as required under Jewish law, if I ever
had a family. If God exists, why did He let this happen to our parents, to our families, to His people, the Jews? None of us had an
answer. So, He probably doesn't exist. Or if He does exist, He
had just forsaken us. All of us asked these questions many times.

In the end, I wasn't so fanatical as to blame God for everything. I knew in my mind that it's not God who does good or bad
things in this world. It's people themselves. It never really occurred to me to completely reject the religion. No matter how
angry I was at God and whether or not I believed in Him, I was
still a Jew. There wasn't something else for me to be. I knew that
the people who had persecuted us were wrong and that their ac-
cusations against us were lies. When the State of Israel was
established in 1948, I saw it as another miracle from God, and it
softened up my anger.

☉ ☉ ☉

WHEN IZAK WENT to Israel in 1948, he found our cousins who had moved to Tel Aviv back in the 1930s, before the war broke out. They were the son and daughter of my Uncle Meir from Mogalnice. They already knew that we'd survived and were living in Stuttgart from the books that the UNRRA distributed all over the world with the names of the Jews from each town in Europe who had survived.

They told Izak that my Uncle Pinchas and his son were killed in Auschwitz, but his wife, Rachel, and two daughters had survived. They'd been hidden by a Catholic family in France.

They also told Aunt Rachel about us, and she wrote us a letter inviting us to visit her in Paris and maybe stay to work in her jewelry store, fixing watches. Mailekh decided to go meet her. Moishe and I didn't want to go to France. We had already decided to go to either Israel or America.

Aunt Rachel's jewelry store in Paris had been taken over by a provisional administrator from the French Vichy government during the war. Later, when the Americans liberated Paris, she went right over and told the provisional administrator to get the hell out of her store! They left, and she took back the store and her home.

Mailekh came back from Paris and told us he'd decided to move there. He didn't say why he was so interested in going to France. It had been such a natural thing for us to promise and risk our lives to stay together in the camps, but as we gradually adjusted to normal life, it felt just as natural for Mailekh to go off on his own. We divided whatever we had among ourselves, and he left. It wasn't a big ceremony.

In Paris, Mailekh changed his name to Marcel and worked in Rachel's store as a watchmaker, but that didn't last long. He didn't get along with her. He wrote us that she provided him with food but didn't pay him a salary. She gave him only a few francs to buy himself cigarettes and acted like she was doing him a favor by allowing him to work for her.

After a short while, he quit and told her that he could make a living anywhere. It was true. Mailekh learned everything fast and became skilled at anything he tried. He also had a good character and a good neshome.

Mailekh decided to go back to his profession as a gemashmak-her, cutting the leather uppers for shoes. He came across someone he knew from Poland and went to work for him in Paris.

⏱ ⏱ ⏱

THE JEWISH ORGANIZATION in Stuttgart coached us on the refugee application process for emigrating to the United States. They told us to be straightforward and simple and only to say things that we could prove. Moishe and I went in together. They asked what happened to us in the war. They wanted to know dates and every little detail about our family life before the war and also why we wanted to go the United States. We told them that we grew up in a religious family and believed in God. We told them that our father was a watchmaker and that he taught us the trade. We told them that we were working as watchmakers in the camps and that we would be able to earn a living as watchmakers in the United States. We told them that we wanted to go to the United States because it was a good, free country.

They gave us an intelligence test and called us in for several interviews over a period of months. We were examined three or four times by a doctor. They were very thorough and asked if we had this or that disease. They didn't want to take sick people. We were young and healthy and strong. While we were waiting, a lot of people were rejected. Finally, the U.S. Consulate called me and said that our applications had been approved.

We had struggled with the decision of whether to go to the United States or Israel. Going to the United States was a once-in-a-lifetime opportunity. I reasoned that I could go to Israel at any time with the fortune I expected to make in the United States. What did I have to lose?

The United States didn't let you in unless you had a sponsor who agreed to support you financially in case you couldn't earn a living. The Americans didn't want refugees to sit in the *goldene medina* (country of gold) and collect welfare payments. The Jewish community in each city of the United States organized volunteers to sponsor Jewish refugees. "One Jew is a guarantor for the other," as the saying goes.[4] The U.S. Consulate notified us that our sponsor was in St. Louis, Missouri, and that's where they would be sending us.

I didn't know about many cities in America, and I had never heard of St. Louis. I asked a G.I. who would trade cigarettes with us. He said, "Oh my gosh! I feel sorry for you. St. Louis is a small, little town with swamps in the area." I walked away from him so depressed. And then I realized that I didn't have to stay there. If I didn't like it, I could go wherever I wanted. When I asked another G.I., he told me that St. Louis was a big metropolitan city. To reassure me, he brought out a map and showed me the dots for the little towns and the circles for big cities.

The application process took about six months. It was March 1949 when we left for America. We had free passage on a military ship with about fifty immigrants from all different nationalities. Eight of us were Jews.

It was President Harry Truman who decided to accept the Jewish refugees into the United States. When our ship arrived at the port of New Orleans and the immigration officers asked us our names, Moishe took the name Morris. I took the name Harry, because of Harry Truman.

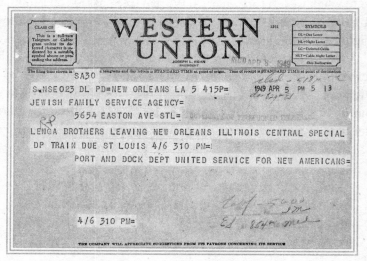

U.S.A.T. "GENERAL HARRY TAYLOR"
Office of the I.R.O. Escort Officer

4 April 1949.

Mr. Lenga Chil

                                   watch maker
For work performed in the   Department.

It has been indeed gratifying to have you aboard the U.S.A.T. "GENERAL HARRY TAYLOR" during the voyage from Bremerhaven, Germany to New Orleans, Louisiana, during the period 22 March 1949 to 5 April 1949.

The wonderful cooperation, the tasks you have undertaken to make this a clean ship, the services you have performed voluntarily for the ship, passengers and crew personnel makes for good citizenship in a new land of great opportunity.

On behalf of the entire ship's staff I wish to thank you wholeheartedly and wish you all health, wealth and happiness in the United States of America.

ERIK WENDT,
I.R.O., Escort Officer

Harry Lenga's ship recommendation, 1949.

WESTERN
UNION

JOSEPH L. EGAN
PRESIDENT

SYMBOLS
DL = Day Letter
NL = Night Letter
LC = Deferred Cable
NLT = Cable Night Letter

CLASS OF SERVICE
This is a full-rate Telegram or Cablegram unless its deferred character is indicated by a suitable symbol above or preceding the address.

The filing time shown in the date line on telegrams and day letters is STANDARD TIME at point of origin. Time of receipt is STANDARD TIME at point of destination

SA30

S.NSE023 DL PD=NEW ORLEANS LA 5 415P=   1949 APR 5 PM 5 13

JEWISH FAMILY SERVICE AGENCY=

      5654 EASTON AVE STL=

LENGA BROTHERS LEAVING NEW ORLEANS ILLINOIS CENTRAL SPECIAL
DP TRAIN DUE ST LOUIS 4/6 310 PM=

      PORT AND DOCK DEPT UNITED SERVICE FOR NEW AMERICANS=

      4/6 310 PM=

THE COMPANY WILL APPRECIATE SUGGESTIONS FROM ITS PATRONS CONCERNING ITS SERVICE

A telegram announcing the departure of the Lenga brothers from New Orleans as they took a train to St. Louis in 1949.

Afterword

by Scott Lenga

AFTER GOING THEIR SEPARATE WAYS in 1948–49, the Lenga brothers went on to marry, have children, and live quiet and uneventful lives in their adopted countries.

Izak worked as a porter at the Haifa port during his early years in Israel and later as a metal worker. Riva worked in their home as a seamstress. Together, they raised three children in Israel—Rosa, Moni (who was born on the train from Russia!), and Michael.

Marcel (Mailekh) established a small factory in Paris that made shoe uppers. In 1969, he won big at the horse races and invested his winnings in a clothing store that he ran successfully with his wife, Violette. They had two daughters—Monique and Patricia.

Morris (Moishe) married a young Shoah survivor named Ann, who had also emigrated to St. Louis, and raised two daughters—Margi and Bobbie. Morris worked as an independent watchmaker and eventually opened a jewelry store of his own. Ann worked as a department manager in a large St. Louis department store.

I knew Ann as the aunt who would pinch my cheek between the knuckles of her dainty fingers until tears welled up in my eyes. But I never doubted her love. To this day, not a Passover goes by for me without a fond memory of her sardonic smile and matzah ball soup. In another darker time, in 1943, she arrived in Auschwitz at age twelve with her mother and eight-year-old brother Henry. She didn't know how they all passed the first selection. Following the routinized cruelty of concentration camp administration, they were separated and sent to different barracks and work assignments. A few months later, an SS officer beat her unconscious for standing on a brick to look taller and more adult-like in a lineup. She woke up in the "hospital" and was able to plead her way into a job carrying a large kettle of soup from the kitchen for children who were kept as "patients." There, she discovered her brother Henry, who was being subjected to medical experiments by Dr. Mengele and his staff. She was helpless to stop the experiments but was able to maintain contact and give Henry extra rations that she stole from the kitchen.

In November 1944, while the "hospital" was being evacuated, Ann and Henry escaped and ran toward another subcamp of Auschwitz called Buna. A Jewish member of the Sonderkommando found them sheltering in an empty barrack. Astonished to see children alive in the camp, he hid them in a basement behind an enclosure that he built from blocks of stored fuel used to stoke fires. He gave them food from his more ample Sonderkommando rations until Auschwitz was liberated by the Russian army on January 27, 1945. Their mother also survived the war, and the three of them reunited in their hometown of Radom, Poland. Threatened with a violent death by the local Polish population if they stayed to reclaim their property, they made their way to Stuttgart and finally emigrated to St. Louis in 1949, where Ann met Morris two weeks later. Ann was nineteen when they married in 1950. By coincidence, the Sonderkommando who had hid Ann and her brother also emigrated to St. Louis. He was part of the community of Shoah survivors but did not want it known that he had worked as a Sonderkommando. Ann kept his secret and didn't reveal his name.[1]

I saw the number on Ann's arm when I was growing up and understood that she had been in Auschwitz, but I knew almost nothing of her backstory until after she passed away.

My dad, Harry (Khil), worked for many years as a watchmaker in a jewelry store, where he met my mom, Dorothy, a local

A poster announcing the 1960 grand opening of Friendly Jewelers, a new business run by Harry Lenga and his wife Dorothy.

St. Louis girl who worked in the same neighborhood. They married and had three sons—Michael, Mark, and Scott (me).

My mom and dad opened a jewelry store of their own called Friendly Jewelers in 1960, a couple of months before I was born. My dad was the watchmaker, and my mom was the salesperson.

After the four Lenga brothers said their goodbyes in Stuttgart, their first and only reunion was in St. Louis at the wedding of my cousin Margi (Morris and Ann's daughter) in August 1975. To everyone's shock, Marcel (Mailekh) died of a massive heart attack only two weeks later.

As far back as I can remember, my dad insisted that something like the Shoah could happen again in America or anywhere else. He never stopped telling his story, and he admonished us to teach the Shoah to our children so they would be able to see the warning signs and understand the dangers of tyranny and anti-semitism. When we were kids and teens, my brothers and I resisted the powerful onslaught of his old country thinking, even as it became part of our being. It seemed stagnant, pessimistic, and sometimes comical—at odds with the foundations of our American self-image. We compartmentalized his worldview and often mocked it. He never backed down, but he accepted our insolence with a touch of good humor and long-suffering disappointment. It is only now that I understand the loneliness he must have felt raising us in an adopted world that so misunderstood him—especially given that the core aspects of his true personality were adaptability and optimism.

The neighborhood on North 14th Street where Friendly Jewelers was located deteriorated and became quite dangerous during the late 1960s and '70s. But my dad endured and continued to make a living there. In his last three years in that store, he suffered four robberies at gunpoint. My dad described one of the holdups to me as follows:

> Two of them walked in and put a bullet in the ceiling
> before they said anything. Your mother started to

scream. They were going to kill her. I started to yell at her, "Please be quiet! Don't do that! Don't yell!" She listened to me, and they backed down.

They put us both facedown on the steps that went up to the back room of the store. They said that if we raised our heads, they would kill us. I told your mother very quietly, "Shhh, if we can live, let's live. Let's not do something stupid. Just lie like this." I thought they would kill us.

They cleaned me out completely. It was right before Christmas. The police were across the street, but they couldn't do anything about it.

Later, my dad got a dog—a white German Shepherd. He thought they would be scared to attempt a holdup if a dog was there. One summer day, I came to spend time with my parents at their store. During lunch, I took a bus to downtown St. Louis to do some shopping. When I returned a few hours later, they had been held up again. Two guys had come in, pointed a pistol at my dad's face, and took all of the money in the cash drawer. My dad laughed when he told me, "The dog stayed asleep the whole time on the steps."

After I heard what happened, I locked the door, hung up the CLOSED sign, and told my parents that the store was finished. We would never open that door for business again. It was several days before I was leaving to move to Berkeley, California, for my last two years of college. I pushed them hard and insisted that we pack up all the merchandise and take it home in two days. That's what we did. In the end, it was my father's decision, of course. It was hard for him to let go, but he knew it was the right thing to do.

He said, "If I stay, there will come another holdup, and another, and another. Eventually, they will kill me. I want to live a little longer. I have enough money to live. I don't need the aggravation and pressure and fear."

My dad spent his retirement during the 1980s and early '90s doing interviews and speaking about his Shoah experiences at schools all over the St. Louis area. One newspaper article reported, "Before he spoke to freshmen students Friday at Melville High School, Harry Lenga thanked them 'for the privilege of letting [him] speak.' But when he finished, it was the students, some with tears in their eyes, who gave a standing ovation to Lenga. They crowded around him afterwards, shaking his hand or giving him a hug and a kiss."[2] I was far away during his retirement years. During my Passover and summer visits, he would tell me about his speeches at school assemblies, but he never showed me the newspaper articles or TV interviews.

Much of my twenties was spent at university and traveling in North America and Asia. I took long wilderness treks and solo hitchhiking trips, driven by the need to "get away" and taste the apparent freedom that was my American birthright. Photos show me happily juggling on a mountaintop, awkwardly trying to sit cross-legged in a Buddhist meditation retreat, and laughing with friends at Disneyland. The camera lens never caught the subtle reverberation of the Shoah. I didn't always notice it or give it a name, but there was always something of it pushing me out the door, showing up along the way, and waiting for me at my destination.

My early career as a corporate lawyer coincided with a long and meandering exploration of my Jewish roots that sparked a desire to interview my dad. He traveled to San Francisco, I took a week off work, and we did more than thirty hours of interviews in my apartment.

Within a couple of years, my dad had fallen ill. I got married and had a couple of kids. When the time came for me to take away his car keys, he and my mom could no longer live independently in the St. Louis suburbs, so I moved them to Israel, where I was already living with my family. Dementia had set in, and a world of memories melted into a melancholy gaze. When my dad stopped talking, I would play him tapes of the interviews we did together. He would sometimes look at his live-in helper and point to the tape player as if to say, "That's who I am, that's what I was." He passed away in 2000 and is buried a short mile from my home.

Sitting down to compile and edit his interview materials for this book some fifteen years later was a journey to the heart of my relationship with the Shoah, intertwined, such as it is, with the relationship between me and my dad. The daily drill-down into the detail and nuance of my dad's story brought an occasional epiphany of closeness to him that went beyond our connection during his life. I am profoundly grateful to him for the privilege to share his legacy with our family and the general public.

May his memory be a blessing to all of us.

My Search for Chassidic Context

by Scott Lenga

STORIES OF MY GRANDFATHER MIKHOEL's discipline and religious austerity loomed large in my childhood growing up in St. Louis, Missouri, in the 1960s and 1970s. They set the boundaries for how I imagined Kozhnitz and the Chassidic Jewish life that surrounded my dad when he was growing up. When I was an adult interviewing my dad for this book, I was surprised to learn about the choices that grandfather Mikhoel had when he was a twenty-year-old watchmaker living in Warsaw in 1908. He had uncles in the United States. His brother Pinchas had moved to Paris, and his other brother Meyer had moved to the Polish town of Mogelnice. Yet, my grandfather decided to move to Kozhnitz in order to be close to the Kozhnitzer Rebbe of his generation and he endured much bitterness to stay there. Why? This question was never answered in my dad's telling of his life story.

My dad never explained the history or teachings of the Chassidic movement or what Kozhnitzer Chassidus meant to grandfather Mikhoel, whom I never met. The wisdom and folklore of the Kozhnitzer Chassidim stood dormant in my dad's memory. It was part of the unarticulated essence of his being that didn't seem relevant to his nonreligious life in America. It had dried up in him, and he never spoke of it. Whoever was paying attention could catch a disconnected glimpse of that spark when my dad and his brother Morris (a.k.a. Moishe) performed the Passover Seder in the old style. He once told me that his Jewish identity was so deeply imprinted on him that he thought it would naturally pass to his kids. He was surprised at how little we had absorbed.

With the help of outside sources and with trepidation due to my limited knowledge, I hope to open a small window for the reader to catch a glimpse of the Chassidic context that imbued my grandfather Mikhoel's religious and spiritual world.

Kozhnitz was a small town surrounded by forests and farms with no industry other than shoemaking. In my grandfather's day, it was famous among all of the Chassidic sects because the holy Rebbe Yisroel Hopshtayn (1737–1814), known as the Maggid of Kozhnitz, had lived there one hundred years earlier, and an unbroken line of his offspring had served in town as Kozhnitzer Rebbes from generation to generation.

The Kozhnitzer Maggid was one of the three "patriarchs" responsible for spreading the Chassidic revolution throughout Poland. He was a disciple of Rebbe Elimelekh of Lizhensk and the Maggid of Mezeritch, the primary disciple of the Baal Shem Tov, the founder of Chassidism. It is said that Rebbe Elimelekh of Lizhensk bequeathed his supernatural powers of perception to the Seer of Lublin and his heart to the Maggid of Kozhnitz.[1]

There were many who feared the Chassidic movement as a clear and present danger to the Jewish religion, believing it to be a foray into the mystical, messianic tendencies of Shabbtai Zevi (1626–1676), who had brought disaster on the entire Jewish world in the seventeenth century. Shabbtai Zevi was a charismatic and perhaps bipolar mystic who was proclaimed to be the Moshiakh (Messiah) in 1665 by his prophet, Nathan of Gaza.[2] Together, they reshaped the wave of enthusiasm for Lurianic Kabbala[3] into an international movement of believers who included a sweeping majority of the rabbinic luminaries and the Jewish masses living in the diaspora.[4]

In 1666, Shabbtai Zevi's apostasy and conversion to Islam under threat of death from the Turkish sultan "threatened to crumble the very bedrock of Jewish belief"[5] and plunged the Jewish world into a profound depression.

The rabbinic establishment responded by imposing strict limits on the study of Kabbala by ordinary Jews. Yeshiva studies were confined to rationalist approaches to the Talmud and other Jewish sources. Study of Kabbala was reserved for elite scholars and select students.[6] Rabbi Aryeh Kaplan describes the impact of this response: "For the average individual, who was neither rabbi nor scholar, this was a time of great spiritual poverty. He was told that the only way he could approach God was through the strictest adherence to the law, but the subject of God Himself was virtually taboo. The feelings of the common man were neglected almost to the point of starvation, and all that he was offered was a dry, formal ritual, without any warmth or inspiration."[7]

The Chassidic movement, from the Baal Shem Tov on, stridently opposed the Shabbtaian teachings but also sought to address the rabbinic backlash to Shabbtai Zevi that had gone too far in the other direction. Many Jews in the towns and villages of Poland and the Russian Pale of Settlement longed for a more heartfelt and spirited Jewish life. The Chassidic movement came to reawaken their spark. Many in the rabbinic establishment, who came to be known as the *misnagdim* (lit., opposers), tried to stop the Chassidic wave of Godly enthusiasm in these downtrodden Jewish communities—and they failed. Marcin Wodziński, a professor of Jewish Studies at the University of Wrocław, relates that "by the mid-19th century [Chassidism] became the most influential religious, cultural, and social force among east European Jews."[8]

The Chassidic masters "stressed the fact that God created the world as an act of altruism and benevolence, and that pleasure, rather than punishment is the goal of man. God Himself is the source of all pleasure, and the greatest delight is therefore attachment [*dvekut*] to God. Why should one sin if doing so will diminish this pleasure, and why mention *Gehenna* [the Jewish concept of hell] when the loss of God's closeness is in itself a much greater punishment."[9]

They also taught that although the one living God is transcendent and beyond human comprehension, He is also immanent in this world. He wears all of heaven and earth as a garment and recreates the world in every moment. Physical existence is nothing more or less than an elaborate filtration of God's light, and each individual is a completely unique filter that has the potential to bring a unique aspect of God's light into the world. The highest form of spiritual endeavor for a person is not to climb the spiritual ladder to heaven but rather to draw the light of God down into our ordinary physical world and relationships. Moreover, a gesture of kindness or an ordinary *mitzvah* (good deed) performed by a simpleton with pure intention can activate the spark of God within him and in others.

None of these ideas were new to Judaism. Rather, the Chassidim brought a radical shift in emphasis to empower the spirit of the common man. Their teachings were "formulated in such a way as to give hope and inspiration to even the lowliest."[10]

The Chassidic masters were exceptional individuals who strived for purity of intent in their scholarship and their deeds and taught this wisdom to the masses with parables and stories. Each one was surrounded by a close circle of gifted disciples and a local community of merchants, tradesman, and water carriers who perhaps were not blessed with brilliant minds or advanced scholarship. All of them, great and small, looked to their Rebbe to activate their holy potential, to guide them, and to intercede with Heaven on their behalf. Chassidim would travel on pilgrimage to see their Rebbe on Rosh Hashanah and other holidays.

The Kozhnizer Maggid was sickly his entire life, and his body was so frail in his later years that he "spent most of his time in bed, wrapped in heavy blankets. For fifteen years, [he] had to be carried to the synagogue to pray. But as soon as he began to worship, a transformation would occur where he would regain all his strength, singing and dancing with flaming passion."[11] He was a towering spirit, a master of Jewish scholarship[12] and the esoteric traditions of Kabbala and a miracle worker who had the power of blessing.[13] He was also a violinist who played at weddings in his youth. He composed *niggunim* (tunes which are often sung without words and sometimes applied to the liturgy) and emphasized music and song in his community as an aspect of dvekut to God.[14]

Jews would come to the court of the Kozhnitzer Maggid from all over Europe for advice and blessings for practical matters such as infertility.

Gentiles in "Polish aristocratic circles also used to tell each other about the Maggid's wonders.... Noblemen used to bow their heads respectfully before the Maggid and ask for his blessing and advice.... It is likely that the Polish defense minister, Josef Poniatowski, was one of the Maggid's Polish adherents, and thanks to this, [the Maggid] succeeded in annulling many decrees which the nobility imposed upon the Jewish population."[15]

Legend has it that the French Emperor Napoleon himself came to meet the Maggid in Kozhnitz on his way to attack Russia.[16]

What follows is the Chassidic story of the birth of the Kozhnitzer Maggid:

The Heavenly Tribunal Danced with Shabbtai the Bookbinder[17]

Shabbtai Hopshtayn was a simple, pious bookbinder in the town of Opatów. He and his wife, Perla, were poor, but they were satisfied with their lot and never complained or told other people about their troubles. The one disappointment of their lives was that they were childless. When they reached their sixties, Shabbtai could no longer work to earn money, and they had to begin selling their possessions in order to buy food. To stretch their resources, they started fasting during the week and had a proper meal only on Shabbos.

Finally, they came to the end of their property. There was nothing left to sell. Friday came and there would be no food for them to eat on Shabbos. Before Shabbtai left for his morning prayers, he told his wife that God would provide if it was His will, and he made her promise not to tell anyone about their plight, lest they become dependent on the charity of other people. They agreed that she would boil pots of water on the stove so the neighbors would think she was cooking for Shabbos.

After Shabbtai left, she started cleaning the house and found an old forgotten blouse behind a piece of furniture. It was laden with buttons of silver. Right away, she went out to sell a few of the silver buttons, and she bought wine and challah and fish and meat to honor the Shabbos. She prepared everything with great joy and gratitude. All the while, she thought about how she would tell her husband, and she decided to surprise him.

When Shabbtai came home from the Friday evening prayers at shul, he saw the beautifully set table and smelled the food. He surmised that his wife had sought help from her friends in a moment of weakness, but he kept silent so as not to taint the Shabbos with any negativity. When she served him a fine portion of fish to begin the meal, she sensed his disappointment and told him all that had happened. Shabbtai was so uplifted with joy at this gift from God that he got up and danced around the table.

In another town on that same evening, the Baal Shem Tov was eating the Friday night meal with his disciples. After kiddish over the wine, he tilted his head back with a smile that expressed profound joy. During the meal, he smiled in the same way a second time and then a third. After Shabbos had ended, one of his disciples asked him what this meant. The Baal Shem Tov instructed him to ready a horse and carriage: they would journey to the town of Opatów, where his question would be answered. Upon arrival in Opatów, they were greeted with honor.

To the dismay of the leaders of the Opatów Jewish community, the Baal Shem Tov asked them to summon Shabbtai the bookbinder. The Baal Shem Tov instructed Shabbtai to relate everything that happened to him on Friday night and not to leave out any detail. Shabbtai told the whole story, including how he got up to dance three times during the meal. The Baal Shem Tov explained to Shabbtai and everyone who was gathered around that the pure, holy joy of Shabbtai's dance with his wife around the table broke through the barriers of heaven and that the Heavenly Tribunal had danced with them those three times. With each dance, the Baal Shem Tov had felt this great joy on high and smiled.

Then the Baal Shem Tov informed Shabbtai that the Heavenly Tribunal would grant him either enough wealth to live out his days comfortably or a child. The choice was his. Shabbtai wished for a son who would be an earnest Jew and a Torah scholar.

"You will have it," said the Baal Shem Tov. "Just as you brought great joy to the heavens, so you shall be blessed with a son who will bring joy and salvation to Jewish hearts.

Within the year, a son was indeed born to Shabbtai and Perla in their old age. The Baal Shem Tov returned and served as the *sandek* (godfather) for the *bris* (circumcision). He advised them to name the child Israel, which was also the name of the Baal Shem Tov. That child grew up to become the Maggid of Kozhnitz.

The story of Shabbtai the bookbinder would certainly have been known to my grandfather Mikhoel and everyone in the community of Kozhnitzer Chassidim. It conveys a taste of Chassidic teachings and offers insight into my grandfather's way of responding to the hardships of his own life (particularly not wanting to take charity and putting pots of water to boil on the stove so neighbors would think his family was cooking for Shabbat).

One can also imagine that my dad struggled with these Chassidic ideas as a teenage boy moving through puberty and trying to find his own way in the 1930s. How did they address the poverty of his family or my grandfather's depressed state of mind? How did they help him and the Jewish community adapt to the great changes that were unfolding in the world? One can only surmise.

APPENDIX B

The Tale of Laizer Yitzkhak Wildenberg

as told by Harry Lenga

MY REAL MOTHER, MALKE REYLE, who died in childbirth in 1924, came from the Wildenberg family, a well-known Chassidic family in Kozhnitz. There was family lore passed down through the generations that her great-great-grandfather, Laizer Yitzkhak Wildenberg, almost became the second Rebbe of the Gerer Chassidim. When he was just a young boy, Laizer Yitzkhak Wildenberg was a *talmid* (disciple) of the Kozhnitzer Maggid when the Maggid was already in his final years. The Maggid foretold that this boy would grow up to be a great scholar and Chassidic master, and indeed, it came to pass. When Laizer Yitzkhak died, he was buried close to the Maggid's grave in Kozhnitz.

The first Gerer Rebbe, known as the Chiddushei HaRim, was raised in the home of the Kozhnitzer Maggid and was also his talmid. When the Chiddushei HaRim was old and approaching death, he told his grandson to take a horse and buggy to Kozhnitz, find Laizer Yitzkhak Wildenberg, and ordain him as the second Gerer Rebbe. Gur, the town that was home to the Gerer Chassidim, is about fifty kilometers north of Kozhnitz. The grandson arrived in Kozhnitz at night and stopped three sep-

253

arate people to ask if they knew Reb Laizer Yitzkhak. All three said they didn't know him. Then the grandson told the wagon driver to turn around and go back home to Gur, saying that if they have such a big *tzadik* (righteous holy man) in their town and they don't even know who he is and where he lives, they don't deserve to have him serve as a great Rebbe. That grandson was nominated to be the second Gerer Rebbe a few years later. He became a great tzadik and the most famous Gerer Rebbe of all. He was known as the Sfas Emes.

That's the story my father, Mikhoel Lenga, told me. If it's true or not, I don't know. I'll tell you one thing I do know. My uncles (my mother's brothers) were Gerer Chassidim, and when they came to the town of Gur before the war, they were invited to sit by the side of the third Gerer Rebbe at his tish. He was the son of the Sfas Emes. That's the honor they gave to my uncles because they were the *kindeskinder* (descendants) of Reb Laizer Yitzkhak Wildenberg. It was not a small thing to be seated next to the Gerer Rebbe in those days. He had the most followers of all the Chassidic Rebbes in Poland. Thousands of people came to his tish every Friday night. It was so crowded that many of his Chassidim who came could hardly see him.[1]

Conflicts Among the Kozhnitzer Rebbes and Their Followers

as told by Harry Lenga

THE KOZHNITZER REBBE AT THE beginning of the twentieth century was Rakhmiel Moishe Hopshtayn, the great-great-grandson of the Kozhnitzer Maggid. My father remembered him from when he was very young. Rebbe Rakhmiel Moishe had three sons—Reb Aharon (Arele), Reb Elimelekh (Mailekh) and Reb Yisroel Eliezer. When the Rebbe died in 1909, his oldest son, Arele, became the Kozhnitzer Rebbe. He got married, but his wife left him right away, and he never remarried.[1]

Bitter arguments arose between him and the middle brother, Reb Mailekh. Some of the Chassidim, including my father, believed that Reb Mailekh should take over as the Rebbe. They thought that Reb Arele was too eccentric and maybe a little meshuga.[2]

Reb Mailekh was a stable person—married, with two daughters and a son. My father was a good friend of his. The supporters of Reb Arele said that he was a holy mystic and that regular people like my father weren't at a high enough level to understand his ways.

Eventually, there was a vote among the Kozhnitzer Chassidim, and Reb Arele won,[3] but a *beis din* (a Jewish religious court) was subsequently convened to hear testimony from a doctor. The beis din decided that Reb Arele was mentally incapable to serve as the Rebbe.

At that time, the Polish authorities also had to approve the appointment of the Rebbe. Normally, this would have been just a bureaucratic formality, but because the local Jews were divided and the beis din had decided that Reb Arele was mentally ill, the Poles had their own doctors examine him, and they confirmed the ruling of the beis din. Reb Arele was rejected.[4]

Reb Mailekh became the Kozhnitzer Rebbe, and my father was part of his close circle of Chassidim.

Before World War I, the youngest brother, Reb Yisroel Eliezer, formed a group called Chevras Avodas Yisroel[5] to buy land in Eretz Yisroel.[6] In 1924, he moved to Eretz Yisroel with some members of that group who set up a communal farm called Kfar Chassidim. It was around the time my mother died in childbirth. They didn't have anything to do with Zionism. The Chassidim believed that emigrating to Eretz Yisroel was worthy but that it was forbidden to re-establish a Jewish State until the coming of the Moshiakh. They claimed that Theodore Herzl, who had established the modern Zionist movement, was an *apicorus* (heretic) and that the Zionists had launched a heretical enterprise.

My father bought a plot of land in Eretz Yisroel with that Chevras Avodas Yisroel group before World War I. When the Depression came in the 1930s, he stopped making his payments. When World War II broke out, everything fell apart.

Jewish Religious and Political Groups in Prewar Kozhnitz

as told by Harry Lenga

IT IS NOT AN EXAGGERATION to say that the Jews and the Poles in pre–World War II Kozhnitz lived in separate civilizations with overlap only where they needed to interact for economic purposes. To the west was Nazi Germany, with its race-based declaration of war on the Jews, and to the east was Stalinist Russia, which made any expression of religion a crime against the state, thereby destroying Jewish culture and religious life for some three million Jews who were living in the USSR.[1]

Among themselves, the Jews in Kozhnitz were split among political parties, ideologies, Zionist groups, and religious groups.

There were Volkissen (assimilationist Jews), Communists (an illegal party in Poland), and Bundists (Jewish social democrats). Those groups were not religious. They opposed Zionism and looked down on the Chassidim as a relic of the ghetto mentality from the times before the Jews of Europe were emancipated. In their eyes, the simple Jewish folk were being led astray with the superstitious, mystical adoration of Chassidic Rebbes who gave *kvitels* (amulets) to heal the sick and open the wombs of barren women.

There were many different groups of Chassidim: Kozhnitzer Chassidim, Gerer Chassidim, Mezricher Chassidim, Piasetzner Chassidim, and many others, too. We also had a small group of misnagdim who opposed the Chassidim on religious grounds. All of these religious groups opposed Zionism, for the reasons described in Appendix C.

Finally, there were the General Zionists who followed Theodore Herzl, the Revisionist Zionists who followed Zev Jabotinsky, and the Mizrachi religious Zionists. The Zionists (and particularly the Zionist youth groups) drew people from many different political, ideological, and religious groups.

We argued with each other and lived together as a community.

I knew boys from these different groups from school and the youth organizations, and I also learned about the groups from my father, who was informed from reading the Yiddish newspaper and his responsibility as a member of the Geminder. My father knew how to get along with different kinds of people, but he was not an official Zionist and didn't belong to any of the political organizations. He was a Kozhnitzer Chassid, and they didn't like the Zionist movement. But as an individual, he sympathized with the Zionists, and others did, too. He used to donate money to Keren Kayemet, the Jewish National Fund,[2] and he was very much interested in moving to Eretz Yisroel.

When I was still in school and going to kheder, my brothers, Izak and Mailekh, and my sister, Khanale, joined Betar—the youth group for the Revisionist Zionist movement established by Zev Jabotinsky, who preached that the Jews can't rely only on diplomacy to achieve an independent Jewish state in Eretz Yisroel. Use of military force would be necessary, and we needed to prepare for it. Betar taught the young generation how to fight—to pack a rifle and shoot like soldiers.[3] It was legal in Poland.

My brother, Izak, was a makher in Betar. He even visited a Zionist collective farm in a different town to learn how to be a farmer—to prepare for life in Eretz Yisroel.

I joined the Noar Hatzioni, the youth group for the General Zionist organization started by Theodore Herzl, and they preached that diplomacy was the only way to get to Israel, not by trying to take it with force.

Testimony of Robert Persinger, the U.S. Army Tank Commander Who Liberated Ebensee

U.S. Army Platoon Sergeant Robert Persinger, Austria, 1945.

ROBERT PERSINGER WAS THE U.S. Army platoon sergeant and the
tank commander of the "Lady Luck," one of the two tanks that liberated Ebensee. Persinger fought in many battles as a part of the
Third Cavalry in Patton's Third Army, including the Battle of the
Bulge. The following testimony was delivered by Persinger in a
May 6, 2005, speech at the site of the Ebensee concentration camp
commemorating the liberation of Ebensee fifty years earlier:[1]

> Our tank platoon arrived in [the town of] Ebensee on
> Sunday May 6th, 1945, and we heard of a concentra-
> tion camp.... My platoon leader Lieutenant Garbowit
> directed me with my [tank and] crew to proceed to the
> gates along with Sergeant Dick Pomante and his tank
> and crew. As we approached on the gravel road to the
> camp, we saw masses of human beings that appeared
> almost like ghosts standing in mud and filth up to their
> ankles behind the high wire fence. They were dressed
> in their filthy striped clothes and some in partial cloth-
> ing, barely covering their bodies. They appeared so
> thin and sickly, it was evident that they were starving.
> Their bodies were just skin and bones. We stopped our
> tank and observed for a period of time trying to decide
> what we would do with the mass of prisoners sur-
> rounding our tanks.
>
> Both tank crews were hesitant to accept or make
> contact with these poor starving individuals. None of
> us had ever seen human beings in this terrible situation
> before. We started to toss rations and energy bars to
> them until our supply was depleted. In all of the confu-
> sion I lit a cigarette and heard someone say, "that it had
> been a long time since he smoked a Lucky Strike." I
> asked him to climb up on the tank so I could give him
> one. This man spoke English so I radioed that informa-
> tion to my Lieutenant, and he told me that we should
> keep him available for future questioning.

This prisoner wanted us to walk around the camp area. At first, we refused because we thought we had seen enough and really didn't want to dismount and wade through the quagmire of mud and around all of the dead bodies. Besides that, the stench of all of the dead bodies made it almost unbearable. He did convince us we needed to see more than we could see from the tank. We were taken to the barracks area, the kitchen which was bare, and then to the crematorium where there were stacks of bodies piled like cordwood one on top of the other completely around the inside walls of the crematorium. If you weren't sick by now you would be before you exited from there. At the same time, you wanted to cry. We had seen terrible sights from combat across Europe but what we were observing was a climax to the things human beings do to their fellow man. It was beyond anyone's imagination that such horrible crimes could be committed.

We returned to the village of Ebensee, to the Post Hotel where our tank company stayed, and started immediately making plans as to how we could get food to at least feed a few of them until our army units could arrive to bring food and hospital units for medical help which was so desperately needed. It was decided to start searching the complete area for food products to make a soup by using the large kettles that they had in their kitchen. We obtained potatoes, cabbage and other vegetables that were available from miles around. All of the bakeries were asked for bread. As an example, Sergeant Pomante used his tank to convince an Ebensee baker to release all of his bakery goods.

We finally got the soup ready but realized that somehow, we had to control the serving. It was decided to fire live ammunition over their heads from our tanks when they started to overrun the soup line. This brought their attention and did provide control. The servings started and some gulped it down so fast that many died from the reaction from it. Their stomachs could not accept the rich hot soup.

The army medical hospitals arrived quickly along with other army quartermaster units to provide services to get the prisoners on the road to recovery. We stayed with them and helped for two weeks to nourish them before we received orders to return to the [United] States and prepare for invading Japan with General Patton and his Third Army.

Glossary

PLACE NAMES

Gorczycki (pronounced Gorchitzki): The name of a Polish company that established a work camp near the village of Wolka. After the German invasion of Poland, the camp became a slave labor camp subservient to German military control but remained under direct management by Polish personnel of the Gorczycki company.

Kozhnitz: Yiddish name for the Polish town of Kozienice.

Schidlovitz: Yiddish name for the Polish town of Szydlowiec.

Shedlitz: Yiddish name for the Polish town of Siedlce.

Starachowice (pronounced Starakhovitse): Polish city. Also the name of a Nazi industrial slave labor camp established at that location in German-occupied Poland.

Tsozmer: Yiddish name for the Polish town of Sandomierz.

Wolanow (pronounced Volanov): Polish town. Also the name of a Nazi slave labor camp established at that location in German-occupied Poland.

NON-ENGLISH WORDS

Aktzion: German army or Gestapo operation to block off a small area of the Ghetto and go from home to home to search for coffee, sugar, money, or other things that violated the anti-Jewish laws. (German)

Aleph-Beis: The Hebrew alphabet.

Aliyah: Immigration to Israel (lit., going up). (Hebrew)

Alte Kockers: Old farts. (Yiddish slang)

Appel: A procedure in the German concentration camps and slave labor camps whereby the prisoners had to line up and stand at attention for roll call. It was routine to have an appel the first thing every morning and before marching to and from work. An appel often involved an inspection or selection of prisoners for execution. (German)

Appel Platz: The clearing in a concentration camp or slave labor camp where the prisoners had to line up every morning for inspection. (German)

Aron Koydesh: Cabinet in the synagogue where they keep the Torah scrolls (lit., holy cabinet). (Hebrew)

Aydele: Refined. (Yiddish)

Baleygert: Under siege. (Yiddish)

Beis Din or **Beit Din:** Jewish religious court. Jewish communities always had a rabbinic court that Jews engaged as a binding arbitrator to resolve disputes of all kinds between themselves. A divorce is not considered valid under Jewish law without a *get* (divorce certificate) from a beis din. (Hebrew)

Beis Medrish or **Beit Midrash:** Study hall dedicated to Jewish studies. Typically, a room filled with holy books in a yeshiva or synagogue. Study is often done aloud, interactively in pairs, so the beis medrish is not expected to be a quiet place. (Yiddish-Hebrew). Kozhnitz was famed for its beis medrishniks, who would sit and learn in the beis medrish from before dawn until late at night. On winter Thursdays, they would stay up all night and learn.... Whoever had the desire to learn found a place.... There were no class distinctions."[1] "The beis medrish in Kozhnitz was a place where "every shade of spiritual and religious life was concentrated." "Whoever had a cold house and a broken oven . . . came to warm themselves by the hot stove on cold winter days. . . . Whomever the poor life had chased from his house, went to the beis medrish."[2]

Block: Barrack. (German)

Blockaltester: An orderly who lived in a German concentration camp or slave labor camp barrack and never left that barrack to go to work. His duty was to guard the barrack from thieves, to clean the barrack, and to carry out administrative functions relating to the barrack. (German)

Bracha or **Brachot** (pl): Blessing. In Jewish practice a bracha is recited before the enjoyment of food, to commemorate a holiday or other auspicious event, in the performance of certain *mitzvot* (obligatory good deeds) or to bless other people. Brachot are recited in public or private and usually begin with the words, "Blessed are you, Lord our God," thereby acknowledging God as source of all blessing. The brachot are intended to draw meaning and holiness down into the mundane actions and events of everyday life.

Bris or **Brit Mila:** The Jewish rite of circumcision whereby a Jewish male is joined to the covenant between God and Abraham that is described in the book of Genesis. The bris is carried out according to Jewish law when a healthy Jewish infant boy is eight days old (the age of Isaac when he was circumcised). If the infant is not strong and healthy enough at this tender age, the bris is postponed until health considerations permit it to be carried out. (Hebrew)

Broyges: A state of mind directed at another person (usually mutual) that reflects a personal relationship which has deteriorated into a constant state of separation, vitriol, and resentment. (Yiddish).

Bubbishe: Grandmother. (Yiddish diminutive)

Chassidim: Followers of the Chassidic movement founded by the Baal Shem Tov. (Yiddish-Hebrew)

Chassidus: The Chassidic teachings and wisdom. Each Chassidic sect developed its own tradition of Chassidus, and each Rebbe would add his unique imprint. It was considered praiseworthy for a Chassid in one sect to study the teachings of other Chassidic Rebbes and sects. (Yiddish-Hebrew)

Cholent: A stew that is prepared before Shabbos and kept on a low heat overnight and served the next day for lunch. There are many variations, but it is typically made with beans, barley, potatoes, and sometimes meat. (Yiddish)

Chutzpa: Bold assertiveness. Can be used in a positive context, like moxie, or a negative context, like gall or brazen nerve. There is no real English equivalent. (Yiddish)

Daven: To pray. Often used to describe praying in a defined prayer service such as the *Shacharit* (the morning service). To **daven hoyakh** is to pray out loud with spirit. (Yiddish)

Dreck: Shit. (Yiddish)

Dreyer: Wily schemer (lit., one who twists or spins things around). (Yiddish)

Droshke: Horse-drawn carriage. (Polish)

Dvekut: Clinging. A term from the Jewish mystical tradition denoting the meditative experience of closeness to God that arises from aligning one's thought, speech, action, and intention with the godly attributes that are within the range of normative human behavior. (Hebrew)

Eretz Yisroel or **Eretz Yisrael:** Land of Israel, where Am Yisroel (the People of Israel) lived and governed themselves during biblical times until the First Jewish Temple built by King Solomon was destroyed by the Babylonian army, and then again under the Jewish Hasmonean kings during the Second Temple Period. When the Roman Legion destroyed the Second Temple (70 CE) and forcibly exiled most of the Jews from Eretz Yisroel after putting down the Bar Kochba Rebellion (c.132–36 CE), the Romans renamed that geographic area Aolea Palestina. (Hebrew)

Farikht: Crazy. (German)

Feldsher: Practitioner of folk medicine who did not have a medical degree but had some apprenticeship experience in the healing arts. Feldshers were commonly found in the small eastern European towns and villages where medical practitioners with formal training were lacking or nonexistent. (Yiddish)

Gemashmakher: Tradesman who cuts the leather upper part of shoes. (Yiddish)

Geminder: Jewish council elected to manage affairs in the local Jewish community. (Yiddish)

Goldene Medina: Nickname for America as a land of opportunity, freedom, justice, and protection from pogroms (lit., country of gold). (Yiddish)

Gonef (pl. Ganuvim): Thief. (Yiddish-Hebrew)

Goy (pl. Goyim): A non-Jewish person. (Yiddish-Hebrew)

Goyish or **Goyishe:** Not Jewish. (Yiddish-Hebrew)

Groshen: Polish currency equal to 0.01 zloty.

Groyse Artik: Distinguished, high class. (Yiddish)

Hefker: Lawless people. (Yiddish-Hebrew)

Judenrat: Jewish council for each city, town, and village that was appointed and controlled by the Germans. Each Judenrat was responsible for taking care of all the basic services in the Ghetto. The Germans wanted a collaborationist Jewish authority to carry out German policies in an orderly way. (German term coined by the Nazis)

Judenrein: Cleansed of Jews. (German term coined by the Nazis)

Kapo: Concentration camp foreman who was also a prisoner and was given privileges in return for supervising prisoner work gangs. A slang term originated by the inmates themselves. (German)

Katzet or **Katzetnik:** Slang term for concentration camp prisoner. (German term coined by the Nazis)

Khametz: Leaven, or the aspect of bread that causes it to rise when baked. During the Jewish holiday of Passover, it is forbidden to eat or use or own any khametz (Exodus 13:6–8). The rabbis taught that khametz represents the egoistic pride that enslaves our souls and that the mundane physical activity of Passover cleaning should be accompanied by a commensurate effort by each individual to liberate himself or herself from spiritual bondage. According to the Ramban, a sage from the thirteenth century, the aim is that khametz not be found "in your mind." (Hebrew)

Khazzan: Cantor. (Yiddish-Hebrew)

Kheder: Primary school for Jewish subjects (lit., room). (Yiddish-Hebrew)

Kibbitz: Chitchat. (Yiddish)

Kiddish: The traditional prayer over wine that is recited in the evening and the morning for Shabbos and holidays. If there is no wine available, the prayer can be made over another type of food or drink. (Yiddish-Hebrew)

Kintsim: Bargaining. (Yiddish)

Kishkes: Intestines, guts. (Yiddish)

Klappen Hertz: A pounding heart. (Yiddish)

Koyakh or **Koakh:** Strength or power. (Yiddish-Hebrew)

Kugel: Traditional casserole, often sweet and made with noodles. (Yiddish)

Loupe: Watchmaker's magnifying glass that you hold in your eye socket. (English)

Luftwaffe: German air force. (German)

Madrikh: Counselor. (Hebrew)

Mager: Thin, malnourished, emaciated. (German)

Makher: A big shot. A guy who gets things done. A **Gansa Makher** is the most important big shot. (Yiddish)

Mameshe: Mother. (Yiddish diminutive)

Mamzer or **Mamzeru:** Mischief maker (lit., a bastard under Jewish law). Often used affectionately to describe a plucky little kid. (Yiddish-Hebrew)

Mazel or **Mazal:** Luck. (Yiddish-Hebrew)

Mensch (pl. Menschen): A decent, moral, upstanding person who can be counted on to do the right thing in the community (lit., man). A parent will admonish his or her kid to behave like a mensch. (Yiddish-German)

Meshuga: Crazy (adj.). (Yiddish)

Metsiye: Good deal, bargain. (Yiddish)

Midrash: Ancient Rabbinic legends and parables that are used to interpret and illustrate concepts in the Torah. It is said that one who believes none of the midrashic legends is a heretic and one who believes all of them is a fool. (Hebrew)

Mikve: A ritual bath. Married Jewish women who observe Jewish law immerse in the mikve every month after their menstrual cycle as a prerequisite to physical reunification with their husbands. It is a custom (but not a legal requirement) for Jewish men in some communities to immerse in the mikve as a purification rite before Shabbos and Jewish holidays. (Hebrew)

Minkha and **Ma'ariv:** Afternoon and evening Jewish prayer services. (Hebrew)

Minyan: Quorum of ten Jewish men, which is required under Jewish law and custom to have a full Jewish prayer service. Why ten men? Because when Abraham bargained with God in an effort to save Sodom and Gomorrah from destruction, he asked God if He would spare the towns if there could be found ten righteous men among them. God answered that He would indeed refrain from destroying the town if there were ten righteous men. God then exited the conversation and proceeded with the destruction. See Genesis 28:20–33. (Hebrew)

Misnagdim or **Mitnagdim:** Orthodox Jews who opposed the Chassidic movement, believing it to be a dangerous foray into mystical, messianic tendencies of Shabbatai Zevi that had ended in disaster in the previous generation (lit., opposers). (Yiddish-Hebrew)

Mitzvah: A meritorious deed that fulfills one's religious obliga-
tions under Jewish law. This is more expansive than it
might seem at first glance. Just as it is a mitzvah to eat
kosher and observe Shabbos, it also is a mitzvah to make
love with one's spouse and to greet every person with a
heartfelt smile and a good word. (Hebrew)

Moshiakh: The Jewish Messiah (lit., the anointed one). (Hebrew)

Muselmänner: A concentration camp inmate who had big eyes,
hollow cheeks, and big teeth. His body was already completely worn out from starvation and hard labor and
didn't have any life in it anymore (lit., a Muslim). (German
concentration camp slang)

Nebekh: Pitiful; such a pity. (Yiddish)

Neshome: Soul (Hebrew)

Niggun (pl. Niggunim): A tune. Also used to refer to Chassidic
melodies that are sung repetitively without words to
create an opportunity for meditative expression of spiritual longing and joy. Each Chassidic sect composed their
own niggunim, which were sung by them and as well
other Chassidic groups. (Yiddish-Hebrew)

Oyshgeshpielt: Spent, used up, and worn out from starvation
and hard labor. (Yiddish)

Passover or **Pesakh:** An eight-day holiday celebrated in March/
April that commemorates the liberation of the twelve tribes
of the Children of Israel from slavery in Egypt. Passover begins with a festive meal called the Seder during which the
story of liberation is told and discussed. Passover begins on
15 Nisan on the Hebrew calendar, which is 30 days after
Purim, 50 days before Shavuot, 163 days before Rosh Hashanah, and 173 days before Yom Kippur. (Hebrew)

Perna: Down comforter. (Polish)

Peyis: Sidelocks. Chassidim and other religious Jews often let
their sidelocks grow to adhere to a biblical injunction
against cutting one's hair in that area. Young boys some-

times wrap their peyis around the sides of their ears. (Yiddish-Hebrew)

Pish: Urinate. (Yiddish)

Purim: A holiday around February/March (14 Adar on the Hebrew calendar) celebrating the rescue of the Jews in the days of the Persian Empire from extermination at the hands of Haman, the chief minister to King Achashverosh of Persia. The story is recounted in the Book of Esther, which is publicly read on Purim. On Purim, it is customary to wear costumes, and getting drunk is extolled as a mitzvah (good deed). (Hebrew)

Rakhmunes: Compassionate pity combined with a charitable act. (Yiddish-Hebrew)

Raus: Out, or get out. (German) The Yiddish variant is *Aroys*.

Rebbe: The rabbi who is the leader of a Chassidic sect. (Yiddish)

Reichsdeutsche: A German who was born and raised in Germany. (German)

Rosh Hashanah: The Jewish New Year. (Hebrew)

Roshe or **Rashah:** Evil person. (Yiddish-Hebrew)

Sandek: At a bris, the baby boy is placed on the lap of the sandek (an adult male who is often a grandfather or other close relative), who holds the baby while another person (the *mohel*) performs the circumcision. The Hebrew term (pronounced 'sandak') is often translated as "godfather," but the meaning carries a uniquely Jewish context that is not included in the English translation. (Yiddish-Hebrew)

Seder: A festive meal conducted on the first and second nights of Passover that includes a formalized retelling of the story of God's liberation of the ancient Hebrews (twelve tribes descended from the sons of Jacob) from Egyptian slavery, which is described in the book of Exodus. (Hebrew)

Sekhel: Common sense, practical intelligence. (Yiddish)

Shabbos or **Shabbat:** The Jewish Sabbath that starts Friday night at sunset and ends Saturday night an hour after sunset. Jews are required under the Ten Commandments to "remember the Sabbath day and keep it holy . . . because for six days, God made the heavens and the earth, the sea and all that is in them, and on the seventh day, he rested." (Exodus 20:8–11.) Jews observe the Shabbos, as required under Deuteronomy 5:12, by refraining from all manner of creative work (Mishnah Shabbat 7:2). (Hebrew)

Shacharis or **Shacharit:** Morning prayer service. (Hebrew)

Shalakh Munes or **Shalakh Manot:** Traditional Purim gifts of fruit, nuts, pastries, and other snacks. (Yiddish-Hebrew)

Shames: Caretaker of the synagogue. (Yiddish-Hebrew)

Shavues or **Shavuot:** A holiday around May/June (6 Sivan on the Hebrew calendar) that celebrates the Summer Harvest and commemorates when all of the Children of Israel "saw the sounds" (Exodus 20:15) of the revelation of God at the foot of Mount Sinai and Moses ascended Mount Sinai to receive the Ten Commandments as an everlasting covenant between God and the Children of Israel. Shavuot falls in the fiftieth day after the first day of Passover. In the Christian tradition, it is known as the Pentecost. (Hebrew)

Shep Nakhes: To take joy and pleasure (different from pride) from the good fortune, happiness, or accomplishment of another person. Most commonly, people shep nakhes from their kids, students, or other people in their close circle of relationships. (Yiddish)

Shisel: Bowl. (Yiddish)

Shiva: Seven-day mourning period under Jewish law. The immediate family sits on low chairs and doesn't leave the house for seven days while family, friends, and other people from the community pay a visit (a shiva call) to comfort the mourners. (Yiddish-Hebrew)

Shmates: Rags. (Yiddish)

Shmir: Wipe. (Yiddish)

Shoah: Holocaust (lit., annihilation). The systematic murder of approximately six million Jews and the near complete destruction of the Jewish communities across German-occupied western and eastern Europe in World War II, with the publicly stated intention to annihilate the Jewish people, the Jewish religion, and the Jewish influence on the world. (Hebrew)

Shoykhet: Someone who slaughters animals for meat in the manner required by Jewish law. (Yiddish-Hebrew)

Shtick Dreck: Piece of shit. (Yiddish)

Shtiebel: A small place (smaller than a synagogue) that is set aside for people to stop in for a communal prayer. The shtiebel was an important gathering place for Chassidic life in Poland. In addition to prayer services, the shtiebel provided an informal community venue for eating, drinking, and lectures. [3] (Yiddish)

Shul: Synagogue. (Yiddish)

Siddur: Hebrew prayer book. (Hebrew)

Sukkes or **Sukkot:** A joyous seven-day holiday that falls in September and/or October on the fifth day after the solemn Holiday of Yom Kippur. Jews are commanded to build temporary booths with thatched roofs and dwell in them throughout the holiday to give thanks for the autumn harvest and to commemorate the sojourn of their ancestors in the Sinai desert after their liberation from slavery in Egypt (Leviticus 23:42). In the Christian tradition, it is known as the holiday of Tabernacles. (Hebrew)

Talmid: A dedicated student, a disciple. (Yiddish-Hebrew)

Talmidey Khakhomim: Torah scholars who are well educated in the interpretation of Jewish law and tradition and who often also obtain rabbinic ordination. (Hebrew)

Talmud: A sixty-three-volume, 6,200-page collection of teachings, debates, and opinions of scores of rabbis on a variety of subjects, including Jewish law, ethics, philosophy, customs, history, folklore, and many other topics. It consists of the Mishnah, which is written in Hebrew, and the Gemora (a commentary on the Mishnah), which is written in Babylonian Aramaic. It was compiled and edited over a four-hundred-year period ending in the fifth century CE. (Hebrew)

Tateshe: Father. (Yiddish diminutive)

Tfilin: Phylacteries. Small boxes made of hardened leather containing specific texts from the Torah that Jewish men fasten to the forehead and arm with leather straps during the morning prayer service. (Hebrew)

Tish: A uniquely Chassidic gathering in which the Rebbe sits at his table and blesses the Chassidim of his community, sings niggunim with them, interprets the Torah, and conveys deeper meanings with parables and stories. It is customary for a Chassidic Rebbe to have a tish on Friday night after the members of the community have finished Shabbos dinner in their own homes. (Yiddish)

Tsures: Trouble. (Yiddish-Hebrew)

Tukhes: Behind, derriere. (Yiddish)

Tzadik (pl. Tzadikkim): A righteous, holy one who successfully applies Jewish law and wisdom with minimized ego to bring his own thought, intention, speech, and action into alignment with the will of God in a manner that expresses the godly attributes such as knowledge, understanding, justice, mercy, and loving kindness in his relationships with other people. (Hebrew)

Tzedoka: Charity. (Hebrew)

UNRRA: United Nations Relief and Rehabilitation Administration, established by the United Nations to provide relief for war refugees.

Verflukhte Hund: Cursed dog. (German)

Volksdeutsche: Ethnic Germans who were born and raised outside of Germany. (German)

Yarmulke: Skull cap worn by religious Jews. (Yiddish). Also referred to as a kippa. (Hebrew)

Yeshua: Savior. (Yiddish-Hebrew)

Yikhus: Notable ancestry, such as well-known rabbis or other Jewish leaders. (Hebrew)

Zecken: Lazy parasites. (lit., ticks) Dehumanizing slang expression used by the original Nazis as well as contemporary Neo-Nazis to refer to people they consider to be from an inferior race, leftist political parties, etc.[4] (German)

Zhid: Derogatory name for Jew. (Polish)

Zloty: Polish currency. A groshen is a coin worth 0.01 zloty.

Zmiroys: Jewish songs that are sung around the table after a Shabbat or holiday meal. (Yiddish-Hebrew)

Sources

Primary Sources

Interview of Harry Lenga (approx. 7 hours), conducted by Vida (Sister) Prince under auspices of the St. Louis Center for Holocaust Studies Oral History Project, 1982–83.

Interview of Harry Lenga (approx. 2 hours), conducted by Vida (Sister) Prince under auspices of the St. Louis Center for Holocaust Studies Oral History Project, 1985.

Interview of Harry Lenga (approx. 30 minutes), conducted by Rabbi Robert Sternberg under auspices of the St. Louis Center for Holocaust Studies Oral History Project, 1987.

Interview of Harry Lenga (approx. 4 hours), conducted by the coauthor, Scott Lenga (his son), 1989.

Interview of Harry Lenga (approx. 33 hours), conducted by the coauthor, Scott Lenga (his son), 1993.

Stories recounted by Harry Lenga to the coauthor, Scott Lenga (his son), throughout his upbringing, 1961–93.

Interview of Hyman (Chaim Meyer) Salzberg (approx. 3 hours), Interview Code 555, USC Shoah Foundation, 1995.

Interview of Ann Lenga (Tape 1, Side B), conducted under the auspices of the St. Louis Center for Holocaust Studies Oral History Project, November 1981.

Affidavit of Wolanow prisoner Jersey Gelnikier, June 17, 1945, sworn in the presence of Reginald C. Borroughs, First

Lieutenant Infantry, Investigator War Crimes Branch, JA Section, U.S. Seventh Army. digital-collections.ww2.fsu.edu/scripto/scripto/diff/324/765/0/10774/10775

Baruch Kaplinski et al., eds., *Memorial Book of Kozienice (Kozienice, Poland): Translation of Sefer Zikaron le-Kehilat Kosznitz,* New York: JewishGen, Inc. 2016. Original Yiddish-Hebrew edition published in New York, 1969; original English edition published in New York, 1985.

  a. Anonymous, "Who is the Kozienicer Who Writes About the Holocaust?" Ringelblum, Archive No. 1, Registration 846, 1942.
  b. Chava Shapiro, "These I Remember Fondly."
  c. Itshe Blatman, "These Are the Kind of Jews That Lived in Kozienice."
  d. Chaim Meyer Salzberg, "Frightful Days and Years."
  e. David Goldman, "The Terrible Nightmare."
  f. M. Sh. Geshuri, "The Heads of the House of Kozienice."
  g. Issachar Lederman, "The Heritage of the Dynasty of Kozienice."
  h. Issachar Lederman, "The Shul and the Beis Medrish."
  i. Yaakov Epstein, "Kozienicer Beis Medrishniks."
  j. Moshe Unger, "The Rebbetzin Perele Davens in a Talus."
  k. Nekhe Katz, "Kozienice Elects a Rabbi."
  l. Leibele Fishstein, "Rabbi Ben Tzion Freilach."
  m. Elimelekh Feigenboim, "A Memorial to My Many-Branched Family."

Moshe Ha-Elion, *The Straits of Hell,* Cincinnati, OH: Bibliopolis and Bowman & Cody Academic Publishing, Inc., 2005.

Robert B. Persinger, Remembering Ebensee, 1945. Speech delivered May 6, 2005, at the annual memorial for the liberation of Ebensee, Ebensee, Austria.

SECONDARY SOURCES

Auschwitz Museum website: auschwitz.org

Yad Vashem: The World Holocaust Remembrance Center website: www.yadvashem.org

United States Holocaust Memorial Museum, online Holocaust Encyclopedia.

Shimon Huberband, *Kiddush Hashem: Jewish Religious and Cultural Life During the Holocaust*, New York: Yeshiva University Press, 1987.

Malka Shapiro, *The Rebbe's Daughter: Memoir of a Chassidic Childhood*, English translation by Nechemia Polen, Philadelphia, PA: Jewish Publication Society, 2002.

Richard Brietman, "Himmler's Police Auxiliaries in the Occupied Soviet Territories," *Simon Wiesenthal Center Annual* 7 (1990).

Arad Yizhak, *The Holocaust in the Soviet Union,* Lincoln: University of Nebraska Press, 2009.

Martin Dean, *Collaboration in the Holocaust: Crimes of the Local Police in Belorussia and Ukraine, 1941–44*, London: Palgrave Macmillan, 2003, 60.

Christopher R. Browning, *Remembering Survival: Inside a Nazi Slave Labor Camp*, New York: W.W. Norton, 2010.

Primo Levi, *Survival in Auschwitz*, New York: Collier Books, 1961.

Peter Longerich, *Holocaust: The Nazi Persecution and Murder of the Jews,* Oxford, UK, and New York: Oxford University Press, 2010.

Roderick Stackelberg and Sally Winkle, *The Nazi Germany Sourcebook: An Anthology of Texts*, New York: Routledge, 2002.

Piotr Hojka and Sławomir Kulpa, *Kierunek Loslau: Evacuation March of Auschwitz Prisoners 1945,* Wodzisław Sląski, Poland: Museum in Wodzisław Śląski, 2016.

Jacqueline L. Longe; Gale Group, "Gale Encyclopedia of Medicine," 3rd ed., Detroit: Thomson Gale, 2006.

Joan Little, "Holocaust, Polish Survivor's Memories Move Students," *St. Louis Post-Dispatch*, June 11, 1984.

Aryeh Kaplan, *Chasidic Masters: History, Biography and Thought*,
New York: Maznaim, 1984.

H. H. Ben-Sasson, *A History of the Jewish People*, Cambridge,
MA: Harvard University Press, 1976.

Gershom Scholem, *Sabbatai Sevi: The Mystical Messiah: 1626–
1676*, English translation by R. J. Zwi Werblowsky, New
Jersey: Princeton University Press, 1973.

Marcin Wodziński, "Hasidism in Poland," Oxford, UK: Oxford
Bibliographies, 2016.

Ezriel Natan Frenk, *Aggadot Chassidim Le Bney Neurim uLeAm
(Legends of the Chassidim for the youth and the nation)*, Warsaw, Poland: Barkai, 1923.

Ezriel Natan Frenk, *Yehudei Polin Bimei Milchamot Napolion
(The Jews of Poland During the Napoleonic Wars)*, Warsaw,
Poland: Hatsfira, 1912.

Hanna Węgrzynek, "Ger Hasidim; Hasidim from Góra Kalwaria," *Museum of the History of the Poland, Virtual
Shtetl*, sztetl.org.pl/en/glossary/ger-hasidim-hasidim-
gora-kalwaria

Menashe Shif, Tzadikei Olam *(Everlasting Righteous Ones)*, Ash-
dod, Israel: Machshevet Publishing, 2009.

Kathleen J. Nawyn, CMH, "The Liberation of the Ebensee Concentration Camp, May 6, 1945," CMH News and Features,
history.army.mil/news/2015/150500a_ebensee.html

Black Five, "The Saint in the Tank" (excerpts from newspaper articles about Robert Persinger and the liberation of Ebensee),
www.blackfive.net/main/2006/03/the_saint_in_th.html

Shaul Stampfer, "How and Why Did Hasidism Spread?" *Jewish
History* 27, 201–219, (2013). doi.org/10.1007/s10835-013-
9186-6

Matthias Heine, "The Tick in the Nazi Mouth, It Couldn't Be More Disgusting," Welt, 23-May-2014. www.welt.de/kultur/article128336389/Die-Zecke-im-Nazi-Mund-ekliger-geht-s-nicht.html.

Endnotes

CH. 1: CHILDHOOD IN THE CHASSIDIC TOWN OF KOZHNITZ (1919–30)

Citations of sources that are abbreviated in the endnotes can be found in full in the Sources section above.

1. The Chassidim are a sect of Orthodox Judaism that was founded in the eighteenth century by Rabbi Israel ben Eliezer, who came to be known as the Baal Shem Tov (master of the good name). Further explanation and a short biography of the Maggid of Kozhnitz is provided in Appendix A, "My Search for Chassidic Context." The details of this betrothal and marriage story have been forgotten and could not be confirmed with available independent sources, though there are known stories that the Maggid of Kozhnitz was sickly and physically disabled and had at least one unsuccessful betrothal before he found the wife who joined him in life and bore him a daughter. See Rabbi Moshe Weinberger, "Kozhnitzer Maggid (1) Introduction to the Life and Teachings of the Kozhnitzer Maggid," August 3, 1998. YUTorah Online, www.yutorah.org/lectures/lecture.cfm/ 823624/rabbi-moshe-weinberger/kozhnitzer-maggid-1-introduction -to-the-life-and-teachings-of-the-kozhnitzer-maggid.

2. The Gerer branch is a different sect of Chassidim. See Appendix B, "The Tale of Laizer Yitzkhak Wildenberg."

3. Preparing for Passover requires a thorough cleaning of the home and special preparation of all cooking and eating utensils for Passover use. This is mandated under Jewish law, which forbids the use

of any *khametz* (leaven or the aspect of bread that causes it to rise when baked) during Passover (Exodus 13:6–8). The rabbis taught that khametz represents the egoistic pride that enslaves our souls and that the mundane physical activity of Passover cleaning should be accompanied by a commensurate effort by each individual to liberate himself or herself from spiritual bondage. According to the Ramban, a sage from the thirteenth century, the aim is that khametz not be found "in your mind."

4. The Shema is the oldest and most widely known Jewish prayer and begins with the most fundamental expression of Jewish monotheism: "Hear, O Israel: The Lord is our God, the Lord is One" (Deuteronomy 6:4–9). Yisroel-Mendele, the teacher of the youngest children, had the exclusive privilege to take his students to recite the Shema for recovering mothers and their newborn babies. Leibele Fishstein, "Rabbi Ben Tzion Freilach," in Kaplinski et al., *Memorial Book of Kozienice,* 342–43. See also Elimelekh Feigenboim, "A Memorial to My Many-Branched Family," ibid., 384–85.

5. It was not the custom of the Kozhnitzer Jews to "run immediately to the local doctor . . . when one didn't feel well. First, all home remedies were tried: a wet towel for a headache; quinine for nausea; an enema for belly-ache; garlic and pepper for a toothache; incantations to ward off an evil eye; and sugar candy for a bad cough or sore throat. When after all these remedies didn't work, we would call upon a barber-surgeon [feldsher] to bang away at varicosities, or place heated cupping glasses upon the affected area. . . . If all this didn't help [and prayer and amulets also didn't work], a rich Jew would call the local doctor or the doctor from Radom. The life of the poor would be extinguished like a candle." Lederman, "Jewish Barber-Surgeons in Kozienice," in Kaplinski et al., *Memorial Book of Kozienice,* 436.

6. There is reference to an "illness called the 'fungus disease' [that] appeared in the throats of newborns" for which the local barber-surgeon "had no cure, so many children died." A local pub owner named Yeshayahu Shabason went to a famous pediatrician in Warsaw who showed him "how to eliminate the fungus. Thanks to him hundreds of children [in the] Kozhnitz region were saved from this terrible scourge." Lederman, "Kozienice Personalities and Figures," in Kaplinski et al., *Memorial Book of Kozienice,* 406.

7. In addition to the religious and spiritual benefits of intensive study, advanced Torah scholars had status that could bring better marriage prospects, social mobility, and associated economic opportunities for a young man. One example was Hirsh Leib, a water carrier in Kozhnitz, who toiled and suffered in the cold months and joked with everyone. He and his wife supported an only son who studied day and night in the yeshiva until he became a recognized scholar and eventually married into a very wealthy family from another town. Many Jews in Kozhnitz "looked on [Hirsh Leib's son] proudly, as if he were city property. Wasn't he the son of the water carrier of all of them?" Shapiro, "These I Remember Fondly, in Kaplinski et al., *Memorial Book of Kozienice*, 443, and Blatman, "These Are the Kind of Jews that Lived in Kozienice," ibid., 456.

CH. 2: TEEN YEARS AND WATCHMAKING (1931–38)

1. Three-card monte is a con game designed to entice people on the street to place losing bets. The rules are very simple. To play, a dealer places three cards face down on a table, usually on a cardboard box. The dealer shows that one of the cards is the target card (e.g., the queen of hearts) and then rearranges the cards quickly using sleight of hand to confuse the player over which card is which. The player is then given an opportunity to select one of the three cards. If the player correctly identifies the target card, the player gets the amount he bet back, plus the same amount again; otherwise, the player loses the money he bet.

2. See Appendix C: "Conflicts Among the Kozhnitzer Rebbes and Their Followers."

3. The Polish Prime Minister Felicjan Sławoj Składkowski delivered this speech to the Polish Parliament on June 4, 1936, after which an economic boycott of the Jews appeared to have the sanction of official government policy. His words were, "An honest host does not allow anybody to be harmed in his house. Economic struggle—yes. But no harm." The Jewish community, including the Jewish press, saw this as a clear reference to the Jews, and the Polish government did not deny it. Joseph Marcus, *Social and Political History of the Jews in Poland 1919–1939*, Berlin: Walter de Gruyter & Co., 1983, 366.

CH. 3: COMING OF AGE IN WARSAW (OCTOBER 1938– SEPTEMBER 1939)

1. In 1939, the population of Warsaw was 1.3 million. "Before World War II, the city was a major center of Jewish life and culture in Poland. Warsaw's prewar Jewish population of more than 350,000 constituted about 30 percent of the city's total population. The Warsaw Jewish community was the largest in both Poland and Europe, and was the second largest in the world, second only to New York City." *United States Holocaust Memorial Museum, "Holocaust Encyclopedia:* Warsaw," encyclopedia.ushmm.org/content/en/article/warsaw.

2. Higher-grade watch movements have traditionally used jewels (originally natural rubies) as bearings for the wheel trains and high-wear parts. Small holes would be drilled into the jewels to house each end of a shaft that would pivot back and forth inside the holes with minimal friction.

3. The *Anschluss* (annexation) of Austria into Nazi Germany took place on March 12, 1938, with no resistance from the Austrian army and widespread support among the Austrian population. The other European powers did not resist the Anschluss even though it violated the Treaty of Versailles (June 28, 1919), which formally ended World War I and forbade the union of Germany and Austria. Israel Gutman, *Anschluss, Encyclopedia of the Holocaust,* New York: MacMillan, 1990, 47–48; and Rosenkranz, *Austria,* 126–32. The Germans took over Czechoslovakia in two stages. Stage one was the infamous Munich Agreement of September 30, 1938, which sought to appease Hitler by giving him the Sudetenland (the German-speaking regions of Czechoslovakia that bordered Germany). Germany negotiated the Munich Agreement with the United Kingdom, France, and Italy (but without any Czech participation). The incorporation of the Sudetenland into Germany began on October 1, 1938, and it left the rest of Czechoslovakia weak and powerless to resist any further encroachment. In stage two, the German army marched in to occupy the remainder of Czechoslovakia on March 15, 1939. *United States Holocaust Memorial Museum, "Holocaust Encyclopedia: Czechoslovakia,"* encyclopedia.ushmm.org/content/en/article/czechoslovakia.

4. Although Poland had the fifth-largest armed forces in Europe, including an army of a million men with almost five hundred tanks, it was unprepared for a modern war. In fact, it still included many

horse-mounted fighting units. Despite the inevitability of war, Poland mobilized late to avoid being blamed for an outbreak of war. Only seventeen of thirty mobilized divisions were fully deployed by August 31. Finally, despite having well-prepared defensive positions, these were dispersed too widely to present a cohesive and viable defense against a mobile fighting force—especially the powerful Wehrmacht. How Stuff Works website, "Buildup to World War II: January 1931–August 1939," history.howstuffworks.com/world-war-ii/buildup-to-world-war-213.htm.

5. *United States Holocaust Memorial Museum, "Holocaust Encyclopedia*: German-Soviet Pact," encyclopedia.ushmm.org/content/en/article/german-soviet-pact.

CH. 4: GERMAN OCCUPATION AND THE WARSAW GHETTO (OCTOBER 1939–MAY 1941)

1. By decree of Reinhard Heydrich on September 21, 1939, councils "composed of 'Jewish elders' were to be set up in each community; they were to be 'fully responsible in the literal sense of the word' for the execution of German orders." These councils allowed the Germans to avoid the burden of front line, day-to-day management and also diverted the anger and resentment of the oppressed Jewish population toward the Judenrat, which added to the demoralization of the Jews. Browning, *Remembering Survival*, 34. The Judenrat councils remain a controversial and delicate subject. The leadership of the Judenrat had to decide whether to comply with German demands. To avoid participation in the roundup of Jews for deportation from the Warsaw Ghetto, Adam Czerniaków committed suicide on July 22, 1942, the day deportations to Treblinka began. *United States Holocaust Memorial Museum, "Holocaust Encyclopedia: Jewish Councils (Judenraete),"* www.ushmm.org/wlc/en/article.php?ModuleId=10005265

2. Here is a sampling of other jokes that were told in the Warsaw Ghetto, from Huberband, *Kiddush Hashem*, 116–17:

   (1) God forbid that the war will last as long as the Jews are capable of enduring.

   (2) The Führer enquires of General Franco, "Comrade, how did you solve the Jewish problem?" Franco answers, "I instituted

the yellow badge." "That's nothing," says Hitler. "I imposed taxes, instituted ghettos, lessened their food rations, imposed forced labor." He goes on, enumerating a long list of edicts and persecutions. Finally, Franco says, "I gave the Jews autonomy and Jewish councils." "Ah," says Hitler, "that's the solution."

CH. 5: KOZHNITZ GHETTO (JUNE 1941–SEPTEMBER 1942)

1. The rabbi they murdered was not the Kozhnitzer Rebbe of the time. He was another rabbi who had the official responsibility for making determinations of Jewish law for the community. The shul that they burned was built by the grandchildren of the Kozhnitzer Maggid. It was located on Maggidtova Street (Hebrew for "the good Maggid"), which was named as such by the Polish authorities who used to seek the Maggid's counsel and held his wisdom in high esteem. The dynasty of Rebbes that descended from the Kozhnitzer Maggid lived in the compound on Maggidtova Street, which was a pilgrimage destination for Chassidim from other places in Poland, Europe, and even Eretz Yisroel. See Shapiro, *Rebbe's Daughter*, 53–64.

2. The Jews living in Germany over the centuries had adapted the German language to Jewish life. They mixed in a lot of Hebrew and Aramaic words from the holy books to express the Jewish religion and culture of their daily lives, and that became Yiddish.

3. On the eve of Germany's invasion of Russia, the British army was alone in fighting the Germans. France and all of western Europe (except the neutral countries) had surrendered. The United States didn't enter the war until six months later, on December 8, 1941. The German surprise attack on Russia, code named "Operation Barbarossa," was the largest German military operation of World War II. More than 3 million German soldiers joined the attack, supported by 650,000 troops from Germany's allies. Much of the Soviet air force was destroyed on the ground, and the Soviet armies were initially overwhelmed. Despite catastrophic losses in the early weeks of the attack, the Soviet Union did not capitulate as expected by the German political and military leadership. By late September 1941, German forces had advanced almost one thousand miles, reaching the gates of Leningrad in the north and moving apace toward Moscow. *United States Holocaust Memorial Museum, "Holo-*

caust Encyclopedia: Invasion of the Soviet Union, June 1941," ency-clopedia.ushmm.org/content/en/article/invasion-of-the-soviet-union-june-1941.

4. "The German occupation authorities periodically demanded that the Judenrat collect sizable financial payments or make specific de-liveries of gold, jewelry, furniture, fur coats, and other valuable items from the Jewish community. The unenviable task of the Ju-denrat was to apportion the obligation among the Jewish commu-nity by estimating each family's financial capacity to pay." Brown-ing, *Remembering Survival*, 36 (describing the role of the Judenrat in Wierzbnik).

5. A midrashic legend relates that Miriam, the sister of Moses, admon-ished her father, Amram, for deciding not to have children in the days when Pharaoh had decreed that all Israelite male children had to be killed at birth. Miriam argued that Amram's decree was harsher than Pharaoh's because while Pharaoh's decree applied only to male children, Amram proposed to withhold life from female chil-dren as well. Amram accepted her rebuke, and the subsequent birth of Moses was credited to Miriam. Babylonian Talmud, Sota, 12a.

CH. 6: GORCZYCKI CAMP AT WOLKA (OCTOBER 1942)

1. Khamaira Salzberg described this scene as follows: "Suddenly there was heard in the [camp] the whistle of a locomotive.... A spe-cial train with many cars had carried away our dearest and most be-loved ... on [Sunday] September 27, 1942. That was the tragic end of Kozhnitz's Jews. To this day the whistle of a locomotive and a train remains for me a nightmare. All were strongly affected by the horrifying news. Many collapsed. Salzberg, "Frightful Days and Years," in Kaplinski et al., *Memorial Book of Kozienice*, 587.

2. Historical sources confirm that "in 1939, [Kozienice] had slightly less than 9,000 inhabitants, of whom roughly half were Jews.... By August 1942, a few weeks before its liquidation, around 13,000 Jews [from the town and surrounding areas] had been assembled in the Kozienice Ghetto, which became immensely overcrowded. The German police conducted the liquidation of the Kozienice Ghetto on September 27, 1942.... The first train to the Treblinka killing center left in the afternoon, and the next, a short time later; there

were 60 railroad cars altogether with approximately 150 people in each car. Railroad documents confirm the exact date on which these special trains (Sonderzüge) from Kozienice arrived at Treblinka." Alina Skibinska, "Kozienice," in Martin Dean and Mel Hecker, eds., *The United States Holocaust Memorial Museum Encyclopedia of Camps and Ghettos, 1933–1945,* vol. 2, *Ghettos in German-Occupied Eastern Europe,* Bloomington: Indiana University Press, 2012, 249–51. Available online at Gale Virtual Reference Library, link.galegroup.com/apps/doc/CX4028000146/GVRL?u=wash137 09&sid=GVRL&xid=6c240745.

3. "The son-in-law of the barber-surgeon, Bendler, was also in the [Kozhnitz] transport [to Treblinka] with his wife and infant child.... With the aid of a miracle, he managed to flee to [the Gorczycki camp].... He told about how our flesh and blood perished." Goldman, "Terrible Nightmare," in Kaplinski et al., *Memorial Book of Kozienice,* 627. See also Tzvi Madanes, "What Fellow-Townsmen of Kozienice Tell," ibid., 733, which confirms that Salke Bendler's husband escaped from Treblinka on a train hidden under packs of clothing that the other workers piled on top of him. "He was able to convey the bitter regards from the huge death-camp, Treblinka. But nobody wanted to believe him. They all said that he must be crazy."

4. Khamaira Salzberg tells the same story about these two men who escaped from Treblinka in his testimony with the Spielberg Project. See Salzberg, Interview Code 555. He tells the story as if it happened in Gorczycki, but then refers to prisoners in Wolanow (the next camp) not wanting to believe their account of extermination in Treblinka. It seems that these two men arrived in the Gorczycki camp, where they first told the story to the group from Kozhnitz, and were later sent to Wolanow with everyone and continued to tell the story in Wolanow. David Bayer, another survivor from Kozhnitz who was in the Gorczycki camp, provided verbal confirmation that these men escaped from Treblinka and arrived in Gorczycki to tell their story. He was never sent to Wolanow. When the Germans evacuated Gorczycki, Bayer was taken to the Pionki slave labor camp.

5. Khamaira Salzberg describes leaving Gorczycki as follows: "On a nice autumn day...a [German] gendarme approached us and ordered to cease our labor and line up in a row. Yisroel Tenenboim's little boy did not line up quickly enough, so the representative of the "master-race" beat him mercilessly. His eyes glazed and he

began to faint—this partially stilled his cries. At the order of the gendarme, we went to the camp. On the way, the gendarme noticed how a Jew was leaving the home of a peasant . . . probably . . . buying some food. . . . He drew his revolver and immediately shot the Jew for his terrible "crime." The one who he shot was Fritz Rozen. . . . In the courtyard of the camp they lined us up and again counted us. Suddenly a Jew stepped backwards and began running. The gendarmes and their helpers chased him. In a few moments they disappeared among the trees. A few shots were heard, and the Jew fell dead. He was a son of Mote Shvartzberg. They gave us ten minutes to take our possessions. In our great hurry and excitement, we left more than half. A few months later, we would become aware of the fact that an undershirt or some other piece of clothing was an unreachable fortune. In four rows they led us to the main road, which was pitted, and there waited for us large transport trucks. During the two-kilometer march to the main road, we were guarded by the Polish overseers. Many used this opportunity to flee. . . . The Polish overseers were helpless. They shouted, "Ya poviem!" which means: "I'll tell on you!" You can ask: "Where was there to run?" We were surrounded by enemies. . . . We passed through our city. This was a last chance to catch a glimpse of the place where we, and also our parents, and grandparents had been born. With great longing and sorrow we looked at the Jewish houses and places of business, that stood empty and orphaned." Salzberg, "Frightful Days and Years," in Kaplinski et al., *Memorial Book of Kozienice*, 589–90.

6. Alina Skibinska, "Kozienice," in Martin Dean and Mel Hecker, eds., *The United States Holocaust Memorial Museum Encyclopedia of Camps and Ghettos, 1933–1945*, vol. 2, *Ghettos in German-Occupied Eastern Europe*, Bloomington: Indiana University Press, 2012, 249–51. Available online at Gale Virtual Reference Library, link.galegroup.com/apps/doc/CX4028000146/GVRL?u=wash13709&sid=GVRL&xid=6c240745.

7. Yad Vashem: The World Holocaust Remembrance Center, "Treblinka," www.yadvashem.org/odot_pdf/Microsoft%20Word%20-%205886.pdf; and Yad Vashem: The World Holocaust Remembrance Center, "Auschwitz-Birkenau Extermination Camp," www.yadvashem.org/holocaust/about/final-solution/auschwitz.html.

8. Longerich, *Holocaust*, 309–10; and Stackelberg, and Winkle, *Nazi Germany Sourcebook*, 345.

9. *United States Holocaust Memorial Museum, "Holocaust Encyclopedia: Killing Centers: An Overview,"* encyclopedia.ushmm.org/content/en/article/killing-centers-an-overview.

CH. 7: WOLANOW SLAVE LABOR CAMP (OCTOBER 1942– JUNE 1943)

1. The Schutz—Schutzmannschaften—was the collaborationist auxiliary force of native policemen serving in the areas of eastern Europe that were occupied by Nazi Germany. During 1942, the Schutzmannschaften expanded to an estimated three hundred thousand men, with mobile commando units that fought partisans and participated in mass murder operations accounting for about a third of the force and the rest serving as guards and police in German camps and occupied towns. Everywhere, local Schutzmannschaft far outnumbered the equivalent German personnel by several times. (In most places, the ratio of Germans to Schutzmannschaft natives was about one-to-ten.) Brietman, "Himmler's Police Auxiliaries; Yizhak, *Holocaust in the Soviet Union*, 107–8; Dean, *Collaboration in the Holocaust*, 60.

2. A Jewish dentist who served as a doctor in Wolanow provided the following account in a 1945 affidavit: "[On] the 21 October, in the morning, the work department ordered all the people to return from work and to gather in the camp.... At three o'clock inspector Rubbe, [a Luftwaffe officer who was the ranking soldier in Wolanow] and [Lagerführer] Bartman arrived and made a selection of the people. All people badly dressed, weak, pale, aged, unshaved and children were driven to a separate place in the camp and guarded by armed Polish men.... There were here about 100 men, women, and children. At 3:15 a lorry arrived with about 20 Ukrainians, SS men.... In two minutes they began shooting and in 15 minutes all the 100 people were killed before the eyes of the other 700 workers. At the order of inspector Rubbe, twenty sick men from the infirmary were transported to the same place and shot. After this action Bartman and Banach personally took control of the dead and took away all together 75,000 zloty, golden watches, and other precious things. The dead were buried in two mass graves." Affidavit of Wolanow Prisoner Jersey Gelnikier.

3. Once a week in Wolanow, on Friday or Saturday, a shower with warm water was permitted.

4. Salzberg, "Frightful Days and Years," in Kaplinski et al., *Memorial Book of Kozienice,* 590–91.

5. "[On] 10 October 1942 I was made physician of the camp.... The same day I was called in by inspector Rubbe and told as there were so many cases of patients with temperature, an infirmary would be installed, and we would be obliged to announce each day the number of patients. [Later,] I myself had a temperature [of] 40° C; [with] typhus spots [in my throat,] but in spite of it, I remained at my work and went every morning to confer with Rubbe." Affidavit of Wolanow prisoner Jersey Gelnikier.

6. Khamaira Salzberg describes the epidemic as follows: "In 1943, there broke out an epidemic of typhus in the camp, and almost all of the Kozienicites 'danced at the wedding' (meaning they came down with the disease). We were afraid to inform that we were ill [for fear of being] shot. Every morning, when they chased us out to work, the rows were filled with sick who had temperature, and could barely stand on their feet. I once worked next to Yakele Shpigel. He was burning up with fever, probably about 40° C (104° F), and was shoveling snow." Salzberg, "Frightful Days and Years," in Kaplinski et al., *Memorial Book of Kozienice,* 591.

7. The hairspring is a flat circular spring that is literally and metaphorically the beating heart in a mechanical watch. It pulsates in a horizontal circle and serves the same function as the pendulum in a clock. The tension in the hairspring must be finely tuned to a beat that drives the watch gears to keep accurate time. This was a brilliant technology invented in 1675 that enabled timepieces to shrink to the size of a wristwatch. Any bend or irregularity in the hairspring will prevent the watch from running. A misguided or overly strong adjustment by a watchmaker can easily ruin a hairspring, making it impossible to repair.

8. The *balance staff*, a watch part, is the shaft that the *balance wheel* and the hairspring are mounted onto. The ends fit into a small hole drilled into a jewel to enable the balance staff (and the other parts that are mounted on it) to pivot back and forth with minimal friction, so as to divide and regulate time equally.

9. The Kiddish is the blessing recited over the first cup of wine that starts the Passover Seder and expresses thanks to God, who liber-

ated the Jews from slavery in Egypt. On that Passover, the Germans had enslaved the Jews and taken away all physical symbols of free-dom and well-being, such as wine. But in that little room in Wola-now, the spiritual freedom of the Jews was asserted with whatever was available—a cup of water. The Passover song, "V'he She'omdo," is translated as follows: "This is what has stood by our fathers and us. For not just one alone has risen against us to destroy us, but in every generation they rise against us to destroy us; and the Holy One, blessed be He, saves us from their hand."

10. While the first half of the Passover Haggadah focuses on the liber-ation of the people of Israel from slavery in Egypt, the second half comprises liturgical praise of God and lively songs that look ahead to the culmination of history in the messianic age.

11. Flash-forward: Privche was in Starachowice and Auschwitz, too. One time, I saw her in Auschwitz walking by the site where I was working. I threw her a piece of bread that I had saved in my pocket. I could have been killed for that. Privche and her sister both sur-vived the war. I saw her after liberation in the Bergen-Belsen refu-gee camp. She married another guy who was in the slave labor camp at Starachowice, and they went to Israel.

CH. 8: STARACHOWICE SLAVE LABOR CAMP (JUNE 1943– JULY 1944)

1. Khamaira Salzberg describes his hospitalization as follows: "A Ukrainian shot me in my left leg . . . while going home from the sec-ond shift in the factory. . . . The guards were 'having a fling,' [and] we heard a shot. . . . I wanted to take a step and felt heat in my leg. I was brought to the camp hospital. My . . . good friends, the three Lenga brothers, were awaiting me. For eight weeks, I lay in the hos-pital. Too much medical help, I didn't get, but I didn't go to work, and the food was a bit better. The head of the hospital was a Jewish doctor from [the town of] Starachowice, a good, upright person. Unfortunately, I can't say this about the hospital aides. They were a privileged group, who had bought their positions for money. One . . . morning . . . we were surrounded by armed Ukrainians . . . and a se-lection began. . . . The fat German [administrator] entered the hos-pital and commanded: 'Everyone out!' [He] questioned me, since I

was first in the line of the sick. . . . I yelled out: 'I'm healthy!' . . . He immediately went to the second one and made a motion with his hand; then to the third, and so on. In short, I was left all alone. The murderers had pushed all of the rest [of the hospital patients] onto the truck [including a Kozhnitzer named Huberman who was in the hospital for an injured finger]. That same day, the murderers brought back the clothing of the victims to the camp warehouse. As to the question: 'Why was I left behind?' I can give but one answer: 'A miracle!'" Salzberg, "Frightful Days and Years," in Kaplinski et al., *Memorial Book of Kozienice*, 595–96.

2. Flash-forward: Khamaira Salzberg was able to survive in the forest. He hid and fought and got a bit of help from a group of Polish socialist partisans. He was liberated by a Russian Army unit. When the Russians met a Jew, they helped him. They knew that a Jew would never betray them to the Germans. The next time we saw Salzberg was in Stuttgart a couple of years after the war ended.

3. The topic of Uncle Yirmia (Jeremiah Wilczek) has also been documented elsewhere: "At the top of the hierarchy [of Jewish authority within Starachowice]—surrounded by a coterie of family, relatives, and supporters, as well as three members of the [previously] disbanded Jewish council—stood . . . Jeremiah Wilczek. This group controlled the camp council (Lagerrat), police (Lagerpolizei), and kitchen. The camp elite enjoyed a number of privileges that the other prisoners did not. They lived in separate housing with their wives and in some cases with their children, whom they had been allowed to bring into camp. They were also able to maintain contact with people outside the camp and even visit them in town in order to conduct business or have access to valuables hidden with friends. In numerous testimonies Wilczek and the camp elite were accused of living and eating well, in effect stealing from the common food and clothing supply while the rest of the camp suffered from hunger and dressed in rags. Two testimonies lodge an even more serious charge: Wilczek and the camp council participated in selections, in effect helping the Germans decide who would live and who would die. The greatest challenge to the camp elite was posed by the Lubliners, the 200 hardened survivors of Majdanek who arrived in Starachowice in spring 1944. The Lubliners openly challenged the Starachowice elite for control of the camp. . . . To some of the prisoners, these Jews were tough veterans and rare survivors of the Lublin

camps; in the words of one admirer, they were 'made out of iron.' To others they were low-class thugs and 'ruffians' grasping for power. In any case, the deep animosity between the Wilczek coterie and the Lubliners remained unabated and ended tragically. When the Starachowice Jews were evacuated to Birkenau in July 1944, several Lubliners slipped into the first train car in which Wilczek and others of the camp elite were riding. Angry words led to a struggle in the suffocating heat and claustrophobic confines of the overloaded railroad car. Wilczek, his son, the head of the camp kitchen, and other members of the camp elite—as well as some who tried to intervene—were strangled. When the train reached Birkenau, their bodies were piled on the ramp for all to see, and the story of their fate quickly spread among the other Starachowice Jews." Christopher R. Browning, "The Factory Slave Labor Camps in Starachowice, Poland: Survivors' Testimonies," in United Stated Holocaust Memorial Museum: Center for Advanced Holocaust Studies, "Forced and Slave Labor in Nazi-Dominated Europe: Symposium Presentations," 69–71, www.ushmm.org/m/pdfs/Publication_OP_2004-02.pdf. See also Browning, *Remembering Survival.*

CH. 9: AUSCHWITZ (JULY 1944–JANUARY 1945)

1. At that time, we didn't know that the Germans were bringing transports of Jews from all over Europe to be exterminated in Auschwitz. These voices were probably speaking Hungarian, which is not Germanic, Latin, or Slavic in origin. "Between May 15th and July 9th, about 430,000 Hungarian Jews were deported, mainly to Auschwitz, where most were gassed on arrival." Yad Vashem: The World Holocaust Remembrance Center, "Historical Background: The Jews of Hungary During the Holocaust," www.yadvashem.org/articles/general/jews-of-hungary-during-the-holocaust.html.

2. Uncle Yirmia had another son, named Adash, who was a policeman in Starachowice. He escaped to the forest with three other Jewish policemen before they took us away on the train. His father probably told them the camp was about to be liquidated. Uncle Yirmia's daughter, Yitka, was sent to Auschwitz on the same train. She was with the women and wasn't in the same boxcar as her father and brother.

Flash-Forward: Yitka and Adash both survived the war. Yitka emigrated to New York. Adash went to Toronto. When I attended Adash's daughter's wedding many years later in Canada, he didn't want to talk about the war years. He said, "I'm glad it's over. Let's forget about it. You lived and I lived, and that's good enough for us." After what happened to us later in Auschwitz and other concentration camps, all of the beatings and abuse committed by the Jewish collaborators in the ghettos and slave labor camps seemed like trivial things. We were happy just to have some family members who survived.

3. "At least six women gave birth in the Starachowice camps. Four survived to give their own accounts. Two others are known only through the testimony of others." In each of these six cases the newborn was murdered at birth. "Another woman became pregnant in Starachowice and gave birth after the evacuation to Auschwitz-Birkenau." Browning, *Remembering Survival*, 185–188. This source confirms the possibility that a woman could have given birth in Starachowice and managed to smuggle a baby on the transport train to Auschwitz-Birkenau.

4. Auschwitz included a group of three different camps. Birkenau (also called Auschwitz II) was the largest camp in the complex.

5. Yad Vashem: The World Holocaust Remembrance Center, "Architecture of Murder: The Auschwitz-Birkenau Blueprints," www.yadvashem.org/yv/en/exhibitions/auschwitz_architecture/overview.asp.

6. To get a shave in Auschwitz-Birkenau, a prisoner would have to pay the "barber" in the barrack with a portion of his bread ration. Primo Levi relates advice he gave to Wertheimer, a recently arrived prisoner: "I told him…he should not forget to have a shave the evening before [the selection], even if it cost him a quarter-ration of bread." Levi, *Survival in Auschwitz*, 114.

7. Excerpts from the "Unisaneh Tokef" prayer are set out below:

> *We shall ascribe holiness to this day.*
> *For it is awesome and terrible.…*
> *The angels are…seized by fear and trembling*
> *As they proclaim: Behold the Day of Judgment!…*
> *On Rosh Hashanah, it is inscribed,*
> *And on Yom Kippur it is sealed.*

How many shall pass away and how many shall be born,
Who shall live and who shall die....
Who shall be at rest and who shall be tormented,
Who shall be exalted and who shall be brought low....
But repentance, prayer and charity avert the harsh decree....
Act for the sake of Your Name and those who sanctify Your
Name (with their martyrdom).

8. "The area adjacent to the Auschwitz camp was flat, without many forests and additionally, there were streams.... All these conditions made it more difficult for prisoners to escape.... A large forest complex was also located about 25 kilometers to the south ... on the slopes of the Beskidy Mountains, visible from ... Birkenau, towards which some of the escapees headed after leaving the camp." Auschwitz-Birkenau Museum, "Escape of Prisoners from Auschwitz," lekcja.auschwitz.org/en_15_ucieczki.

9. Reichsführer-SS Heinrich Himmler was the head of the SS and commander of all of the concentration camps in Poland, including Auschwitz. He was part of the inner circle of Nazi leadership and had operational responsibility and command over the systematic genocide of the Jews of Europe.

10. Since each person is created in the image of God according to the Jewish sources, your life cannot be viewed as your property that can be destroyed by means of suicide. Maimonidies, Mishneh Torah, Hilchot Rotzeiach Ushemirat Nefesh, 1:4 and 2:2, 1180 CE.

11. For a detailed description of concentration camp badges, see United States Holocaust Memorial Museum, "Holocaust Encyclopedia: Classification System in Nazi Concentration Camps," encyclopedia.ushmm.org/content/en/article/classification-system-in-nazi-concentration-camps.

CH. 10: DEATH MARCH, MAUTHAUSEN, AND MELK (LATE JANUARY 1945–APRIL 1945)

1. United States Holocaust Memorial Museum, "Holocaust Encyclopedia: Death Marches," encyclopedia.ushmm.org/content/en/article/death-marches-1.

2. Hojka and Kulpa, *Kierunek Loslau.*

3. United States Holocaust Memorial Museum, "Holocaust Encyclopedia: Death Marches," encyclopedia.ushmm.org/content/en/article/death-marches-1.

4. Several kilometers from Melk, Project Quartz was a huge tunneling project initiated to expand the underground production area of the Steyr-Daimler-Puch armaments factories to sixty-five thousand square meters, with slave labor by prisoners from the Melk concentration camp. MERKwürdig. Eine Veranstaltungsreihe wider Gewalt und Vergessen, "History," www.melk-memorial.org/en/history. Regarding work conditions in the Melk concentration camp, see Ha-Elion, *Straits of Hell*, 59–60.

5. Co-author Scott Lenga's note: My dad never went back to see that castle. I traveled there with my oldest daughter, Talia, and another time with my youngest daughter, Yael, to fulfill my dad's concentration camp dream and visit the Austrian camps where the Lenga brothers were imprisoned during the war. Melk was and is to this day a charming tourist town on the Danube River in the scenic Wakau valley. The "castle" is actually a renowned and still active monastic abbey known as Stift Melk and is considered to be one of the world's best examples of baroque architecture. It is located on a prominent hill, so anyone strolling on the terrace enjoys a 360° view of the Danube River, the entire town, and the now indiscernible site of the concentration camp, Konzentrationslager (KZ) Melk, just as the prisoners at KZ Melk could see Stift Melk.

CH. 11: EBENSEE AND LIBERATION (APRIL 1945– OCTOBER 1945)

1. See also Ha-Elion, *Straights of Hell*, 64–66, regarding food rations in the Ebensee concentration camp. "The bread we received [at Ebensee] . . . was baked from a flour that was a mixture of bran and sawdust. . . . The daily portion reached barely 100 grams . . . instead of the [250 gram ration] at Auschwitz."

2. In Ebensee, slave laborers from the concentration camp dug an underground tunnel network of approximately seventy-six thousand square meters for industrial production. Work continued on the Ebensee tunnels right up to the end of the war. Zeitgeschichte Museum Ebensee und KZ-Gedenkstätte Ebensee, "History,"

memorial-ebensee.at/website/index.php/en/history. For detailed information on the Ebensee tunnels with photos and plans, see Geoff Walden, "Ebensee, Austria: Underground Factory Projects; 'Dachs/Zement' and Concentration Camp Site," Third Reich in Ruins website, www.thirdreichruins.com/ebensee.htm.

3. Zeitgeschichte Museum Ebensee und KZ-Gedenkstätte Ebensee, "History," memorial-ebensee.at/website/index.php/en/history; Jewish Virtual Library: A Project of AICE, "Concentration Camps: Ebensee (Austria), www.jewishvirtuallibrary.org/ebensee-austria.

4. "A bloated stomach and swelling in the legs are symptoms of starvation," Gale, *Gale Encyclopedia of Medicine*. Now we know that Mailekh's symptoms were caused by starvation, not excessive drinking of water. Encyclopedia.com, s.v. "Starvation," www.encyclopedia.com/medicine/diseases-and-conditions/pathology/starvation .

5. See also Ha-Elion, *Straights of Hell*, 65, regarding prisoners eating coal to pacify intense hunger in Ebensee. "The stuff we ate regularly was train coal that was found abundantly at the work site. The coal, which was sweetish, sufficiently brittle, and easy to chew, was apparently satiating too.... [Eating coal] caused a violent desire to give off excrement [combined with] acute constipation." After a few days, the constipation gave way to acute long-term diarrhea accompanied by sharp abdominal pain and bloody stools.

6. See Appendix E: "Testimony of Robert Persinger, the U.S. Army Tank Commander Who Liberated Ebensee."

7. "The Hatikva" was the Zionist anthem that was later modified and adopted as the national anthem of the State of Israel. The version they sang in 1945 is translated as follows:

> As long as in the heart within,
> The Jewish soul yearns,
> And toward the eastern edges, onward,

> An eye gazes toward Zion.
> Our hope is not yet lost,
> The hope that is two-thousand years old,
> To return to the land of our fathers,
> The city where David encamped.

For another description of this event. see also Ha-Elion, *Straits of Hell*, 71.

8. See also Ha-Elion, *Straights of Hell*, 70, regarding revenge taken on the cruelest kapo in Ebensee and Melk: "He was caught by a group of Russian-Ukrainian Jews who were soon joined by many, many others.... They beat him until he collapsed.... At one point a Russian lifted up a heavy stone and smashed it upon the kapo's head." Thinking he was dead, they proposed to burn his body in the crematorium. When he began to show signs of life, they hesitated until the mob resolved to burn him alive. Upon arrival at the furnace, he regained his strength and began to struggle and scream for help. The crowd beat him heavily and pinned him to the carriage mechanism at the door to the furnace. "Someone took the long bar, which served for pushing the corpses from the carriage into the oven and thrust the hook into the kapo's groin and pushed the body into the oven. At the same time somebody else pulled back the carriage. The door of the oven was shut. The cries were no more heard."

9. During the war, the Germans called a Jew "verflukhte Jude" (cursed Jew) or "verflukhte hund" (cursed dog).

10. "Shema Yisroel" is a Hebrew phrase from a Jewish prayer.

11. United Nations Archives and Records Management Section, "Fonds AG-018—United Nations Relief and Rehabilitation Administration (UNRRA) (1943–1946)," search.archives.un.org/united-nations -relief-and-rehabilitation-administration-unrra-1943-1946; and United States Holocaust Memorial Museum, "Holocaust Encyclopedia: United Nations Relief and Rehabilitation Administration," encyclopedia.ushmm.org/content/en/article/united-nations-relief-and-rehabilitation-administration

CH. 12: POSTWAR EUROPE (OCTOBER 1945–MARCH 1949)

1. The touchstone gold purity test has been in use since ancient times. The gold is scratched across a dark hard stone with a finely grained surface and leaves a visible line. By observing the color on the line, an experienced jeweler can tell the purity of the gold.

2. United States Holocaust Memorial Museum, "Holocaust Encyclopedia: The Survivors," encyclopedia.ushmm.org/content/en/article/the-survivors.

3. Moishe went back to Kozhnitz in the 1980s and was depressed for months afterward. None of the other Lenga brothers ever went back.

4. "*Kol Yisrael arevim zeh bazeh*," meaning all Jews are responsible for each other. Talmud, Shevuot, 39a. This well-known quote is a cornerstone of Jewish communal life.

AFTERWORD

1. Interview of Ann Lenga.
2. Little, "Holocaust, Polish Survivor's Memories Move Students."

APPENDIX A: MY SEARCH FOR CHASSIDIC CONTEXT

1. Aryeh Kaplan, *Chasidic Masters*, 133.
2. See Scholem, *Sabbatai Sevi.*
3. Isaac Luria (1534–1572) expounded a systematic and comprehensive interpretation the Jewish mystical tradition of Kabbala that is widely accepted as the definitive approach to this subject.
4. See Scholem, *Sabbatai Sevi*, 601 and 693.
5. Kaplan, *Chasidic Masters*, 1.
6. "The reaction to [the Shabbataian crisis] was swift and decisive. If Kabbalah and mysticism could result in such calamity, then its study would be proscribed and its dissemination forbidden. If Shabbatai Zevi could find justification for the abrogation of the [Jewish] law, then its hold would be tightened and made all the more strict. If [religious] joy and ecstasy could be perverted, they would be banned altogether." Ibid., 1–2.
7. Ibid., 2.
8. Marcin Wodziński, "Hasidism in Poland," Oxford Bibliographies, August 18, 2016, www.oxfordbibliographies.com/view/document/obo-9780199840731/obo-9780199840731-0133.xml.
9. Kaplan, *Chasidic Masters*, 4–5.
10. Ibid., 4.
11. Ibid., 135.
12. "It is reported that he once met Rabbi Chaim Voloziner, [one of the great rabbinic scholars of his generation who] was a fervent opponent of Chassidism. Rabbi Chaim had a lengthy Talmudic discussion with [R. Israel when he was a young man before he became the Kozhnitzer Maggid] and later said that [the Kozhnitzer Mag-

gid] knew the entire Talmud, along with its major commentaries, by heart, word for word." Ibid., 134.

13. "The reputation of the Kozhnitzer was that of a wonder worker without equal. . . . Many people called him the second Baal Shem Tov." Ibid., 133.

14. Geshuri, "Heads of the House of Kozienice," in Kaplinski et al., *Memorial Book of Kozienice*, 114.

15. Lederman, "Heritage of the Dynasty of Kozienice," in Kaplinski et al., *Memorial Book of Kozienice*, 168–69.

16. The Maggid opposed the Enlightenment and political emancipation of the Jewish communities in Napoleonic Europe. He believed that the resulting assimilation would do severe damage to the Jewish people. The Maggid warned Napoleon not to invade Russia and admonished him to his face: "You maniac, you egoist. What are you striving for? You think that this world has lost its balance and you can conquer it? You believe you can fling nations around and destroy religions? God is in heaven. You are on earth." Frenk, *Aggadot Chassidim*, 142. In Frenk, *Yehudei Polin*, 50, the author adds that on the order of the Polish Prince Czartoryski, the Maggid prayed for the success of the emperor. See also Lederman, "Heritage of the Dynasty of Kozienice," in Kaplinski et al, *Memorial Book of Kozienice*, 168–69.

17. This is a shortened and edited version of "The Heavenly Tribunal Danced with Shabtai the Bookbinder" story, which is found in Menachem Mendel, *Der Maggid fun Kozhnitz*, Jerusalem: Ateret Publishing, 1987. English translation by Rikee H. Gutherz-Madoff, "Tales of the Maggid of Kozhnitz," master's thesis, Concordia University, 2000.

APPENDIX B: THE TALE OF LAIZER YITZKHAK WILDENBERG

1. Independent historical sources relate that after the Chiddushei HaRim's death in 1866, his Chassidim wanted his eighteen-year-old grandson, Rabbi Yehudah Aryeh Leib Alter, to succeed him. When the grandson refused to accept this position, most of the Chassidim became followers of another Chassid called Rabbi Levin. When he died four years later in 1870, Rabbi Yehudah Aryeh

Leib (who became known posthumously as the Sfas Emes) agreed to become their next Rebbe to succeed the Chiddushei HaRim. See Arthur Green, "Ger Chassidic Dynasty," The YIVO Encyclopedia of Jews in Eastern Europe, Chassidyivoencyclopedia.org/article .aspx/Ger_Hasidic_Dynasty; Hanna Węgrzynek, "Ger Hasidim; Hasidim from Góra Kalwaria," *Museum of the History of the Poland, Virtual Shtetl,* sztetl.org.pl/en/glossary/ger-hasidim-hasidim-gora -kalwaria, and Menashe Shif, Tzadikei Olam (Everlasting Righteous Ones), 27–35.

APPENDIX C: CONFLICTS AMONG THE KOZHNITZER REBBES AND THEIR FOLLOWERS

1. See also Lederman, "Heritage of the Dynasty of Kozienice," in Kaplinski et al., *Memorial Book of Kozienice,* 172; and Unger, "Rebbetzin Perele Davens, ibid., 189.

2. Reb Arele drove away the old Chassidim, the scholars, and the wealthy men, and he focused on simple people. Lederman, "Heritage of the Dynasty of Kozienice," in Kaplinski et al., *Memorial Book of Kozienice,* 172

3. See Katz, "Kozienice Elects a Rabbi," in ibid., 217.

4. Reb Arele left Kozhnitz after this ordeal and wandered from place to place. "The Rebbe was a good fiddler and would not move without a fiddle. [Eventually] he settled in [the town of] Otwock where he conducted his court [and] befriended simple people, artisans and laborers.... Chassidim told of Reb Arele's bizarre miracles, and of how he used his path to attract the vulgar and make them repent.... From time to time, he came to Kozhnitz, and each time he did so he threw the town into turmoil. Fistfights almost broke out between his Chassidim and those of his brother Elimelekh." Reb Arele was killed by the Germans in World War II. Lederman, "Heritage of the Dynasty of Kozienice," in Kaplinski et al., *Memorial Book of Kozienice,* 172–74, 188–89. See also Yitzkhak Gochnarg, "Still Greater in Death: In Memory of the Kozhnitzer Rebbe, Reb Arele," ibid., 190–91.

5. "Avodas Israel" was also the title of the seminal work of the Kozhnitzer Maggid.

6. What's in a name? Use of the name Eretz Yisroel (Land of Israel) derives from biblical references and Jewish liturgy and carries the implication of a God-given right of Jews to a homeland and a nation state in the Holy Land. There were bitter disagreements between the Zionist movement (which was secular in nature) and the Chassidim over the lack of divine intervention in the Zionist initiative to establish a Jewish state, even though there was broad agreement between them regarding the covenantal rights of the Jewish people to Eretz Yisroel. The name Palestine (originally Syria Palestina) was imposed on the province by the Roman General Hadrian "in an effort to wipe out all memory of the bond between the Jews and the land," after he put down the Bar Kochba Jewish Revolt (c.132–36 CE) and exiled the vast majority of Jews from the area. Ben-Sasson, *History of the Jewish People*, 334.

APPENDIX D: JEWISH RELIGIOUS AND POLITICAL GROUPS IN PREWAR KOZHNITZ

1. "The [Soviet] census of 1939 reported a population of 3,028,528 Jews, representing 1.78 percent of the country's total numbers." Yaacov Ro'i, "Union of Soviet Socialist Republics." The YIVO Encyclopedia of Jews in Eastern Europe, yivoencyclopedia.org/article.aspx/union_of_soviet_socialist_republics#idoeaaae.
2. Karen Kayemet, the Jewish National Fund, was created by the Zionist movement in 1901 to purchase and develop land in Eretz Yisroel, which was then under the control of the Ottoman Empire, and after World War I, under the control of the British Mandate.
3. The British had already backtracked on their commitments under the Balfour Declaration. After the Arab pogroms in 1929, the British gave fewer and fewer certificates for Jews to emigrate to Palestine. They issued a new policy called the White Paper to discourage and prevent Jewish emigration. Jabotinsky used to say that the ground in Europe was burning under our feet—that we should get up and walk to Palestine with or without a permission certificate from the British.

APPENDIX E: TESTIMONY OF ROBERT PERSINGER: THE U.S. ARMY TANK COMMANDER WHO LIBERATED EBENSEE

1. Persinger, Remembering Ebensee. See also Nawyn, "Liberation of the Ebensee Concentration Camp"; and Black Five, "Saint in the Tank."

GLOSSARY

1. Epstein, "Kozienicer Beis Medrishniks" in Kaplinski et al., *Memorial Book of Kozienice*, 219.
2. Lederman, "The Shul and the Beis Medrish," in Kaplinski et al., *Memorial Book of Kozienice*, 257
3. Shaul Stampfer, "How and Why Did Hasidism Spread?" Jewish History 27, 201–219 (2013). doi.org/10.1007/s10835-013-9186-6
4. Matthias Heine, "The tick in the Nazi mouth, it couldn't be more disgusting," Welt, 23, May 2014. www.welt.de/kultur/article128336389/Die-Zecke-im-Nazi-Mund-ekliger-geht-s-nicht.html

Photo Credits

IN-TEXT MAPS AND DOCUMENTS

1-A   Prewar Poland. Creative Commons.
3-A   German-Russian Invasion of Poland. United States Holocaust Memorial Museum.
4-A   Warsaw Ghetto. United States Holocaust Memorial Museum.
6-A   Train Schedule. Memorial Book of Kozienice.
6-B   Extermination Camps. United States Holocaust Memorial Museum.
8-A   All Nazi Camps in Occupied Poland. United States Holocaust Memorial Museum.
9-A   Auschwitz-Birkenau. United States Holocaust Memorial Museum.
10-A Death Marches. United States Holocaust Memorial Museum.
11-A Austrian Concentration Camps. United States Holocaust Memorial Museum.
11-B DP Camps in Italy. United States Holocaust Memorial Museum.
12-A Major DP Camps. United States Holocaust Memorial Museum.
12-B Harry Lenga Ship Recommendation. Lenga family collection.
12-C Telegram: Lenga Brothers on Train to St. Louis. Lenga family collection.
Afterword-A Friendly Jewelers Grand Opening. Lenga family collection.
Appendix E   A U.S. Army Platoon Sergeant Robert Persinger, Austria, 1945.

Photo Insert

p. 1 Mikhoel Lenga, 36, with sons Mailekh (*left*), 10, and Itshele (*right*), 11, in 1924, when the boys were leaving their home in Kozhnitz to go to yeshiva in Shedlitz, 127 kilometers away. Lenga family collection.

p. 2 Hirsh Leib, a water carrier in Kozhnitz, circa 1938. According to other Kozhnitzer townspeople, Hirsh Leib toiled and suffered and joked with everyone. United States Holocaust Memorial Museum, courtesy of Sabina and Samuel Goldstein.

Friends seeing off Tsvi Madanes before he made *aliya* (immigration) to Eretz Yisroel, 1933. Mailekh Lenga is at the far left in the back row, and Izak Lenga is fourth from the right in the back row. *Memorial Book of Kozienice.*

The large dots on this watch movement are jewels that serve as bearings for the high-wear moving parts. A small hole would be drilled into the jewel to house each end of a shaft that would pivot back and forth inside the hole with minimal friction. Photo by Andrzej Tokarski.

p. 3 A Jew being abused by Germans who are cutting his hair and sidelocks, circa 1939. This photo is reported to have been taken in Kozhnitz, Poland. Yad Vashem Photo Archive, Jerusalem. CAS-325667.

Moishe Lenga (*above*) and Mikhoel Lenga with his daughter Khana Lenga (*below*) in Kozhnitz, circa 1940. These photos were among a collection of negatives found in Kozhnitz in the early 2000s. This is the only existing photo of Khana. Photos by Haim Berman.

p. 4 Jewish men in Kozhnitz taking off their hats when they pass German soldiers, as required by law, circa 1940. Note the sign on the top left with the photo of a clock (and the blowup of that section below). The left side says WATCHMAKER in Polish, and the right says JEWELER. Across the bottom it says MICHAL LENGA. This was the family store at 35 Radomska Street, where the Lenga family worked and lived in Kozhnitz. Babyn Yar Holocaust Memorial Center.

p. 5 Khil Lenga (*left*) with his best friend Khamaira Salzberg (*right*) during the summer of 1941 in the Kozhnitz Ghetto. Lenga family collection.

Typical watchmaker's workbench with the array of tools used in the trade. Photo by Niels Vrijlandt.

p. 6 Jews from the Kozhnitz Ghetto at forced labor digging a canal in the nearby village of Wolka, circa 1942. They are working for the Gorczycki company, which was building the canal. United States Holocaust Memorial Museum, courtesy of Sabina and Samuel Goldstein.

Watch hairspring—the beating heart in a mechanical watch. It pulsates in a horizontal circle and serves the same function as the pendulum in a clock. Photo by Richard Keller.

Stock photo of a watchmaker wearing a magnification loupe in his eye socket and holding a hairspring in his tweezers. Photo by Jan Faukner.

p. 7 Jews from Hungary arrive by train and undergo a Selection on the ramp at Auschwitz-Birkenau, May 1944. Photo by Bernhardt Walter/Ernst Hofmann. United States Holocaust Memorial Museum, courtesy of Yad Vashem.

Harry Lenga, in 1993, shows the number tattoo—A19367—that he received in Auschwitz-Birkenau upon arrival in July 1944. Photos by Scott Lenga and David Oughton.

Watchmaker's screwdriver and tweezers, made in Auschwitz from materials available in the camp by Chaim Shtatler, a Jewish prisoner. Photo by Scott Lenga.

p. 8 *De Intérieur d'un Block* (The interior of a concentration camp barrack). Daniel Piquée-Audrain, *Never Again!*, 22 pen drawings, 1945–1947, Paris, copyright Amicale de Mauthausen.

Travaux d'avancement (Work in progress). This drawing depicts prisoners digging a tunnel with electric jackhammers at the Melk concentration camp. Daniel Piquée-Audrain, *Never Again!*, 22 pen drawings, 1945–1947, Paris, copyright Amicale de Mauthausen.

p. 9 *Traveux Extérieurs en Hiver* (Outside work in winter). This drawing depicts prisoners carrying steel rails in winter outside the tunnel at the Melk concentration camp. Daniel Piquée-Audrain, *Never Again!*, 22 pen drawings, 1945–1947, Paris, copyright Amicale de Mauthausen.

Stift Melk, 2012, the "castle" that was visible to the prisoners at the Melk concentration camp. Photo by Bertl123. iStock.

View of the Melk concentration camp, 1948. United States Holocaust Memorial Museum, courtesy of Instytut Pamieci Narodowej.

Scott Lenga viewing the town of Melk from the terrace of the "castle" (Stift Melk), 2015. It is located on a prominent hill, so anyone strolling on the terrace enjoys a 360° view of the Danube River, the entire town of Melk, and the site of the Melk concentration camp. Photo by Yael Lenga.

p. 10 *Travaux dans une Galerie (Work in a tunnel)*. This drawing depicts one of the tunnels that housed underground armaments factories. Daniel Piquée-Audrain, *Never Again!*, 22 pen drawings, 1945–1947, Paris, copyright Amicale de Mauthausen.

View of the Ebensee concentration camp, May 1945. United States Holocaust Memorial Museum, courtesy of Gisela Wortman.

U.S. Army Sergeant Dick Pomante (*left*) and Platoon Sergeant Robert Persinger (*right*), Germany, 1945. They were the commanders of the two tanks that liberated the Ebensee concentration camp.

p. 11 A crowd of survivors gather in the main square of the Ebensee concentration camp, May 7, 1945, one day after liberation. Photo by Arnold E. Samuelson. United States Holocaust Memorial Museum, courtesy of Arnold E. Samuelson.

Survivors of Ebensee concentration camp pose undressed for a U.S. Army photographer to show the effects of malnutrition, May 8, 1945—two days after liberation. Khil Lenga is the marked person closer to the right. Moishe Lenga is the marked person closer to the center. At liberation, Khil weighed seventy-five pounds, and Moishe weighed seventy. Photo by J. Malan Heslop. United States Holocaust Memorial Museum, courtesy of U.S. National Archives and Records Administration, College Park.

p. 12 UNRRA ID confirming Khil Lenga's internment in the Ebensee concentration camp. Note the entry NATIONALITY: STATELESS. Lenga family collection.

Uniform patch for the Palestine Jewish Brigade soldiers of the British Army in World War II. Photo by Wim Leydes.

From the left: Moishe, Mailekh, and Khil Lenga in either Rome or Stuttgart, circa 1945. Lenga family collection.

p. 13 Certificate of Professional Competence in Watchmaking issued to Khil Lenga, May 26, 1948. This was required for his emigration application to the United States. Lenga family collection.

From the left: Moishe, Khil, and Izak Lenga in Stuttgart, circa 1947, during the period when all four of the Lenga brothers were reunited after the war. Lenga family collection.

From the left in the car: Izak, Khil, and Moishe Lenga in Stuttgart, circa 1947. Lenga family collection.

p. 14 Wedding of Harry and Dorothy Lenga, St. Louis, Missouri, 1950. Photo by Edwin H. Balk.

Wedding of Morris and Ann Lenga, St. Louis, Missouri, 1951. *From the left*: Dorothy, Scott, Michael, Harry, and Mark Lenga at Michael's bar mitzvah, St. Louis, Missouri, 1964. Photo by Edwin H. Balk.

p. 15 *From the left*: Margi, Morris, and Bobbie Lenga, St. Louis, Missouri, 1966.

From the left: Marcel, Monique, Violette, and Patricia Lenga, Quiberon, France, circa 1966.

The four Lenga brothers reunited for the wedding of Morris and Ann Lenga's daughter, Margi, to Michael Kahn, St. Louis, Missouri, 1975. *Front row*: Morris, Ann, Margi, Bobbie, Dorothy, and Harry Lenga. *Second row*: Marcel, Violet, Yitzkhak, and Riva Lenga. *Back row*: Monique, Mark, Patricia, and Scott Lenga. Photo by Joel Marion.

p. 16 The four Lenga brothers at the wedding of Margi Lenga and Michael Kahn, St. Louis, Missouri, 1975. *From the left*: Morris, Marcel, Harry, and Yitzkhak Lenga. This was their first and only reunion after they said their goodbyes in Stuttgart around 1948. Photo by Joel Marion.

Harry Lenga, St. Louis, Missouri, circa 1985. Photo by David M. Henschel.

Harry Lenga and his son Scott Lenga in San Francisco, California, 1993, during the week of intensive interviews that formed the basis of this book. Photo by Carrie Lenga. Lenga family collection.

In memoriam. Gravestone of Harry Lenga, Raanana, Israel. Photo by Scott Lenga.

Acknowledgments

I WOULD LIKE TO EXPRESS my deepest gratitude to Vida (Sister) Prince and Rabbi Robert Sternberg, who were the driving forces in getting my dad to speak to school groups in the St. Louis area under the auspices of the St. Louis Holocaust Center Oral History Project. They arranged his speaking engagements, picked him up, and often joined him on the assembly stage to speak with students. Ms. Prince also conducted about ten hours of taped interviews with my dad from 1982 to 1986. This initiative was part of a coordinated "Never Again" response to the Holocaust denial narratives that gained notoriety in the late 1970s,* and it provided my dad with meaning and purpose during his retirement years, when there were no kids at home to listen to his stories. Ms. Prince's interviews served as one of the primary sources for this book and inspired me to do my own set of comprehensive interviews with him. I was finally introduced to Rabbi Sternberg when this book was nearing publication, and he jumped in to provide Yiddish language and editing consultation with a warmth and love for my father that shines through every time I speak with him.

---

* See United States Holocaust Memorial Museum, "Holocaust Encyclopedia: Holocaust Denial: Key Dates," encyclopedia.ushmm.org/content/en/article/holocaust-denial-key-dates.

Doris Klippen, my late, beloved "favorite mother-in-law," volunteered to transcribe my dad's interview tapes at my first mention of their existence and, in effect, kicked off this project.

My wife, Carrie, never wavered in her encouragement and generous moral support. Moreover, she read every draft, contributing detailed comments with love (some of it tough) at each stage. Her collaboration has been invaluable.

My daughters, Talia, Orli, and Yael, grew up hearing my dad's stories. The roots trips that I took with each of them, at age fifteen, to visit sites in Poland and Austria where my dad and his brothers were interned in World War II solidified the emotional and conceptual platform I needed to begin writing this book. Each of my daughters relates to my dad's legacy in her own way, and all of them provided encouragement and valuable input to the project. My daughter Orli is off the charts in terms of her connection to the Shoah in general and the stories of my dad and his brothers in particular. She rightly counts this book as a personal achievement for her in driving me to start and complete it. I can't say for sure, but perhaps this book would not have been written without Orli's passion and persistence.

Mourning for my brother Michael (a lost child of the 60s who was ten years my senior) after his untimely death in 2014 sparked a sense of urgency in me to start working on this book. His crazy wisdom and lessons derived from his profound journey have had a far-reaching influence on my thinking and will remain with me always.

My brother Mark (eight years my senior) was a parent-like figure to me. In addition to reading the manuscript and responding with nuanced, insider comments, he provided me with consistent encouragement and support for this project, as he has done with all my endeavors.

My first cousins, Margi, Bobbie, Monique, Patricia, Rosa, Moni and Michael are all integral parts of the second-generation story that extends beyond the timeline of *The Watchmakers*. This project has brought me closer to all of them, and I hope this book will strengthen the connections within our family.

Nathan Marx, Michael Clerizo, Sharona Berken, Stan Hoffman, and Michelle Orrelle watched this project take shape from its early stages and read chapter after chapter in the rough. They were incredibly generous with their time, providing coaching and editorial suggestions with kindness and validation of the intrinsic value of my dad's story.

Beyond the many hours Michelle Orrelle spent reading drafts of the manuscript and providing comments, she personifies the character trait called *firgun* in Hebrew which means to take joy from another's good fortune and accomplishments. Always available to give sage advice and a concise list of action items for both her and me, every interaction with Michelle included a distinct measure of grace and inspiration to strive for the next milestone.

Stan Hoffman, Itamar Kadosh, Susan Hochstadt, Jim Appelbaum, Uri Lenga, Abigail Hirsch, Shuki Sheinman, Steve Tamsky, Josh Teitelbaum, Josh Goldberg, Nico Israel, Ian Tick, Mark Sherman, Hilton Damelin, Lori Banov Kaufmann, Brad Fetterman, Jim Gammon, John Burns, Randy Tischler, David Ehrlich, Adrian Schrek, Robert Berken, Betsy Berken-Zaslav, my brother Mark Lenga, and others read my work at key junctures and responded with enthusiasm and encouragement that lit my way forward.

Dan Cohen was introduced to *The Watchmakers* at a barbeque that coincided with my first efforts to talk up the book in social settings. Dan graciously offered to help and has been a masterful PR advisor and coach in this adventure.

Finally, James Abbate, my editor at Kensington Publishing, infused every step of the publication process with enthusiasm, creativity, the highest level of responsive professionalism, and respect for my father's legacy.

I am deeply thankful to all of them.

Index

Adela, 42, 54
Aktzion, 49, 75, 87, 263
Aleph-beis, 9, 264
Aliyah, 215, 264
Allied invasion of Italy, 134
Alte kockers, 196, 198, 264
Alter, Yitzchak Meir (Chiddushei HaRim), 253–54
American liberation of camps, 197–209, 260–62
American refugee application process, 234–35
Amram and Miriam, 289n
Anschluss (annexation) of Austria, xix, 43, 286n
Antisemitic laws, 21–22, 48–49, 54, 56–57, 70, 77
Antisemitism, 18–19, 23–24, 31–33, 47–48, 52, 68, 71–72, 130
Appel, 103, 147, 264
Appel platz, 102, 195, 197, 264
Arbeit Macht Frei, 165
Armbands, 48–49, 55, 62, 64, 79–80, 85, 119
Aron koydesh, 69, 264
Assimilation, 37–38
Asylum in U.S., 234–35
Auerbach, Mr., 38–39
Auschwitz-Birkenau, xvii, 135, 138–68, 238
    barbers and shaving, 159, 297n
    barrack attendants, 145–46
    episodes of despair, 163–64
    food and nutrition, 147, 158–59, 169

holidays, 161
ID numbers, xvii, 142, 143, 150
inspection and showers, 141–44
layout of, 144–45, 146
Moishe and missing shoes, 166–68
"orchestra" at, 148
prisoner status, 164–65
risk-taking, 155–58
Russian liberation of, 238
selections, 139–41, 147–48, 159–60
Sonderkommando bombing, 161–63
Sonderkommando's list, 152–55
suicides, 146–47, 164
train transport to, 135–39
watchmaking, 150–51, 157–58
work, 148–50, 151–52
Austria. See also Ebensee concentration camp
    Anschluss (annexation) of, xix, 43, 44, 286n
    border crossings, 216, 225–26
Ausweis, 50
Aydele, 15, 264

Baal Shem Tov, 246, 247, 250–51, 283n
Balance staffs, 86, 119, 293n
Baleygert, 45, 264
Balfour Declaration, 305n
Bar mitzvahs, 28
Barter, 132
Bartman, 104, 110–20, 125–26, 131, 292n
Bednarski Street, 40
Beis din, 256, 264

Beis medrish, 8, 28, 29, 69, 264–65
Bendler, 290n
Betar, 31, 32, 258
Black market, xviii, 58, 59, 75, 132
Blockaltester, 265
  at Auschwitz, 143, 145–46, 150–51, 152,
    156–57
  at Melk, 183–89
  at Wolanow, 98
Border crossings, 56, 217, 225–26, 229
Bracha, 33, 265
Bread, 7–8, 15, 30, 47–48, 58, 83, 100, 158,
  159, 169, 178, 181
Brenner Pass, 217, 225
Bris, 251, 265
British Army, 214
British Mandate, 215
Bronshtein, Moishe, 73–74, 76
Bronshtein, Moshe, 82
Broyges, 11, 265
Buna, 238

Candy, 59
Cannibalism, 194
Challahs, 30
Chassidim, 26–27, 257–58, 265, 302–4n.
  See also Kozhnitzer Chassidim
  author's search for Chassidic context,
    245–52
Chassidus, 245, 266
Chevras Avodas Yisroel, 256
Cholent, 27, 266
Christian Sabbath, 27
"Christ killers," 23–24, 52
Cigarettes, 132, 159, 202–3, 207, 208, 209–
  10, 213, 218, 225
Coal, 3, 76, 128–29, 132, 135, 300n
Coffee, 98–99, 103–4, 112, 147, 158, 178
Coke, 128–29
Concentration camps in Poland, 95, 95.
  See also Auschwitz-Birkenau; Tre-
  blinka extermination camp
Corbinus, 105–9
Czechoslovakia
  German occupation of, 43, 286n
  Izak and border crossing, 229
  train transport and generosity of
    Czech peasants, 174
Czerniaków, Adam, 55, 287n

Danube River, 188, 193
Daven, 5, 28, 31, 124, 266
Death March, 169–73, 177, 178
  third night and shelter in basement,
    171–73
Disneyland, 242
Displaced Persons (DPs), 211–12, 215, 217–
  21, 224, 227
Dreyer, 126, 266
Drimmel, 173, 266
Droshke, 41, 266
Dvekut, 248, 249, 266
Dysentery, 194, 199, 206–7
  Eastern Front, 134, 164, 193
  Russian advances and Auschwitz, 157
  Russian advances and Melk, 187, 188–89
  Russian bombing of military installa-
    tions, 188–89
  Russian liberation of camps, 198, 238

Ebensee concentration camp, 191–215,
  192
  liberation of, 197–209, 260–62
  revenge, 301n
  revenge against Germans, 198–99
  stay in SS barracks, 209–11, 213–14
  watchmaking, 200–202, 206–10, 212
Education, 8–11, 17–24
Endeks Party, 32–33
Eretz Yisroel, 31, 32, 214–17, 256, 258, 266
Extermination camps in Poland, 95, 95.
  See also Auschwitz-Birkenau; Treblinka extermination camp

Farbrente, 130, 266
Farikht, 106, 118, 188, 267
Feldsher, 11, 267
Final Solution, 95
Folk remedies, 78–79
French Jews, 194–95
Friendly Jewelers (St. Louis), 239, 239–41

Gambling, 24–25
Gansa makher, 74, 268
Ganuvim, 218, 267
Gemashmakhers, 14, 267
Geminder, 26, 55, 258, 267
  Kozhnitz, 26, 68–69, 70, 274
General Zionists, 31–32, 258

Geneva Convention, 44
Gerer Chassidim, 2, 253–54, 257–58
German annexation of Austria, xix, 43, 286n
German invasion of Poland, 43–45, 46, 286–87n
German invasion of Russia, 72–73, 230, 288–89n
German language, 288n
German occupation of Czechoslovakia, 43, 286n
German occupation of Poland, xviii, xix, 47–65. See also Kozhnitz Ghetto; Warsaw Ghetto
   beating by German military police, 49–52
   bread incident, 47–48
German Shepherd, 241
German siege of Warsaw, 43–45
German SS. See SS
German surrender, 198–99
Gestapo, 88, 163, 204
Glass watch crystals, 86
Glossary of terms, 263–75
Gold, 48, 64, 79, 90, 141, 142, 224–25, 231
Goldene medina, 235, 267
Gold test, 301n
Gorczycki Camp, 80, 83, 87–93, 263
   arrival at, 87–88, 89
   food and nutrition, 89
   return to Kozhnitz, 93–94
   Treblinka escapees, 89, 91–92
   work, 88–89
Goyishe, 8, 267
Great Depression, 36
Groshen, 3, 267
Groyse artik, 41, 59, 267

Haftarah, 28
Hager, Yisroel, 256
Haggadah, 33, 120, 294n
Hairspring, 115, 116, 293n
Harvey, 207–9, 212–13
"Hatikva, The" (anthem), 197–98, 300n
Head lice, 15, 113, 160
Health insurance, 42
Hebrew, 8–9, 10, 58, 214
Hebrew calendar, 161
Hefker, 218, 267

Heiger Heine, 105–6, 110
Herzl, Theodore, 31, 256, 258
Heydrich, Reinhard, 287n
Himmler, Heinrich, 163, 298n
Hitler, Adolf, 31–32, 36, 43, 45, 72–73, 214, 223, 232
Holocaust Memorial Museum, U.S., 95
Holocaust trains to Treblinka, 81, 89–91, 289–90n
   train schedules, 94, 94
Hopshtayn, Yisroel (Maggid of Kozhnitz), 1–2, 246–52, 283n, 302–3n
   tale of Laizer Yitzkhak Wildenberg, 253–54
Horse meat, 58
Hoyakh, 124, 266

ID tattoo, 142, 150, 185
Immerglick, Zygmunt, 111, 116–17
Italy, 217–21, 223–27
   Allied invasion of, 134

Jabotinsky, Zev, 31, 258, 305
Jewish Brigade, 214–17
Jewish Quarter (Warsaw), 49, 50, 52, 53
Judenrat, 53–54, 55, 57–58, 69–70, 73–74, 78, 267
Judenrein, 88, 267

Kabbala, 246–47
Kalisch, 77
Kapos, 138–41, 148, 149, 150, 267
Katzet, 211, 221, 267
Kaufman, Meyer, 224
Kaufman, Mortra, 224–25
Kennedy, John F., xvii
Kennedy, John F., Jr., xvii
Khale mit yagdes, 12–13
Khametz, 267–68, 284n
Khayala, 37
Khazzan, 76, 268
Kheder, 8–9, 10, 17, 28, 268
Khumash (Chumash), 10
Khutzpa, 185, 268
Kibbitz, 25, 123, 268
Kiddish, 28, 30, 120, 268, 293–94n
Kinstim, 86, 268
Kishkes, 199, 268
Klappen hertz, 123, 268

Koyakh, 150, 170, 172, 268
Kozhnitz
    birth and early life in, 1–8
    brothers learning a trade, 14–15
    brothers move to Warsaw, 32–33
    education in, 8–11, 17–24, 28
    father's charity in, 29–31
    father's illness, 11–12
    father's remarriage, 12–14
    market days, 24–25
    mother's death, 3–6
    move to Warsaw, 35–36
    during World War I, 2–3, 71
Kozhnitzer Chassidim, 1–2, 25–27, 245–
    58, 283n
    author's search for Chassidic context,
        245–52
    burning of rabbi to death, 69
    conflicts among rebbes and followers,
        255–56
    religious and political groups, 257–58
    tale of Laizer Yitzkhak Wildenberg,
        253–54
Kozhnitzer Rebbe (Reb Mailekh), 25–26,
    27, 255–56, 288n
Kozhnitz Geminder, 26, 68–69, 70, 274
Kozhnitz Ghetto, 67–84
    burning of rabbi to death, 69
    cleansing of, 81–82, 87–88, 89, 92, 94
    curfew, 74–75, 78
    escape from, 82–87
    father's watchmaking business, 76–78,
        81–82
    first days, 68–69
    German restrictions, 69–70
    Jewish police in, 69–70, 73–74, 75–76,
        81, 85
    return from Gorczycki, 93–94
    return to, 67–68
    sealing of, 74–75
    train transport to Treblinka, 89–91, 94,
        289–90n
    typhus epidemic, 78
    weddings, 78
Krakowska, 40
Krolewska Street, 61–62, 62
Kugel, 27, 268

Leather-cutters, 15, 29

Leib, Hirsh, 285n
Lenga, Ann, 237–38
Lenga, Dorothy, xviii, 239–40
Lenga, Khanale
    death of mother, 3–6
    early life of, 6–7, 11, 16, 258
    fate of, 94, 101
    marriage to Toyvia, 70–71, 81
Lenga, Mailekh
    at Auschwitz, 142–43, 149, 151–52, 155–
        58, 164
    Death March, 171–73, 174
    death of mother, 4–6
    as displaced person, 219–20
    at Ebensee, 191–92, 193–94
    escape from Kozhnitz Ghetto, 82–84,
        86–87
    firerebombing of Warsaw, 44
    ID tattoo number A19366, 142, 185
    Jewish police abduction of, 75–76
    in Kozhnitz Ghetto, 67–68
    later life of, 237, 240
    learning a trade, 15, 29
    liberation of Ebensee, 202–3, 205,
        206–9
    at Mauthausen, 175–78
    at Melk, 179–80, 182–89
    move to Warsaw, 32–33, 36–37
    name change to Marcel, 237
    in Paris, 233–34, 237
    at Pionki, 76, 81, 97, 126
    return from yeshiva, 14–15
    return to Kozhnitz, 53
    in Rome, 220–21, 223–25, 226–27
    at Starachowice, 127, 131–32, 134–36
    in Stuttgart, 227–29, 231–32
    at Wolanow, 97–103, 110–11, 115
    yeshiva education of, 8, 11
Lenga, Malke Wilczek (stepmother), 12–
    17, 25, 30
    cooking of, 27
    in Kozhnitz Ghetto, 67–68, 78–79, 83–
        84, 92
    photo at Auschwitz, 141
Lenga, Malke Wildenberg
    death of, xvii, 3–6
    family background of, 2, 253–54
    marriage to Mikhoel, 2
Lenga, Meyer, 233

Lenga, Mikhoel
  charity of, 29–31
  death of first wife Malke, 3–6
  education of children, 9, 21–22, 28
  illness of, 11–12
  Kozhnitzer Chassidim and, 1–2, 25–27,
    245–46, 252
  in Kozhnitz Ghetto, 67–68, 70, 71–72,
    75, 76–78, 80, 83–87, 92
  letters of, 60
  marriage to Malke Wildenberg, 2
  photo at Auschwitz, 141
  remarriage to Malke Wilczek, 13–14
  Shabbos, 26–27, 30–31
  sons move to Warsaw, 33, 35–36
  watchmaking business of, 1, 15, 29–30,
    43, 73, 76–78, 81–82, 83
Lenga, Moishe
  at Auschwitz, 142–43, 149, 151–52, 154–
    58, 159, 164, 166–68
  birth and early life of, 3, 6–7
  Death March, 171–73, 174
  death of mother, 3–6
  as displaced person, 219–20
  dysentery of, 194, 199, 206–7
  at Ebensee, 193–94
  escape from Kozhnitz Ghetto, 82–84,
    86–87
  at Gorczycki, 80, 87
  ID tattoo number A19368, 142, 185
  illness of, 14
  Jewish police abduction of, 75–76
  later life of, 237
  learning a trade, 15, 29
  liberation of Ebensee, 202–3, 205,
    206–9
  at Mauthausen, 175–78
  at Melk, 181–87, 198
  name change to Morris, 235, 237
  return from yeshiva, 14–15
  at Starachowice, 127, 131–32, 134–36
  in Stuttgart, 227–29, 231–32
  at Wolanow, 99–103, 110–11, 113–16
  yeshiva education of, 8, 11
Lenga, Pinchas, 233–34, 245
Lenga, Rachel, 233–34
Lenga, Riva, 229–31, 237
Lenga, Yitzkhak "Itshele" "Izak," 22, 258
  birth and early life of, 2, 4

emigration to Israel, 233
escape to Russian side of Poland, 56–
  57, 72–73, 228, 230
firerebombing of Warsaw, 44
later life of, 237
marriage of, 55–56
move to Warsaw, 32–33, 36–37
reunion with, 228–31
in the Warsaw Ghetto, 51, 53, 55
yeshiva education of, 14
Lenga Kahn, Margi, 240
Lescinski, 83, 87
Levi, Primo, 297n
Levinson, 40–44, 45, 47, 51–54, 57, 60, 61
Liberation, 197–209, 260–62
Lice, 15, 113, 160
Lola, 42, 53, 54, 61
Lubelski Street, 75, 76–77, 93
Luftwaffe, 99, 105, 119, 125–26, 151, 157,
  164, 268
Luria, Isaac, 302n
Lurianic Kabbala, 246–47

Madrikh, 73–74, 268
Mager, 149, 268
Maggid of Kozhnitz. See Hopshtayn, Yis-
  roel
Makhers, 61–65, 126, 268
Mamzeru, 12, 268
Mauthausen concentration camp, 175–78,
  192
  barracks, 176–77
  inspection and showers, 175–76
  train transport to, 174–75
Mazel, 58–59, 167, 269
Melk castle, 182–83, 299n
Melk concentration camp, 178–89
  barracks, 183–86
  food and nutrition, 178, 181, 182, 186–
    87
  selections, 187–89
  work, 178–79
Melville High School, 242
Mengele, Josef, 139, 147, 238
Mensch, 10, 269
Meshuga, 118, 163, 255, 269
Mestlik, 228
Metsiye, 37, 269
Midrash, 33, 269

Mikve, 26, 269
Minyan, 269
Miriam, 289n
Misnagdim, 247, 258, 269
Mitzvah, 248, 270
Modena, Italy, 217–20
Molotov-Ribbentrop Pact, 45, 46
Moshiakh, 246, 256, 270
Munich Agreement, 286n
Muselmänner, 159, 203, 270

Napoleon Bonaparte, 73, 249
Nathan of Gaza, 246–47
National Antisemitic Democratic Party
    (Endeks Party), 32–33
Nebekh, 41, 270
Neshome, 129, 270
New Orleans Port, 235
Niggunim, 249, 270
Noar Hatzioni, 31, 258

Occupation of Poland. See German occu-
    pation of Poland
Operation Barbarossa. See German inva-
    sion of Russia
"Oyfn Pripetchik" (folk song), 9–10
Oyshgeshpielt, 159, 270

Palestine, 121–23, 215–19
Paris, 194, 233–34, 237, 245
Passover, 6, 120–21, 246, 270, 283–84n
Penicillin, 115
Perna, 86–87, 271
Persinger, Robert, 259, 260–62
Peyis, 10, 21–22, 270
Pilsudski Street, 43–44, 49, 53
Pionki labor camp, 76, 81, 82, 97, 126,
    290n
Piyutim, 161
Plastic watch crystals, 86
Poland
    extermination camps in, 95, 95. See
        also Auschwitz-Birkenau; Tre-
        blinka extermination camp
    German invasion of, 43–45, 46, 286–
        87n
    German occupation of. See German
        occupation of Poland; Kozhnitz
        Ghetto; Warsaw Ghetto

Jewish population of, xviii, 72, 286n
    Russian invasion of, 45, 46, 164
Polish language, xxi, 17–18, 22
Polish Parliament, 32, 52
    beating by German military police,
        49–52
Polish resistance movement, 105, 134, 135,
    295n
Postwar Europe, 223–35
    American refugee application process,
        234–35
    move to Stuttgart, 227–29, 231–32
    reunion with Izak, 228–31
    in Rome, 223–25
    smuggling operation, 224–27
Privche, 125, 294n
Project Quartz, 299n
Prostitution, 37, 77
Purim, 5, 271

Radios, 48
Radom, 4, 60–61, 65, 119–20
Radom Ghetto, 119
Radomska Street, 26–27, 76
Rakhmunes, 10, 271
Ration cards, 57–58
Raus, 89, 271
Reb Mailekh (Kozhnitzer Rebbe), 25–26,
    27, 255–56, 288n
Red Cross, 44, 206
Reichsdeutsche, 129, 165, 181–82, 186, 271
Revisionist Zionism, 31, 258
Rome, 220–21, 223–25, 226–27
Rosen, Ezra, 11
Roshe, 117, 271
Rosh Hashanah, 161, 271
Rubbe, 119, 121–23
Russian front. See Eastern Front
Russian invasion of Poland, 45, 46, 164
Russian labor camps, 230–31
Russian-occupied Poland, 56–57, 72–73,
    228–29
Russian prisoners, 176–78, 194, 198–99,
    204

St. Louis, 235, 238–43
Salzberg, Khamaira
    at Gorczycki, 88, 290–91n
    in Kozhnitz, 22, 27, 30, 31, 73–74, 75

Salzberg, Khamaira, *cont.*
  in Starachowice, 133, 294–95n
  Starachowice escape, 134, 295n
  on Treblinka, 289n, 290n
  in Wolanow, 123, 293n
  in Zionist youth group, 31, 73–74
Sandek, 251, 271
Schidlovitz, 70–71, 263
Schidlovitz Jews, 70–71, 81, 94, 101, 123
Schmaltz gribene, 127
Seder, 6, 14, 120–21, 246, 271
Sekhel, 7, 271
September campaign. *See* German invasion of Poland
Shabason, Benny, 228–29
Shabbos, 26–27, 30–31, 271–72
Shabbtai Zvi, 246–47
Shalakh munes, 5, 272
Shavues, 161, 272
Shedlitz, 8, 11
Shema, 9, 284n
Shep nakhes, 272
Shisel, 98, 272
Shiva, 5, 272
Shmates, 207, 272
Shmir, 141, 272
Shoah, xvii–xviii, 272–73
Shoemaking, 13, 15, 36, 37, 78
Shoes, 13, 86–87, 132, 145, 166–68
Shoykhet, 26, 273
Shpigel, Yakele, 293n
Shtick dreck, 73, 273
Shtiebel, 26, 29, 273
Shul, 6, 26, 27, 69, 273
Siberia, 57, 72–73, 228, 230
Siddur, 124, 221, 273
Siege of Warsaw, 43–45
Sikolowski, Kashie, 19
Skarzysco Slave Labor Camp, 126
Skladkowski, Felicjan Slawoj, 285n
Sleepers, 38–40
Smuggling, 224–27
Soviet Union. *See* "Russia" *entries*
Sports, 18
SS (*Schutzstaffel*)
  at Auschwitz, 138–40, 141, 143, 147–52, 155, 157–63
  beating at Polish Parliament, 50–52
  burning of rabbi to death, 69

Death March, 170–71, 174
  at Ebensee, 196, 198
  at Gorczycki, 93
  living in Ebensee barracks of, 209–11, 213–14
  at Melk, 178, 179–81, 183, 185, 187–89
  patrol of Warsaw Ghetto, 54
  at Starachowice, 130
  train to Treblinka, 89–91
Stalin, Joseph, 45
Stalingrad, 164
Starachowice (city), 128, 263
Starachowice Slave Labor Camp, 126, *126*, 127–36, 224
  arrival at, 127–28
  escape plans, 134–35
  evacuation from, 135–36
  food and nutrition, 127, 159
  "hospital," 133
  Khamaira's escape, 134, 295n
  Uncle Yirmia at, 126–29, 131–32, 133, 135
  watchmaking, 130–31
  work, 128–29
Starvation, 59, 75, 78, 158–59, 199
Stuttgart, 227–29, 231–32
Sugar, 69, 92, 134–35
Sukkes, 36, 81, 273

Talmid, 253, 273
Talmidey khakhomim, 14, 273
Talmud, 17, 273–74
Tarfon, Rabbi, 191
Tfilin, 31, 274
Three-card monte, 24–25, 285n
Tish, 27, 274
Torah, 18, 25, 28, 69
Toyvia, 70–71, 81, 94, 101
Treblinka extermination camp, 89–91, 289–90n
  Jews of Schidlovitz, 81, 94, 101
  Kozhnitz trains to, 89–91, 94, 289–90n
  two escapees, 89, 91–92, 290n
Truman, Harry, 1, 235
Tsozmer, 16, 263
Tsures, 22, 30, 107, 147, 274
Tukhes, 142, 194, 274
Typhus, 78, 113–16, 133, 160
Tzadikkim, 26, 274
Tzedoka, 29–31, 274

Tzileger Batreeb, 157
Tzukerinian, 79

Ukraine, 80, 99
Ukrainian Schutz, 99, 102, 292n
"Unisaneh Tokef," 161, 297–98n
United Nations Relief and Rehabilitation
    Administration (UNRRA), 210, 211–
    12, 217–21, 220, 224, 226–28, 274

Vasser treyger, 3, 274
Vistula River, 36, 41
Volksdeutsche, 71, 129, 274
Voloziner, Chaim, 302–3n

Wannsee Conference, 95
Warsaw
    brothers' move to, 32–33, 36–37
    German siege of, 43–45
    move to, 35–36
Warsaw Geminder, 26, 258
    Warsaw Ghetto, 53–65, 228
    curfew, 54, 56
    dead bodies in, 59
    diet, 58–59
    escape from, 60–65
    food rations, 57–58
    Jewish police in, 55
    laws, 54–55
    map of, 62
    order to move, 53–54
    sealing of, 54–55, 57
Watchmaking
    at Auschwitz, 150–51, 157–58
    at Ebensee, 200–202, 206–10, 212
    of father, 1, 15, 29–30, 43, 73, 76–78, 81–
        82, 83
    in Kozhnitz Ghetto, 72, 76–78, 81–82
    at Starachowice, 130–31
    for UNRRA staff and British soldiers,
        219
    in Warsaw, 35, 38–44, 61
    at Wolanow, 105–13, 115–20, 121–22
Watchmaking tools, 40, 83, 86, 107, 150–
    51, 201

Weiss, Khil, 39–40, 41–42, 51, 52–53
Wilczek, Adash, 127–28, 296–97n
Wilczek, Avramele, 127–28, 139
Wilczek, Jeremiah "Uncle Yirmia," 126–
    29, 131–32, 133, 135, 139, 295–97n
Wilczek, Liba, 79–80, 83–84
Wilczek, Slova, 16–17, 67–68, 79
Wilczek, Yitka, 127–28, 296–97n
Wildenberg, Aharon, 23
Wildenberg, Feyge, 3–8, 11–12, 14
Wildenberg, Fishel, 3–4
Wildenberg, Laizer Yitzkhak, 2, 253–54
Wildenberg, Perla, 7–8, 12, 14
Wodziński, Marcin, 247
Wolanow (town), 263
Wolanow Slave Labor Camp, 97–126
    arrival at, 97–98
    Corbinus and the watch, 105–9
    digging a tunnel, 123–25
    food and nutrition, 98–99, 100–101,
        112
    ID numbers, 103
    Moishe and typhus, 113–16
    Passover Seder, 120–21
    Rubbe and Palestine list, 121–23
    trip to Radom, 119–20
    watchmaking, 105–13, 115–20, 121–22
    weekly selections, 102–5, 110–11, 128
    work, 99–100, 105–9, 292n
Wolka. See Gorczycki Camp
World War I, 2–3, 71

Yarmulke, 18, 274
Yellow badges (armbands), 48–49, 55, 62,
    64, 79–80, 85, 119
Yeshua, 205, 274
Yiddish, xxi, 17–18, 140, 208
Yikhus, 2, 275
Yom Kippur, 75–76, 161
Yontiff dika, 84

Zecken, 112, 116, 275
Zhid, 23–24, 275
Zionist youth movement, 32, 73–74
Zmiroys, 26–27, 275

About the Authors

HARRY LENGA was born in 1919 to a family of Chassidic Jews in Kozhnitz, Poland, where his father taught him and his brothers the watchmaking trade that would save their lives during the war. Harry was working in Warsaw when the Germans invaded Poland in 1939, and escaped from the Warsaw Ghetto in 1941 to reunite with his family in the Kozhnitz Ghetto. The night before the Germans murdered its entire Jewish population—including his remaining family members—Harry and two of his brothers escaped Kozhnitz to a nearby Polish-run labor camp. From there, the three brothers were transported between 1942 and 1945 to the camps in Wolanow, Starachowice, and Auschwitz, and then to the Austrian concentration camps of Mauthausen, Melk, and Ebensee. All three brothers were liberated by the U.S. Army on May 6, 1945. In 1949, Harry immigrated to St. Louis, Missouri, where he married, had three sons, and went on to have grandchildren. He continued working as a watchmaker for nearly thirty years before retiring and later moving with his wife to Israel. Harry Lenga died on January 2, 2000 at the age of eighty.

SCOTT LENGA is the son of Harry Lenga. A native of St. Louis, Missouri, he holds a BA in economics from UC Berkeley and a law degree from UCLA. He and his wife live in Israel, where they raised three daughters who grew up listening to stories about the grandfather they never really knew. In addition to writing and speaking about his family's experiences during and after World War II, he serves as a corporate and intellectual property lawyer for technology companies. Visit him online at ScottLenga.com.